ARIZONA GOES *to* WAR

★

ARIZONA GOES *to* WAR

THE HOME FRONT AND THE FRONT LINES DURING WORLD WAR II

EDITED BY

BRAD MELTON AND DEAN SMITH

WITH A FOREWORD BY SENATOR JOHN McCAIN
AND AN INTRODUCTION BY MARSHALL TRIMBLE

THE UNIVERSITY OF ARIZONA PRESS

TUCSON

The University of Arizona Press
© 2003 The Arizona Board of Regents
First printing
♾ This book is printed on acid-free, archival-quality paper.
Manufactured in the United States of America
08   07   06   05   04   03   6   5   4   3   2   1

Library of Congress Cataloging-in-Publication Data
Arizona goes to war : the home front and the front lines during World War II / edited by Brad Melton
and Dean Smith, with a foreword by Senator John McCain and an introduction by Marshall Trimble.
        p.   cm.
Includes bibliographical references and index.
    ISBN 0-8165-2189-1 (cloth : alk. paper)—ISBN 0-8165-2190-5 (paper : alk. paper)
    1. World War, 1939–1945—Arizona.   2. Arizona—History—1912–1950.   3. World War,
1939–1945—Personal narrartives, American.   I. Melton, Brad, 1971–   II. Smith, Dean, 1923 Apr. 3–
D769.85.A7 A75 2003
    940.53'791—dc21

                                                                              2002013833

British Library Cataloguing-in-Publication Data
A catalogue record for this book is available from the British Library.

In January 1986 the Papago Indian Tribe of Arizona formally changed its name to the Tohono O'odham
Nation. Because of this, historical references in this book are to the Papago, while contemporary references
are to the Tohono O'odham.

Publication of this book is made possible in part by the proceeds of a permanent endowment created with
the assistance of a Challenge Grant from the National Endowment for the Humanities, a federal agency.

Dedicated to the Arizona men and women
who served their country in so many ways during World War II,
as well as to those other military personnel from other states
and many Allied nations who trained here.

★ ★ ★

To Gary,
I'n appreciation for
all of your help
and friendship,
Andy Russell

Contents

FOREWORD

SENATOR JOHN McCAIN

THE SUBJECT OF Arizona history evokes a number of immediate images: from the Wild West of Tombstone and the timeless peaks of Monument Valley to the snow-tipped red rock of Sedona and the mirrored high-rises of Phoenix. Yet many Arizonans, and most Americans lucky enough to have visited our state, do not know that modern Arizona was forged from her unique role in a nation at war.

In this book, the authors tell the story of Arizona's transformation during the war years in rich detail and with a native eye for local color. Thanks to the activity of wartime mobilization, the strategic value of our state to the war effort, and the industriousness of our people, what was in the 1930s a young desert state remote from the federal government became by 1945 a bustling center of national life.

The *Arizona Republic* distilled the hopes and fears of a nation on the eve of its greatest trial, forecasting what lay ahead for its readers in a prophetic editorial on December 4, 1941: "[This year's] New Year's Eve ceremony will bring to an end an eventful year in the annals of American history. It will herald the beginning of a new one that is likely to be epochal in the historical records of the nation. . . . It will mark the beginning of an era in these United States of America in which democracy will be put to its severest test. The entire future of the nation will depend upon the philosophy of life that Americans develop in the next year. We think America will emerge from this trying period far better than it was when the test began."

Modern Arizona was born in war. A great nation rallied to defeat nefarious enemies, and Arizona was integral to its victory. During the war years, the military bases familiar to Arizonans today—Davis-Monthan, Luke, the air station at Yuma—were built, along with dozens of other military facilities that sustained our war effort in the Pacific. "All Arizona became an armed camp between 1940 and 1946," writes Dean Smith.

Indeed, more than a million American and Allied troops served in or passed through Arizona during the war years. Many of these soldiers were so enchanted by our state's climate, spaces, and people that they settled here after the war, providing, as Smith points out, "the biggest impetus for growth of any event in Arizona's long history." This included not just Americans from other parts of the country but also citizens of Britain, Australia, China, and other nations.

Wartime made common heroes out of Arizona's uncommon stock, such as an Army Air Corps lieutenant at Luke Field named Barry Goldwater, who barreled his way into military service despite poor eyesight. Lieutenant Colonel John Rhodes, executive officer of Williams Field and later minority leader in the U.S. House of Representatives, says of his wartime service, "It was my assignment to the base that introduced me to Arizona and made me an Arizonan for the rest of my life."

Courage required no fame for its finest expression. Eight Arizonans are entombed in the USS *Arizona*; their loss was Arizona's first sacrifice of the war. In 1992, Lura Skeen White, the last of Arizona's Gold Star Mothers—so named for the gold star a grieving mother would place in her window after losing a son in the war—died on the birthday of her son Harvey, whose grave is the ship named after his beloved state.

Private First Class Silvestre Herrera's gallant service against the German army in the forests of France earned him our nation's highest military recognition. "I'd rather win the Medal of Honor," said President Harry S. Truman to the Arizonan at his White House awards ceremony, "than be President of the United States."

Perhaps the most riveting story of Arizona at war is that of the American

Indians who answered their country's call to arms. That country had not been kind to them: Only eight decades before the war, the U.S. government had usurped their land and freedom. When World War II began, American Indians still did not have voting rights. Nonetheless, no other ethnic group in the United States made a greater per capita contribution to wartime service. Ninety-nine percent of all eligible American Indian men had registered with the selective service by 1942. If the entire eligible U.S. population had enlisted for military service in the same proportion as American Indians, there would have been no need for any draft at all.

The Navajo code talkers earned a fame from their war service commensurate with their key role in winning it. The story of how an enterprising World War I veteran developed a code in the Navajo language that was used in every marine assault in the Pacific is legendary. The heroes were the Navajo code talkers themselves, who made not a single error in the transmission of any message between 1942 and 1945. One of them recalls, "Sometimes we had to crawl, had to run, had to lie partly submerged in a swamp or in a lagoon, or in the dead of heat, pinned under fire. But there was no problem. We transmitted our messages under any and all conditions." The code talkers were called "Arizona" in battlefield shorthand.

During the epic battle of Iwo Jima, six networks of "Arizonas" sent eight hundred flawless messages over the course of a staggering month-long struggle for control of the island. When the marines raised the Stars and Stripes on the summit of Mount Suribachi, the talkers announced the victory in Navajo code: "mouse-turkey-sheep-uncle-ram-ice-bear-ant-cat-horse-itch" (Mt. Suribachi). One marine officer who was there says, "Were it not for the Navajos, the marines would never have taken Iwo Jima." Read their story and be awed by what they did for America.

This volume also contains important chapters on the detention in Arizona of prisoners of war, the contributions of Japanese Americans despite reprehensible prejudice against them, and the remarkable contributions of Arizona's women to the war effort. Throughout, the forces that shaped our state's character and conscience make for fascinating reading.

When Raymond Carlson transformed *Arizona Highways* early in the war years from a drab engineering pamphlet into an expression of the lore of the American West, he touched the spirit of Arizona in a founding editorial: "This

humble journal dedicates itself to the task of telling you something of one corner of America, this land of ours called Arizona. We will speak of roads and
where they lead and we will tell you something of the people who live along
those roads. We will bring you tales of long ago and we will have you meet some
of our neighbors. We'll invite you to come and 'sit a spell.' And, most of all,
these pages will reflect our pride in our land and our pride in America, of which
we are all a part." This book reflects that founding spirit in a way that cannot
fail to make America proud.

PREFACE

BRAD MELTON

FROM THE SINKING of the USS *Arizona* during a surprise attack on Pearl Harbor to the Navajo code talkers who frustrated Japanese code breakers to the Japanese Americans who were incarcerated by their own country, Arizona stands out as one of the most fascinating chapters of the American World War II experience. In this book, some of the state's best known journalists and historians have joined forces to bring readers an engaging and informative look at Arizona's role during World War II. Beginning with a snapshot of Arizona on the eve of war to the dramatic transformation of the state throughout and following it, the book not only tells what happened in Arizona during the war, but also personalizes the experience by sharing the stories of some of its sons and daughters who answered their country's call in a variety of ways.

More than sixty years ago the United States was attacked by the Japanese Empire and became a full participant in World War II. The war was portrayed as a worldwide struggle between good and evil. The United States and its allies wore the white hats in their response to Axis aggression, but that doesn't mean our country was immune from mistakes and dark alliances: America had policies of institutionalized racism that subjugated many African Americans to a lower status than even German prisoners of war; old-fashioned political and business opportunism abounded in the roundup and incarceration of Japanese

Americans; and our ally by necessity, Joseph Stalin, was perhaps a greater butcher than even Adolph Hitler, Benito Mussolini, and Emperor Hirohito combined. Still, the imperfections of our society then were outweighed by the ideal that we aspired to as a nation—to be a land of opportunity and a beacon to all freedom-loving peoples.

Revisionist historians reflect back with the benefit of hindsight, but also with the baggage of their own generation's perspective. This book is written by historians and journalists from nearly all generations now living, and to a greater or lesser extent reflects that in its organization and treatment of the material. Even so, efforts were made to tell these stories with an appreciation for the mood of the times written about and a respect for the generation that lived through these days of uncertainty.

It is nearly impossible to follow a chronological thread with a work such as this, but the chapters are in a sensible structure loosely based on the order in which events occurred. Each of these chapters contributes to the understanding that World War II was a watershed event in Arizona that dramatically brought about changes in a few short years that would have taken decades to accomplish—a population boom occurred when large numbers of servicemen who had served in the state later returned to settle down; manufacturing, military, and high-tech industry diversified the economy and brought the state out of its reliance on extractive resources; Arizona's political landscape began its change from a Democratic stronghold to a Republican one; and the state graduated from its reliance on eastern capital to an increased reliance on the federal government. Even so, it was the New Deal programs of the 1930s that paved the way for securing gains, and the decades-long Cold War following V-J Day that ultimately maintained those gains.

Despite these themes and their theoretical implications, this book is neither an exhaustive history nor a scholarly tome—cold, impersonal, and distant. World War II in Arizona is a reality woven into the fabric of the personal lives of men and women from communities across the state, and is best understood in terms of their experiences.

It is the story of Luther Flick, who learned about the attack on Pearl Harbor around seven o'clock that night while standing on a street corner in Phoenix. "There was a special edition of the newspaper, and I had never seen a special edition," he says. "I was eighteen and didn't know where Pearl Harbor was." Luther joined the navy in September 1942 and served in distant places, such as the Marshall Islands, the Marianas, Okinawa, and Iwo Jima, which left him with an incredible empathy for those who suffered and an understandable bitterness toward war in general. "War is hell," he says. "I saw planes hit the water. I saw dead men in the water. I saw men killed. And those memories don't go away."

It is also the story of Vernon Fairchild, who left his home in the Iowa countryside in 1943 so he could participate in the navy's V-5 program, which brought him to Arizona State Teachers College (Northern Arizona University) in Flagstaff. While studying to become a pilot, he was invited by a buddy to the First Baptist Church on South Beaver Street, where the congregation fed him and other servicemen. On one of these occasions a pretty young lady, Betty Jean Rawson, invited him over to make homemade ice cream—they would marry in October 1945, and he would become one of the thousands of servicemen to relocate to the state following the war.

This book draws on contemporary newspapers, oral histories, interviews, and secondary sources for stories like these of Luther Flick and Vernon Fairchild to create an engaging account of Arizona's World War II experiences—a work of public history.

Learning about World War II has been a lifelong interest of mine that started in first grade when I began reading the Cornerstones of Freedom series from Children's Press. One of these books featured the story of the USS *Arizona*, and another featured the battle for Iwo Jima. Ironically, the first involved a ship named for Arizona and the second included Ira Hayes, a Pima Indian from Arizona who helped raise the flag on Mount Suribachi. So, it is only fitting that this book brings me full circle—back to the stories that first sparked my interest in the subject.

Acknowledgments

BRAD MELTON

A WORK OF this scope would not be possible without the efforts of many individuals and institutions. First, Dean and I would like to thank the writers. History should capture the imaginations of young and old alike—that's the premise I started with at the genesis of this project—and along the way I was fortunate to find fellow journalists and historians who agreed. Not a single writer among us has not been humbled by the men and women portrayed in this volume, but I must also say that I've been humbled by the writers who joined me in this cause. All of them had competing priorities that would have remained insurmountable had the subject been different, but they cast aside all other considerations because they knew that this story was bigger than all of us. No matter what challenge arose, the writers always faced it with great faith and commitment, and I am in their debt. Second, many thanks to Patti Hartmann and her colleagues at the University of Arizona Press for their immediate excitement, patience, and ongoing support of this worthwhile project.

A word of special appreciation goes to the Arizona Historical Foundation at Arizona State University, the Arizona Historical Society (Central and Southern Divisions), the Arizona Collection at Arizona State University, Special Collections at the University of Arizona, the McFarland State Historical Park Library and Archives, *Arizona Highways* magazine, the Arizona Military

Museum, Colonel Dave Manning, Joe Alman, Special Collections at Northern Arizona University, Corbis, and Scottsdale Community College's Center for Southwest Studies, all of whom were instrumental in providing the book's stunning imagery.

This book would not exist without the help of numerous librarians, archivists, journalists, and historians who provided essential expertise, advice, and contacts. The book is in many ways a collaborative project involving all of these individuals and the institutions they represent. They include Lee Pierce, Steve Hoza, Mary Melcher, and Renee Immel of the Arizona Historical Society's Central Arizona Division; the National Archives in Washington, DC; the Special Collections Department at the University of Arizona; Christine Marin of the Arizona Collection in the Hayden Library at Arizona State University; the Cochise County Historical Society; the Pimería Alta Historical Society; the Arizona Historical Foundation at Arizona State University; the Arizona Historical Society's Southern Arizona Division; Donald Langlois of the Arizona Department of Library, Archives and Public Records; Bob Fessler; Art Hansen of California State University, Fullerton; The Arizona Chapter of the Japanese American Citizens League; the *Arizona Republic;* James McBride; Bing Brown; Louise DeWald; Lloyd Clark; Sam Brunetto; Sam Lowe; Betty Cornelius; Nelda Crowell; Wallace Flannery; Janice Griffith; Richard Lord; John Lynch; Mike Thompson; Barbara Yost; and Gustave Vinas.

Throughout this project, many individuals who recounted their war and stateside experiences for this book or for other oral history projects aided the writers. They include but are not limited to Donna Cosulich, Yndia Moore, Harry Maryan, Jack Kennedy, the Honorable John J. Rhodes, former Arizona Governor Evan Mecham, Rhea Robinson, Jayne Drotning, Abe Chanin, Dianne Bret Harte, James Turner, Susan Garland, James R. Finley, Helen Stout, Lynda Reithmann, Josephine Soza Michalec, Raquel Soza, Ruth Petry, Margaret Tamplin, Roy Petsch, Donna Petsch Donavan, Susie Sato, Bill Kajikawa, Michiko Tadano, Bill Butler, Stan Turley, Silvestre Herrera, Joe Abodeely, Vernon Fairchild, Luther Flick, Maxine Perkins, Laura Harris, Dora Mendoza Gomez, Dot Wilkinson, Annie Garcia Redondo, Joe Torres, Eleanor Curran, Janette Arkie, Elizabeth Blanton, Dorothy Cady, Rose Cahall, Georgiana Garland, Edna Gleim, Evelyn Jackson, Fran McClendon, the Honorable Polly Rosenbaum, Charlotte Wiehrdt, Gertrude Williams, Josephine Michalec, Byrd

Granger, Agnes Begay, Ruth Reinhold, Dorothy Wood, Lillie Skinner, and Laura Celaya.

I would especially like to thank Dean Smith for his uncommon professionalism, generosity, and humility in his roles as co-editor and contributing writer; Marshall Trimble for his early "count me in" attitude that caught the imagination of other great writers; John McCain for penning the book's foreword; Jack August, Carol Osman Brown, Bob Farrell, James McBride, and Jeb Stuart Rosebrook for their friendship, encouragement, and advice; Noel Stowe, Beth Luey, Robert Trennert, and Bradford Luckingham at Arizona State University for the training without which this book would have remained nothing more than an idea; and purveyors of quality popular history—for their inspiration. After all, the most influential history will always be told as a story.

Finally, I would like to thank my wife, Jennifer, for her sacrifice and understanding through the endless hours I spent tucked away in our home office. Family is so much more important to me than any book, and I would have handed it off to someone else had she asked me. Still, she consented because she knew how important it was to me, and she knew that the book would become a valuable addition to the literature about Arizona's colorful past.

INTRODUCTION

MARSHALL TRIMBLE

OFFICIAL ARIZONA STATE HISTORIAN

SOMEDAY IN THE future, historians will divide Arizona history into two parts: pioneer history and modern Arizona. World War II will be the event that separates these two periods.

When the war began, the population of the state was less than a half-million. Phoenix was a dusty cow town with a population of 65,414 residents. The metropolitan area, including Mesa, Glendale, Tempe, and Scottsdale, boasted 186,000. Tucson had 36,818 residents. Almost overnight, military bases sprang up all over the state. On weekends Arizona's towns and cities were bursting at the seams with young men and women in uniform out for a good time before shipping out overseas. Arizona became both an armed camp and an arsenal for democracy. Army experts found more perfect flying weather in Arizona than anywhere else in the United States. Even before the war, the government began constructing army air-training bases such as Luke Field west of Phoenix, Davis-Monthan Field at Tucson, and Williams Field east of Chandler. Before long pilots were being trained at fields from Kingman to Douglas. The skies were so full of planes that one reporter was prompted to write, "a red-tailed hawk had to look twice before going upstairs to stretch its wings."

Pilots from England to China came to train in the desert, where flights cancelled by the weather were rare indeed. British student pilots arrived in the desert community of Mesa to train at Falcon Field still wearing their heavy woolen uniforms. Many had never driven an automobile, much less flown an airplane. The British pilots had a slogan, "From plow jockey to pilot in twenty-nine weeks." Buzzing Camelback Mountain was a favorite diversion among the young English fliers until local residents complained. "If you got caught scratching the camel's back," recalls one cadet, "you would be washed out and sent back to England."

A Chinese cadet became lost on a cross-country flight from Luke in 1942. Short of fuel, he made an emergency landing near Kingman. This was brought to the attention of the local sheriff, who arrived to see an Asian peering at him from inside the cockpit. The sheriff drew his six-shooter on the pilot, who was armed only with a card explaining who he was and why he spoke no English.

By the end of the war more than sixty thousand American, British, and Chinese pilots had earned their wings in the skies over Arizona. Besides being an ideal location for training airmen, the dry, hot, inhospitable deserts of western Arizona became a training ground for the campaign in North Africa. Track marks from General George Patton's tanks are still visible today. Bottles of beer sold at the post exchange were so hot, soldiers claimed, that a bottle under a hundred degrees was considered a "cold one." Ironically, two infantry divisions who endured the hot, blistering desert wound up fighting in the steamy jungles of the South Pacific.

General George "Blood and Guts" Patton wanted the training to be as realistic and rigorous as possible. At the same time he was a stickler for spit and polish, insisting his men dress properly. Patton told of an incident that happened when he was in the desert near Yuma: When he came upon a man stripped to the waist, working on a telephone pole, the general walked over to the pole, looked up, and yelled, "Get your ass down here and explain this to me." The man climbed down, and Patton said, "Stand at attention. Give me your name, rank, and serial number." "My name is John Smith," came the reply, "and I work for Mountain States Telephone Company, and you can go to hell."

The economy in Arizona changed dramatically during the war, bringing an end to the Great Depression. Everyone had a job, and people were putting money in the bank again. Cotton and copper returned to boom times. Farmers doubled the amount of land they planted in Pima long-staple cotton. The copper mines operated in high gear. Cattlemen found an eager market for their livestock. Huge government contracts gave rise to the manufacturing industry. The Del E. Webb Corporation received large government contracts to build military installations in the state. Allison Steel Company made portable bridges. The Garrett Corporation, later Allied Signal, made parts for B-17 bombers. The Goodyear Aircraft Corporation had large contracts with the navy and eventually evolved into Goodyear Aerospace Corporation. ALCOA ran the world's largest aluminum plant, which later became Reynolds Aluminum.

When the war ended, many of the young men who had trained in Arizona decided to return with their families and take up residency. Footloose veterans had learned they didn't have to live where they were born. Arizona was young and vibrant, a good place to raise a family. In 1949, Dan Noble opened the first of several Motorola plants in Arizona. By 1950, Arizona's population had grown to 750,000 residents. Encouraged by the state's famous climate, along with tax incentives, other corporations—including Hughes Aircraft, General Electric, Honeywell, Sperry, and IBM—quickly followed. By the 1960s manufacturing had become the state's number one income-producing industry, and soon thereafter metropolitan Phoenix became the nation's third largest high-tech area. Coinciding with all this was the advent of affordable air conditioning.

All the ingredients were in place to transport Arizona into the modern period of its illustrious history.

ARIZONA GOES to WAR

★

1

Prelude to War

BRAD MELTON

IN THE EARLY hours of September 19, 1934, three separate dynamite explosions shattered the stillness in the vicinity of Japanese homes and farmland in Arizona's Salt River Valley. Two of the bombs landed approximately eighty to a hundred feet away from the targeted residences of Fred Okuma and Ryemon Asano; and at Frank Sugino's farm near Mesa, a blast tore out a floodgate, inundated twenty acres of land, and slightly damaged his roof and a window screen. One week earlier another farmer, Tadashi Tadano, was tending a floodgate on his farm when fifteen masked men in six automobiles approached, pulled pistols, and ordered him to raise his hands. The men left only after firing two shots over Tadano's head and two into his truck, which they had shoved into an irrigation canal.

According to historian Jack August, these and other acts of terrorism against Japanese farmers in the Salt River Valley were caused when local white farmers, suffering from depressed economic conditions and angered by alien agricultural excellence, organized a movement to oust all Japanese farmers from the valley in 1934 and 1935. Trying to capitalize on the "yellow menace" for the September 11 elections in 1935, politicians had also hurled accusations at Japanese farmers in an opportunistic effort to gain favor among white constituents. Soon after the September 19 incidents, an *Arizona Republic* editorial condemned the agitators: "The fools who have been recklessly tossing dynamite about are yet to learn that grievances cannot be adjusted by terrorism. They will learn before this incident is closed that dynamite possesses an even greater explosive quality than they had supposed. They will know that the detonation has been heard as far to the west as Tokyo, and; [*sic*] to the east as far as Washington. Dynamite is a weapon peculiarly, of cowards and criminals."

After further terrorist attacks, pressure from both Japan and the U.S. federal government finally forced cooler heads to prevail. Terrorist acts eventually subsided into dialogue and enforcement of the alien land laws, which were designed to prevent non-Americans from purchasing land. Unfortunately, Jack August notes, nearly one-third of the Japanese farmers in Arizona left the state during the 1930s, and hearts hardened so much against those who remained that many Arizonans supported Governor Sidney P. Osborn's 1942 protest to the federal government against the use of Arizona as a "dumping ground" for incarcerated Japanese Americans.

★ ★

THE MAN WHO KILLED SANTA CLAUS

It was the height of the 1932 Christmas shopping season, and merchants in rural Tempe and Mesa (yes, rural) were suffering from slack sales due to the Great Depression. So John McPhee, the colorful editor of the *Mesa Tribune,* concocted a scheme involving Santa parachuting out of a plane to generate interest in the Christmas parade, which would lead hundreds of shoppers downtown. In his millennial history of Arizona, Marshall Trimble writes that the crowd cheered as the plane's doorway opened and Santa appeared. The crowd's cheery mood quickly changed to horror, however, as "Santa began to tumble end over end, down, down, down, like a lead balloon. *Splat.* Santa landed facedown in the field. Mothers covered their children's eyes. Fathers stared in disbelief."

Fortunately, the parachutist planning to jump as Santa Claus that day had not shown up, so the figure in the red suit was actually a department store mannequin. Even so, outraged onlookers loaded up their families and headed back to their farms, and vocally upset merchants returned to empty stores. Thirty-six years later, the front page of the *Mesa Tribune* noted the editor's passing with this headline: "John McPhee, The Man Who Killed Santa, Dies."

In addition to its adverse effects on the state's agriculture, the Great Depression had wreaked havoc on Arizona's mining, construction, and transportation industries. In his groundbreaking history of Phoenix, historian Bradford Luckingham writes that copper mining in Arizona experienced a decline when consumption decreased, sending copper from 18.1 cents a pound in 1929 to 5.6 cents in 1932. Thousands lost their jobs and began tapping savings accounts, which forced banks to liquidate their assets to meet cash demands. Homeowners could not renew their mortgages and faced foreclosure. Salaries paid to Arizona workers dropped by nearly half from $253 million in 1929 to only $132 million in 1933, driving down the average annual income per person from $592 to $321. The state's population also dropped from 435,573 in 1930 to 380,000 in 1933, primarily due to the evacuation of mining towns.

The enormity of the depression forced Arizona's governors to seek federal support. President Herbert Hoover's Republican administration provided several million dollars, but it was under President Franklin Delano Roosevelt (who swept Hoover out of office in 1933) that the federal government stepped in and truly began to alleviate the crisis in Arizona. A spirit of optimism prevailed throughout the state as Roosevelt began to push unemployment insurance, retirement programs, wage and hour laws, housing for the poor, federal relief projects, and local welfare boards—all as the responsibility of the federal government. Arizona Democrats outnumbered Republicans by 3 to 1 during the 1930s, which smoothed implementation of the president's New Deal.

Among the many federal programs created by the New Deal was the Civilian Conservation Corps (CCC). Composed mainly of young men between the ages of sixteen and twenty-four, the CCC worked in twenty-seven camps of two hundred men each, usually in the mountains and national forests. From there the CCC teams worked on a variety of projects designed to prevent soil erosion, increase forest and grazing lands, develop infrastructure, and promote tourism. One of these projects included an effort, launched in 1938 by Flagstaff's 20-30 Club, to improve access to the Arizona Snowbowl ski run. In 1939 and 1940, CCC crews built a nine-mile cinder-surfaced road to the ski run, and also built a log cabin. With the threat of war increasing, however, the CCC shifted its energy to programs that related directly to military preparedness. In addition to the economic benefits, reserve officers who commanded CCC camps found their experiences tremendously beneficial once hostilities began.

With the CCC geared to help teens and young adults (unskilled laborers), the Works Progress Administration (WPA) was designed to employ skilled adults. The WPA's work program included building, professional, and women's projects. Most of the WPA building projects in Arizona related to school and road improvements, but the list also included park development, public building construction and improvement, water and sanitation improvement, and irrigation projects. The professional projects included musical and stage performances, public art commissions, writing assignments, health services improvement, and educational service projects. The projects geared for women included sewing rooms, household labor training, and nursery work. Some prominent WPA projects include the Desert Botanical Garden in Papago Park, Phoenix Junior College, Encanto Park in Phoenix, and Grand Canyon improvements, as well as *The WPA Guide to 1930s Arizona.*

Reclamation projects were also among those sponsored by the federal government, and Arizonans soon benefited from jobs provided by the building of Hoover (1936), Parker (1938), and Imperial Dams (1938) on the Colorado River, and Bartlett Dam (1939) on the Verde River. However, Arizona governor George W. P. Hunt and his successor Benjamin B. Moeur opposed the building of the Colorado River dams due to issues surrounding water rights for the seven states that drain into it. The governors knew that Arizona was losing out because the lion's share of the water trapped behind the dams would go to

One of the most successful of the New Deal economic recovery programs of the 1930s was the Civilian Conservation Corps (CCC). Its camps, such as this one at Portal, Arizona, provided work and self-respect for many thousands of young Americans.

California. Lake Mead, which was created by the Hoover Dam on the Arizona-Nevada border, was tapped by California's Imperial and Coachella Valleys by way of the All-American Canal, but there was no provision made to pump any of the water into Arizona. According to historian Marshall Trimble, this prompted critics to claim that although California profited from the project, "she didn't give a dam site for it." Further down the Colorado River, the Parker Dam near Yuma was built for the express purpose of delivering water to California.

In 1939, a year after the completion of Parker Dam, workers were transforming the mountains west of Tucson into a world-renowned movie set, Old Tucson, for the epic motion picture *Arizona*. The film stars William Holden and Jean Arthur and tells the story of a determined pioneer woman trying to bring civilization to the Arizona

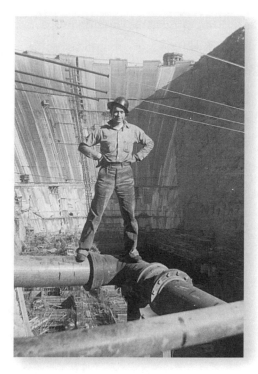

ABOVE: During the Great Depression of the 1930s, Arizonans watched with pride the construction of Hoover Dam on the Colorado River. The hydroelectric capability of the dam was a boon to World War II industry in the Far West.

Territory. Meanwhile in Monument Valley, director John Ford had teamed up with a young actor named Marion Michael Morrison (John Wayne) on an adaptation of a short story, "Stage to Lordsburg" by Ernest Haycox, which he had read in *Collier's* magazine. The film, *Stagecoach,* went on to win two Academy Awards and gross well over a million dollars in its first year while competing with such notable rivals as *Gone with the Wind, The Wizard of Oz,* and *Mr. Smith Goes to Washington.*

Ford was originally attracted to this remote location along the Arizona-Utah border through the tireless efforts of Harry Goulding, who co-owned a trading post there and wanted to jump-start the local economy. Goulding contacted his friend Josef Muench and borrowed some of his stunning black-and-white photographs of the monoliths and volcanic plugs dotting the area to convince Ford to film there. Beginning with *Stagecoach,* Ford's love affair with Monument Valley continued for decades, and the valley became the backdrop for such masterpieces as *The Searchers* and *My Darling Clementine.* Consequently, Monument Valley would become one of the most recognized symbols of the American West. Muench would also go on to make a name for himself as a first-rate photographer on the pages of *Arizona Highways* magazine.

Raymond Carlson, the editor of *Arizona Highways,* often promoted Arizona's perfect winter climate, which encouraged vacationing at the state's dude ranches and desert resorts. In fact, it is estimated that thirty-five thousand

THE ARIZONA NAVY

In response to California's power politics with the building of Parker Dam near Yuma to deliver water to Los Angeles, Governor Moeur sent the Arizona National Guard to the east bank of the Colorado River and set up machine gun emplacements, which prohibited construction workers from continuing on the project. According to historian Marshall Trimble, "one night a party of guardsmen borrowed a couple of relic steamboats . . . and headed toward the 'enemy' shores of California. Unfortunately, the 'Arizona Navy' got tangled in some cables and had to be rescued by the 'enemy.' The incident made the nation's newspapers and caused a few red faces."

RAYMOND CARLSON

★ ★ ★

Raymond Carlson, long-time editor of *Arizona Highways,* guided the magazine to prominence among the nation's state journals.

Raymond Carlson, a.k.a. Mr. Arizona, became the sixth editor of *Arizona Highways* in 1938. Launched in April 1925, the magazine began with the express purpose of propagating the building of new and better roads. It was a drab engineering pamphlet laced with ugly black-and-white construction advertisements. Arizona, like many western states, saw tourism as an important resource but did not have the roads necessary to take advantage of America's dependable new automobiles and increased leisure time. The Good Roads movement reached its peak in the 1930s when the federal government began funding large transportation projects. The New Deal brought Arizona the road construction it requested and gave *Arizona Highways* a new cause in tourism.

The Great Depression shrank advertisers' budgets and forced several Arizona-based travel magazines to either cease publishing or transform their missions. *Arizona Highways,* which survived because of a state subsidy, was then able to pursue the wide open tourist market. In 1939, Carlson stopped selling advertising space in order to improve the publication's visual appeal and avoid competition for advertising dollars with other Arizona-based publications. In his fifth year as editor, Carlson became the magazine's philosophical architect when he laid out his vision: "This humble journal dedicates itself to the task of telling you something of one corner of America, this land of ours called Arizona. We will speak of roads and where they lead and we will tell you something of the people who live along those roads. We will bring you tales of long ago and we will have you meet some of our neighbors. We'll invite you to come and 'sit a spell.' And, most of all, these pages will reflect our pride in our land and our pride in America, of which we are all a part."

In the months following the attack on Pearl Harbor, Carlson published a series of letters (actually poorly disguised editorials) in the front of *Arizona Highways* issues. The first letter, "Greetings from Arizona to the Emperor of Japan," struck a pseudo-friendly tone and spoke of several things that reminded Carlson of Emperor Hirohito. The first thing was the sound of planes flying and soldiers marching with a warning that "trouble is coming for you and your boys." The second thing was a letter from a corporal in the Marine Corps who enjoyed his monthly copy of *Arizona Highways* so much that he wanted to read it to the "Japs in the public square of Tokyo." Carlson's letter concludes, "You'll learn a lot more about these boys, Mr. Hirohito, when they come marching up Main Street in Tokyo some day, Stars and Stripes heralding the victory of free peoples everywhere."

Shortly thereafter, Carlson himself put his body where his pen was and enlisted in the armed forces. Following the war, he returned as editor of *Arizona Highways* and through his folksy demeanor, homespun superlatives, and zealous use of scenic color photography, transformed the magazine into the best known and most widely circulated state-owned magazine. He retired in 1971.

---

visitors came to the Phoenix area in the winter of 1939–1940, which was brought on by improved economic conditions and the elimination of Europe as a tourist destination due to the war. Even so, summer life in Phoenix, Tucson, and other desert communities before the invention of air conditioning and evaporative coolers was miserable. Wealthy Phoenix families traveled north to Prescott while their Tucson counterparts summered on nearby Mount Lemmon to escape the heat. Working husbands commuted from outlying areas to the cities, spending weekends with their families, then driving or catching a train for the work week. Those who could not afford to leave the cities dragged their beds outside and slept under wet sheets to keep cool. Fortunately, evaporative cooling was discovered in the early 1930s, and air conditioning followed less than a decade later, which provided much-needed relief and enabled the postwar population boom.

FOR DECADES ARIZONA'S economy was based primarily on cattle, copper, citrus, and cotton. As America's involvement in the war grew, however, Arizona's warm weather, clear skies, great expanses of unoccupied land, good railroad connections, low taxes, cheap labor, and proximity to California made the state attractive to both the military and private manufacturing companies alike. The resulting location of military bases and related industries brought jobs, money, and prosperity, which created boom times unprecedented in Arizona history for once sleepy towns like Glendale and Flagstaff. Federal statistics show that in 1940 the gross income from manufacturing in Arizona was $17 million, while in 1945 the figure reached $85 million.

Phoenix, particularly, benefited from the influx of federal bases and private industry. In February 1941 the city purchased 1,440 acres of land for forty thousand dollars, which it then leased to the federal government for one dollar a year. On March 29 the Del E. Webb Construction Company began excavation there on what would become the largest fighter-training base in the world. Luke Field, which was named for Lieutenant Frank Luke, Jr., Arizona's ace of World War I fame, was built at a cost of $4.5 million to provide advanced flight training for thousands of pilots. Soon after, the Goodyear Aircraft Corporation established a large plant west of Phoenix to build parts for combat aircraft, and the Garrett Corporation built its AiResearch plant at Phoenix Sky Harbor Airport to manufacture parts for B-17 bombers. Other incoming manufacturers included the Allison Steel Company and the Aluminum Company of America (ALCOA).

Glendale, like Phoenix, gained from nearby Luke Field as well as from its own air field. Founded in the 1880s as a temperance colony by entrepreneur W. J. Murphy, Glendale, northwest of Phoenix, was the perfect site for flight training. In his centennial history of Glendale, *Glendale: Century of Diversity,* Dean Smith notes that Thunderbird Field, located at 59th Avenue and Greenway Road today, was laid out in early 1941 to resemble a Thunderbird, an Indian god of thunder. Smith writes that "the observation tower was its head, the administration building its body, the barracks its wings, and the gardens its tail feathers." Built in five months at a cost of five hundred thousand dollars, Thunderbird Field held its dedication ceremony in May and started training pilots for the impending conflict. On November 5 fifty Chinese aviation cadets arrived at Thunderbird Field near Glendale for training as combat pilots. By the

★ ★

EVAPORATIVE COOLERS

Evaporative coolers had been around since the early 1930s, but they were new to twelve-year-old Illinois resident Maxine Perkins when she visited family in Phoenix in 1940. She remembers that their cooling system was a box in the kitchen window that was covered with burlap and had a fan on the back of it. "Every day the iceman came and delivered a block of ice, which was placed in the box in such a way that the melting ice dripped down into the burlap, the fan blew the cooled air into the room, and—voila!—probably the first swamp cooler!"

Flying cadets from many nations trained at Arizona air bases during World War II. This Chinese cadet earned his wings at Luke Army Air Field.

end of the war more than ten thousand American, British, and Chinese pilots had passed through Thunderbird. In its first few months as an air base, the field was also the site of a movie, *Thunderbirds (Soldiers of the Air),* starring Preston Foster and Gene Tierney. Across the Valley of the Sun, Arizonans' epithet for Phoenix and surrounding areas, other communities landed air fields: Mesa (Falcon), Scottsdale (Thunderbird Number 2), and Chandler (Williams).

The city of Tucson and the surrounding area also benefited from military buildup and private investment. In August 1940 the federal government announced its intention to transform Davis-Monthan (D-M) Field, which was Tucson's airport, into an army air base. The plans were to expand the three hundred–acre airport to sixteen hundred acres in order to handle the largest bombers as well as three thousand men. The city and army worked alongside each other for a while, but the army soon realized that it needed all of the facilities, actual or potential, and evicted the city on December 8. Tucson would have to find, pay for, and build a new airport. Consolidated Aircraft established a plant at D-M to modify bombers flying in from San Diego, Fort Worth, and Detroit. Two other air installations were also built nearby: Ryan Field to the west, and Marana Army Air Field to the north. Farther south, historic Fort Huachuca was the state's only major army base, which housed a full regiment by the fall of 1940. Days before the attack on Pearl Harbor, the War Department disclosed plans to expand Fort Huachuca to provide for an additional 11,309 men, bringing the strength of the post to 17,903.

As war approached, the mountain town of Flagstaff was already benefiting from the training of National Guard troops every summer at Fort Alexander M. Tuthill. The fort was named for the brigadier general who would soon lead Arizona and Colorado troops in the war. The month after Japan's sneak attack, the War Department decided to site a huge ordnance depot west of town. The $30 million Navajo Ordnance Depot required the labor of eight thousand workers to build and would eventually employ more than two thousand people, including many American Indians.

Hitler's invasion of Poland in September 1939 prompted President Roosevelt to proclaim a limited state of emergency. Following the collapse of France a year later, Congress federalized the National Guard, approved a $5 billion defense bill, and passed the Selective Training and Service Act, which required all males between the ages of twenty-one and thirty-five to register for military conscription with the goal of inducting enough men to create a 1.5 million–member armed force by mid-1941. A national registration day was declared on October 16, 1940, and civilian boards were created statewide to both register eligible Arizonans and supervise the draft.

In Arizona these actions resulted in the Arizona guard being called to active duty with the 158th Infantry Regiment, or "Bushmasters." The nickname came from a deadly snake that haunted the jungles of Panama where the regiment trained. The unit later became famous as it fought in General Douglas MacArthur's island-hopping campaigns in the South Pacific and earned another hard-won nickname, "Butchers of the Pacific," from the Japanese.

★ ★

NOISY NEIGHBORS

The dramatic increase in noise pollution brought on by the arrival of military aircraft at air bases around Phoenix caused a brief stir in the months preceding the attack on Pearl Harbor.

The *Arizona Republic* weighed in on October 26 by asking the aviators not to zoom down near the housetops. A like-minded reader responded, "The constant drone of airplane motors over Phoenix is a damned nuisance. Moreover it is wholly unnecessary. We are blessed with more open space in Arizona than any other section of the nation perhaps. The training ships might just as well roar where nobody is annoyed."

However, several readers supported the cadets, with one saying, "Of course, we wish they wouldn't 'zoom' over our houses, but don't take them where we can't see them and thank God they are American planes. And if they 'zoom' too close and knock the bricks off our chimneys, at least it will be an accident and not a well-placed bomb."

This Reg Manning cartoon, published March 17, 1941—before the United States entered the war—expressed Manning's belief that the United States stood in the way of Axis domination.

Published October 3, 1941, in the *Arizona Republic,* this cartoon by Reg Manning accurately predicted America's entry into the war.

Another consequence of the draft occurred as a result of misunderstanding and fear. Following the Selective Service and Training Act, attempts were made to register all American Indian men of draft age. A Papago leader named Pia Machita refused to allow his young men to register because he considered himself a citizen of Mexico and did not recognize the United States. Federal officials knew that his youth were illiterate and could not be drafted, but Pia was unaware of this fact and resisted. In an early morning raid on October 16, federal officials attempted to arrest Pia for draft evasion, but the officers were beaten up and bruised by his defiant tribe. A manhunt followed and eventually led to Pia's capture and incarceration.

IN SEPTEMBER 1940, with a Gallup poll showing 62 percent of the American public supporting him, President Roosevelt transferred fifty World War I–era destroyers to the British navy in exchange for British military bases in the Americas. The following year Roosevelt declared Iceland a part of the Pan-American Security Zone and landed 4,095 marines there to solidify the claim. American warships also began escorting Britain-bound convoys to a point south of Iceland where British warships resumed protection of the convoys. Reg Manning, the editorial cartoonist for the *Arizona Republic,* saw that the United States was swiftly moving on a collision course with the Axis powers, and his prophetic cartoon, "A Glimpse of the Future," appeared in the newspaper on March 17, 1941.

These and other actions of false neutrality by the United States were enough for Adolf Hitler to declare war, but he forbade his naval forces from initiating an attack at sea on American vessels. An editorial in the *Arizona Republic* later stated that "many of the steps we have taken to giving aid to England and later to Russia have virtually been acts of war. They have been steps we normally would have taken had we declared war. There is no denial that all of these things have brought us closer and closer to active participation in the struggle." However, even with Hitler's self-serving desire to keep America officially out of the war, darkness and poor weather conditions often made it difficult for German submarine commanders to identify the nationality of ships, and it wasn't long before warlike incidents began to occur.

On September 4, 1941, a German submarine launched two torpedoes at the U.S. destroyer *Greer,* which was traveling near Iceland. The torpedoes missed, and the *Greer* responded by launching eight depth charges. The attack enraged Roosevelt who issued "shoot first orders," which created an undeclared state of war between the United States and Germany. On October 17, 1941, the U.S. destroyer *Kearny* was torpedoed while protecting a convoy near Iceland. The crew suffered eleven dead and twenty-two injured, but the ship itself was able to limp back to port. Two weeks later on October 31 the destroyer USS *Reuben James* was attacked and sunk while on escort duty six hundred miles west of Ireland. The attack killed 115 servicemen and prompted the United States to almost drop its "short of war" policy. Woody Guthrie, who joined the merchant marine three times during the war, memorialized the incident with a song, "Sinking of the Reuben James."

On November 5 seventeen more Americans were killed when the British ship they were being transported on was sunk. The Americans had enlisted into the British technical corps for various kinds of noncombat service in England. The U.S. Congress responded by amending the nation's Neutrality Law, which

REG MANNING

★ ★ ★

Throughout the Great Depression and World War II, Arizonans were treated to the talents of one of the best editorial cartoonists in the business. Reg Manning began his lifelong relationship with the *Arizona Republican,* then its successor the *Arizona Republic,* in June 1926, at the age of twenty-one. Even so, Manning had already cut his artistic teeth when Governor George W. P. Hunt hired him in the fall of 1924 (the year of Manning's graduation from Phoenix Union High School) to pen several political campaign cartoons.

Reg Manning, Pulitzer Prize—winning political cartoonist for the *Arizona Republic,* portrayed the saga of World War II, especially events in Arizona, for many thousands of readers.

In his book *The Best of Reg,* historian Dean Smith writes that Manning first achieved national visibility in 1934 with his memorable editorial cartoon "I Cover the Waterfront," which showed Death stalking the strike-torn San Francisco docks. The following year, so many newspapers were reprinting his cartoons that the Phoenix Republic and Gazette Syndicate was created to distribute them for a fee. The client list eventually included seventy newspapers.

The Great Depression was a favorite subject for Manning, who attacked Roosevelt's New Deal as an unnecessary growth of the federal bureaucracy. Even so, it was Manning's ability to forecast several World War II events with uncanny accuracy that was most remarkable. The first, "A Glimpse of the Future," occurred on March 17, 1941, and showed exasperated Axis leaders huddled around a crystal ball that revealed the face of a stern Uncle Sam. According to Dean Smith, however, the most spectacular forecast occurred on April 17, 1942, in a cartoon "which showed Emperor Hirohito quaking with fear about the possibility of an American bomber raid on Tokyo. Since there were no apparent means of bombing Japan, such a thing seemed impossible. Yet, the following day, April 18, Jimmy Doolittle and his airmen from the carrier *Hornet* rained bombs on the Japanese capital." In March 1942, Manning introduced "Little Itchy Itchy," a homely Japanese youth who was always offering a hara-kiri sword to Japanese military leaders. This humorous character became a fan favorite and the subject of a future book by Reg.

By the end of his career decades later, Manning had crafted more than fifteen thousand cartoons, covered three wars, and won the Pulitzer Prize and scores of other awards, and his name was familiar to millions around the world.

left the legislation a hollow shell. An *Arizona Republic* editorial on November 9 said, "More and more throughout the nation there is a growing feeling that the time has come to openly declare war against Germany and to join Britain and Russia in putting down Hitlerism. The sinking of the U.S. destroyer *Reuben James,* and the several American merchantmen, as well as the attacks on two naval vessels, seem to have given impetus to a feeling that has slowly been growing for some months."

Far to the west the U.S. Pacific Fleet was stationed at Pearl Harbor in the Hawaiian Islands to serve as a deterrent to Japanese aggression. A smaller fleet, along with ground forces under the leadership of General Douglas MacArthur, defended the Philippines. On November 6 Arizona Senator Carl Hayden told members of the University of Arizona student body that by entrenching itself in the Philippines, the United States could protect its interests in the Pacific and obstruct any Japanese expansion in the direction of the oil- and rubber-rich Dutch East Indies.

Relations between the United States and Japan were strained due to the

THE AMERICA FIRST COMMITTEE

In late October 1941, the isolationist America First Committee launched a fight to prevent the repeal of the Neutrality Law. The campaign was to last for two weeks and include thirty meetings. An editorial in the November 1 *Arizona Republic* responded, "Merely as an observation, we believe the nation is already in an undeclared 'shooting war' so it makes little difference so far as this country is concerned whether the neutrality act is repealed, amended or left as it now stands." In addition, the editorial board criticized famed aviator Charles Lindbergh (an America First Committee spokesperson) for being naïve and threw down the gauntlet by saying, "We have reached that point in world affairs where we either must permit Hitler to tell us what we may or may not do, or assert ourselves and tell him what we are going to do. In short, we're faced with being appeasers and thus running the risk of suffering the same fate as the others who have tried to appease this power-mad man or standing up and stamping out that which threatens our peace and security."

latter's aggression in China and the United States' response in freezing Japanese assets and halting the export of much-needed fuel to Japan. In an act of subterfuge the Japanese government sent a special envoy, Saburo Kurusu, to the United States to purportedly try to iron out the countries' differences. However, a news article in the November 9 *Arizona Republic* was pessimistic: "The United States as well as Japan would like to work out an agreement. But the policies of the two countries are so diametrically opposed that an agreement seems impossible without considerable backing down by one nation or the other. And the United States is not backing down."

In August 1941 powerful isolationists in the U.S. Senate accused the Hollywood film industry of expounding pro-war propaganda and being a willing puppet of President Roosevelt's interventionist policies. A special subcommittee, which was stacked with four self-proclaimed isolationists and a little-known freshman senator from Arizona named Ernest W. McFarland, was established to determine the feasibility of a full Senate investigation. Elected to the Senate just six months earlier, McFarland was expected to maintain a low profile throughout what was supposed to be the beginning of a full-scale smear campaign. However, Mac (as he was affectionately known) was a tough-minded attorney as well as a staunch supporter of President Roosevelt's foreign policy. Just a few weeks earlier McFarland had given a speech to a crowd at a Democratic rally in Wisconsin. "If Hitler wins in Europe," he said, "the United States will be an armed camp for years to come. A constant threat of war would curb our personal liberties. This nation can never be safe as long as men like Hitler are in power."

The isolationists began the hearings by not only using hearsay to slander Hollywood, but also refusing to allow the motion picture industry's attorney, Wendell Willkie, to cross-examine witnesses. Therefore, McFarland stepped in as cross-examiner and skillfully waded through testimony to separate facts from fiction. "While a senator ought to kinda take it easy at first, see what's what and everything," said McFarland, "I couldn't very well just sit there and let that kind of testimony be accepted. Wasn't facts at all."

The national press loved the David and Goliath struggle. The *New York Times* remarked that McFarland had attracted "more favorable attention from the country than has fallen to the lot of any first year senator in years." The *Washington Post* proclaimed that the Arizonan "has stamped himself as a senator to be reckoned with." Meanwhile Arizona newspapers included headlines such as "Arizona's Freshman Senator Steals Movie Inquiry Show" and "McFarland Throws Wrench in Film Quiz." Following the attack on Pearl Harbor, the subcommittee was canceled, the Senate isolationists faded into obscurity, and McFarland was re-elected to a second term in the Senate before serving as Arizona's governor from 1955 to 1959 and Supreme Court justice from 1965 to 1971.

On Saturday, November 1, 1941, Governor Sidney P. Osborn proclaimed the week of November 11–16 as Civilian Defense Week in Arizona in conjunction with the president's call for every American to become better acquainted with their civilian defense program. The observance opened on Armistice Day. November 12 was designated War Against Waste Day; November 14 as Health and Welfare Day; November 15 as Civilian Protection Day; and November 16 as Freedom Day.

THE WEEKEND OF Japan's surprise attack on Pearl Harbor, football reigned in Arizona. On Friday, December 5, the St. Mary's Knights captured the state prep football championship by staging a sensational fourth-quarter rally to defeat the Mesa High School Jackrabbits 19 to 13. On Saturday the University of Arizona Wildcats lost 12 to 6 in a well-played home game against Utah, and the Arizona State Teachers College Bulldogs (the predecessor to the Arizona State University Sun Devils) lost 20 to 0 at home to the hard-riding Cowboys from Hardin-Simmons. The following morning on Sunday, December 7, Arizonans awoke to newspaper headlines that declared "Pacific Peace Hope Fades."

At Safeway in Phoenix three 14.5-ounce cans of Carnation milk cost 23 cents; sugar, 56 cents for 10 pounds; prime rib, 22 cents a pound; butter, 35 cents a pound; Tovrea's Morning Glory sliced bacon, 25 cents a pound; and a 12-ounce bottle of Pepsi cost 5 cents. The Boston Store sold women's fur-trimmed coats for $29.95, women's dress shoes for $4.49 a pair, men's wool suits for $22.50, and men's silk neckties for 97 cents. A 35mm camera at Montgomery Wards sold for $15.50, and down comforters cost $16.50 at Penneys. A Chevrolet with all accessories cost less than $1,000. Just a month earlier, couples were charged $1.10 to dance to the music of Lyle Smith and his orchestra at Riverside Park in Phoenix. The Arizona State Fair ran from November 8 to November 16 with tickets selling for a quarter.

In December 1941, television was still in its infancy, with radio and movie theaters competing for audiences. Radio listeners in Phoenix were treated to episodes of *The Lone Ranger* and *The Green Hornet* on KTAR, *Tailspin Tommy* and *Blondie* on KOY, and the sweet sounds of Glenn Miller's orchestra on KPHO. Other big music stars of the day included Duke Ellington and Jimmy Dorsey. Meanwhile filmgoers across the state watched major motion pictures such as *Keep 'em Flying,* starring Bud Abbott and Lou Costello, and *One Night in Lisbon,* featuring Fred MacMurray and Madeline Carroll, at such theaters as Tucson's Fox, Flagstaff's Orpheum, and Phoenix's Rialto. Sadly, even as African Americans were about to be called upon to defend their country, they were still relegated to segregated seating if they wanted to watch a movie.

On December 4, 1941, as Japanese aircraft carrier fleets sailed toward Hawaii, the *Arizona Republic* published a prophetic editorial: "[This year's] New Year's Eve ceremony will bring to an end an eventful year in the annals of American history. It will herald the beginning of a new one that is likely to be epochal in the historical records of the nation. . . . It will mark the beginning of an era in these United States of America in which democracy will be put to its severest test. The entire future of the nation will depend upon the philosophy of life that Americans develop in the next year. We think America will emerge from this trying period far better than it was when the test began."

And in Honolulu, in the early morning of December 7, Admiral Husband Kimmel and Lieutenant General Walter Short were preparing to meet for a round of golf.

2

DAY OF INFAMY

JANE EPPINGA

"ALL MILITARY PERSONNEL report back to your base!" Arizonans listened intently to their radios as the story unfolded that Japan had attacked Pearl Harbor in the early morning hours on December 7, 1941. Fear rose that the Japanese would attack the U.S. mainland along the coasts or by coming up through Mexico.

In Hawaii it promised to be another beautiful Sunday until 7:53 A. M., when Commander Mitsuo Fuchida broke radio silence with the code phrase *Tora! Tora! Tora!* (Tiger! Tiger! Tiger!). With these words, Fuchida informed the Japanese navy that Japan would make a surprise attack on Pearl Harbor. Five minutes later U.S. Navy Lieutenant Commander Logan C. Ramsey sent the radio message, "Air raid on Pearl Harbor! This is no drill!" At the sound of eight bells the American flag rose on the USS *Arizona*. Sailors topside spotted aircraft approaching.

During the next two hours brutal torpedo strikes, deadly dive bombing, and constant strafing essentially destroyed the U.S. Pacific Fleet and the U.S. military installations on the Hawaiian Island of Oahu. The ship that has come to symbolize this terrible attack is the *Arizona*.

In Arizona the air corps immediately alerted Luke, Williams, and Davis-Monthan military bases. Three days after the Pearl Harbor bombing, B-18s left

The USS *Arizona* under attack on December 7, 1941, at Pearl Harbor.

Tucson for the Pacific. At Luke Field the windows were covered with tar paper as concealment against a Japanese attack. However, on December 8 Tucson's *Arizona Daily Star* acknowledged that "Actual bombing of Japanese planes is not anticipated here." The late Senator Barry Goldwater had been assigned as an infantry lieutenant to Luke Field three months before Pearl Harbor. He was playing golf on December 7, 1941. When he heard of the bombing, he quit the game and called his headquarters, which confirmed the attack. During World War II Goldwater traveled from base to base, training the military in air-to-air gunnery.

In Tucson, Mayor Henry Jaastad asked for guards to protect telephone and gas lines, railroad bridges, dams, and reservoirs. Jaastad ordered the erection of a six-foot wire-mesh fence topped by barbed wire around water storage facilities. The guards, headed by William "Scrap" Roberts, called themselves the Tucson Vigilantes. Police Chief Harold C. Wheeler offered to deputize these volunteers. Within the next few days, three hundred Tucson women poured into the Red Cross office to offer their services as volunteers.

Students for the most part had deserted the campus of the University of Arizona on that deceptively serene Sunday. With much of the country blan-

SALUTING MAN'S BEST FRIEND

Davis-Monthan's commander, Colonel Lowell Smith, was well known for his big Irish setter, who loved to ride with the commander. Military pedestrians, seeing a figure in Smith's car, often snapped to and saluted. Then they would swear, "Oh (bleep), I've saluted that damn dog again."

keted in snow and shivering in the cold, it was a great day to pack a picnic basket and go see the university polo game. It would be the last peaceful Sunday for several years.

At dawn on December 8, the university campus and Tucson were stunned to see that a Japanese flag, crudely fashioned with pillowcases and red crayons, had been run up the university flagpole. Because the halyard had been cut, the Tucson Fire Department volunteered its services with hook and ladder.

In an interview, Abe Chanin recalls well that day of infamy. He had been at the Rialto Theater in Tucson watching a matinee movie when the lights came on and an officer stood up and made an announcement: "All soldiers report to Davis-Monthan." Abe, a University of Arizona student, was also working at the *Arizona Daily Star* at the time. He ran all the way to the *Star* office, where the Associated Press bells were ringing with the news of the Pearl Harbor bombing. He described the flag incident as a "stupid prank."

ABE CHANIN

★ ★ ★

Abe Chanin, left, sells war bonds in Tucson on Bill Bishop Day. Bishop was the first University of Arizona casualty of World War II.

Abe Chanin, a journalist for almost half a century, was an editorial director and sports editor for the *Arizona Daily Star* and was editor-publisher of *The Arizona Post* and *Collegiate Baseball*. This grandson of a Russian Jewish rabbi graduated from the University of Arizona, where he taught journalism and served as director of Southwest Jewish Archives. He organized the Bill Bishop War Bond Day in honor of the first University of Arizona student to be killed during World War II.

Chanin also served as editor of the *Wildcat*, the student newspaper. He got into trouble with university officials for writing an editorial criticizing the Board of Regents for not allowing American Japanese to take correspondence courses, and the Tucson police for raiding a university fraternity for hoarding gasoline. He was threatened with expulsion but it came to nothing because he was drafted in 1943.

Young and old alike exhibited strong patriotism. General John J. "Black Jack" Pershing, who had once chased Pancho Villa from his headquarters in southern Arizona, wrote to President Roosevelt, while in poor health at age eighty-one, that he "was one of millions of Americans who wanted to be of help in the fight."

Mr. and Mrs. J. R. Vensel of Winslow were delighted to receive a letter from their son, who had been in Hawaii during the attack. Ray Vensel wrote his parents: "Don't worry about Marge and Frisky [his wife and child]. They are all in one piece. . . . When the war is over the Stars and Stripes will still be flying higher than ever. I was in Pearl Harbor during the attack and can tell you this without fear of censor, I saw [the] Japs' planes come in but I saw darn few leave. They were shot down all over the island."

Eight Arizona families received sad news of loved ones who went down with the *Arizona*. These sailors included Apprentice Seaman James Van Horn of Tucson; Seaman Second Class George Allen Bertie, Jr., of Phoenix; Seaman First Class Louis Edward Cremeens of Yuma; Chief Gunner's Mate James William Horrocks of Nogales; Coxswain George Sanford Hollowell of Phoenix; Seaman First Class James Joseph Murphy of Bisbee; Seaman Second Class Harvey Leroy Skeen of Miami; and Fireman First Class Roy Eugene Wood of Yuma. A ninth man, Harold "Pat" Patterson, had attended school in Yuma.

THE BATTLESHIP USS *Arizona* had a long, proud history. Her keel was laid on March 16, 1914, and she was launched on June 19, 1915, from the Brooklyn Navy Yard with thousands of onlookers and a host of prominent Arizonans in attendance. William Ross, a pharmacist and former captain of the Arizona territorial militia, suggested that Governor George W. P. Hunt select his daughter, seventeen-year-old Esther, to christen the battleship. For several days Esther practiced in her Prescott backyard by breaking syrup bottles full of water across the fence. She developed a strong, accurate swing.

On the day of the christening she wore a long white dress, white shoes, and a floppy white hat and clutched a bouquet of American Beauty roses. In a clean swing she broke two bottles across the ship's bow. One contained American champagne and the other was filled with water from Roosevelt Lake. The bottles were encased in a filigree of Arizona-mined silver.

The state of Arizona had collected enough money, including nickels and dimes from school children, to present the new battleship with an eighty-piece silver service to be used in the officers' mess. After the war the silver service, along with the bell and ship's anchor, were retrieved.

Among the people who witnessed the launching were Secretary of the

YNDIA SMALLEY MOORE

★ ★ ★

Yndia Smalley Moore at age 94 with her daughter, Dianne Bret Harte.

By the time Yndia Smalley Moore, local historian, died on January 13, 1997, she had seen great changes come to Tucson and remembered the day, February 14, 1912, when Arizona Territory received statehood status.

After graduation from the University of Arizona, she married James P. Moore, an army officer who served as a member of General Dwight D. Eisenhower's staff during World War II. They traveled widely during this time, but after her husband's death in 1946, Yndia returned to Tucson.

During her working years, she served as the first paid employee of the Tucson Fine Arts Commission (now Tucson Museum of Art), curator and executive director of the Arizona Historical Society, and history editor for the *Tucson Citizen*.

On the day of the Pearl Harbor bombing, Yndia and her daughter, Dianne, had remained in Tucson while her husband, Jim, an army captain, traveled to his next duty station. He had just left Hawaii in October.

On that fateful day, Yndia had decided to go to Nogales with her father, George Smalley, to do some Christmas shopping. She says in interviews, "Jim had left in the morning and I was feeling very bereft." They found Nogales, Mexico, full of rowdy drunks, so Smalley decided they should eat at the Montezuma on the U. S. side.

When they heard the news of the bombing on the hotel radio, they immediately returned to the Mexican side of the border to get their car. Because their car still had army license plates from her husband's recent assignment in Fort Devens, Massachusetts, soldiers walked up to Smalley and said, "Sir, report to your station immediately," and then they saluted. Smalley replied, "Okay, boys." After two hours they were on their way back to Tucson.

★ ★

VOICE FROM THE ARIZONA

by Jack F. Langham, United States Navy (Retired) Deceased

It's time to break the silence
I have kept for many years
I want to send a message
To dry away your tears.

Let my story be heard by mothers
Whose sons I still enfold,
And to tell the wives of loved ones
Who defended me brave and bold

To you who've served in battle ships
Or perhaps you shipped with me
You might be mourning a shipmate
Who is resting beneath the sea.

My story began in Brooklyn
Nineteen-sixteen was the date
They christened me *Arizona*
After the sunny baby state.

I was a proud ship *Arizona*
And my commissioning became complete
The day I took my place in line
With the mighty U. S. Fleet.
My bow cleaved through the water
My sisters steamed at my side
I was part of the greatest navy
That ever graced a tide.

If you have been a son of mine
You've helped me earn my fame
You served me well and faithfully
I'll always cherish your name.

The years sped by—too fast, it seems,
And this lady was growing old;
Then infamy at Pearl Harbor
My destiny did unfold.

That tranquil Sunday morning
Found me secured in battle ship row;
Then without a sign of warning
I suffered my first blow.

My crew rushed to battle stations
And valiantly began to fight
The aggressors came on relentlessly
Attack! Attack! with no respite.

My boilers blew with a resounding blast
When a bomb dropped down my stack
The magazines were next to go
A blow that broke my back.

Colors flying—a last salute,
And with twisted and burning steel
I gave in to merciful waters
And felt mud engulf my keel.

Now I rest beneath the waves,
Embracing my beloved crew
Almost the entire complement;
One thousand, one hundred and two.

Though our worldly days are over,
Don't for the moment be misled;
The spirit within me is still alive,
Kindled by the gallantry of my dead.

We receive your prayers and tributes,
We hear you toll our bell;
We thank you for your reverence,
Much more than words can tell.

If we could ask one thing of you,
Our sole request would be;
Do everything within your power
To keep our nation strong and free.

Navy Josephus Daniels, Governor George W. P. Hunt, Senator Henry Ashurst, Major General Leonard Wood, and Vice Admiral Henry T. Mayo. At the request of Dwight B. Heard, editor of the *Arizona Republican,* Ashurst telephoned his eleven-hundred-word speech sentence by sentence to a stenographer who transcribed and transmitted it to Phoenix.

The navy commissioned the *Arizona* on October 17, 1916. Her armament included twelve fourteen-inch guns in four turrets, twelve five-inch guns, eight anti-aircraft guns, and two three-pound saluting guns. Her quarters were designed to accommodate eighty-four officers and one thousand enlisted men, but she carried at least twelve hundred men at the time of the Pearl Harbor attack.

On November 30, 1918, she joined the battleships *Utah* and *Oklahoma* in Portland, England. A few weeks later she proceeded with other Atlantic Fleet vessels to sea, where they met the USS *George Washington* with President Woodrow Wilson on board ready to present a treaty that would "guarantee peace." The ships escorted the transport with the president to Brest, France.

The fleet then returned to New York for review by the Secretary of the Navy. For the next four years the *Arizona* saw service in Europe, Asia, the Panama Canal Zone, and along the United States west coast. Never did she fire her guns in anger. In 1929 she joined the fleet in Hawaii.

In Hawaii, on December 7, 1941, American navy personnel stared in horror as the *Arizona,* with other distressed vessels, emerged through the inferno of fire and smoke. Pounded with a barrage of torpedoes and bombs, the *Arizona* rose out of the water, shuddered violently, and sank. Rescuers struggled to fish hideously burned survivors out of the Pearl Harbor waters. Throughout the carnage, the Rising Sun insignia appeared on Japanese planes that flew so low, navy men on deck could see the faces of their assailants. Of the *Arizona's* crew, fewer than two hundred survived the attack.

In Phoenix, Governor Sidney P. Osborn assembled a defense council and doubled the guards at the Mexican border. Within two weeks, Osborn asked the state's congressional delegation to request the Secretary of the Navy to christen one of the new battleships *Arizona.* The new ship would commemorate the distinguished service of the ship that had been so treacherously sunk. Osborn said the state of Arizona was appalled and saddened by the attack, but it had an effect that the Japanese had never anticipated: It united Americans. Following the attack on December 7, 1941, Don Reid and Sammy Kaye produced one of the most memorable patriotic songs in American history. "Remember Pearl Harbor" became the slogan and battle cry of World War II.

IN 1936, JAMES Van Horn's family moved to Tucson from Dallas, Texas. His father taught chemistry at Tucson High School. In 1941, James Van Horn, an athletic seventeen-year-old, wrestled with the decision as to whether he should go back to Tucson High School for his junior year or join the navy. Van Horn decided to join the navy.

After completing basic training in San Diego, Van Horn went straight to the *Arizona* without a furlough. In his last letter to his mother on November

★ ★

USS *ARIZONA* MEMORIAL

The USS *Arizona* Memorial grew out of a wartime desire to establish some type of memorial at Pearl Harbor to honor those who died in the attack on December 7, 1941. Suggestions began in 1943, but it wasn't until 1949, when the territory of Hawaii established the Pacific War Commission, that the first steps were taken to bring it about. President Dwight D. Eisenhower approved the creation of the memorial in 1958, and construction was completed in 1961. The 184-foot-long memorial spans the mid-portion of the sunken battleship. It has three main sections, including a shrine room, where the names of those killed on the USS *Arizona* are engraved on a marble wall.

The USS *Arizona* Memorial, in the waters near Honolulu, Hawaii, has come to commemorate all military killed in the Pearl Harbor attack on December 7, 1941. It straddles the sunken hull of the battleship, which was hit by a bomb at 8:10 A. M., exploded, and sank in less than a minute with 1,177 crewmen aboard. The memorial was dedicated in 1962 and became a National Park Service area in 1980.

26, 1941, he promised to send pictures and Christmas gifts. Van Horn had KP duty in the ship's kitchen on December 7. The Van Horn family waited anxiously for news of the son who was known to be on board the *Arizona,* but they did not learn of his death until late December. The first notice said he was missing in action, and the second announced that he was presumed to have been killed in action.

IN BISBEE, HOME of Seaman First Class James Joseph Murphy, another casualty aboard the USS *Arizona,* the unions and Phelps Dodge personnel resolved to put aside their differences and unite in the war effort. Copper production went into high gear, and throughout Arizona, miners started seven-day work weeks. The price for copper held at twelve cents per pound. Bisbee's Civilian Defense Council urged every able-bodied man and woman in the Bisbee district to register for possible emergency duty.

James Joseph Murphy was Bisbee's first casualty when he went down with the *Arizona.* His parents, Richard and Mary Jackson Murphy, had emigrated to the United States from England in 1923. They settled in Bisbee where Richard found work with Phelps Dodge. James joined the navy on January 31, 1941, and went through boot camp at San Diego. He served briefly on the USS *Enterprise* before transferring to the *Arizona.* On December 20, Richard and Mary Murphy received a telegram confirming their son's death:

> *The Navy Department deeply regrets to inform you that your son James Joseph Murphy, Seaman First Class, USN, is missing following action in performance of his duty and in the service of his country. The Department appreciates your great anxiety and will furnish you further information when it is received. To prevent possible aid to our enemies, please do not divulge the name of his ship or station.*
> —Rear Admiral Randall Jacobs, Chief of the Bureau of Navy Information

LURA SKEEN ALSO received the distressing news that her son, Harvey, had gone down with his ship. When Lura Skeen White died on January 26, 1992, at the age of ninety at the Miami Inspiration Hospital, she was the last of Arizona's Gold Star Mothers. These women were given gold stars to put in their windows after they lost sons in the war. Lura died on the birthday of her son, who had gone down with the *Arizona* just seven weeks short of his twenty-eighth birthday.

On February 3, 1942, Lura had received official notification from Rear Admiral Randall Jacobs that "After exhaustive search it has been found impossible to locate your son Harvey Leroy Skeen and he has therefore been officially declared to have lost his life in the service of his country as of December 7, 1941. The department expresses to you its sincerest sympathy."

TWO FAMILIES WAITED anxiously in Nogales for news after the bombing of the *Arizona*. Esther Ross Wray, who had originally christened the vessel, now lived in Nogales, where her husband was a wholesale dealer in Mexican native artwork. Virginia Horrocks was the wife of Chief Gunner's Mate James William Horrocks. She received a letter from him postmarked December 2 stating that he expected war to break out any minute. Then on December 22 Horrocks, who had served in the navy for nineteen years, was officially declared missing in action.

YUMA, WHICH WOULD become a training ground for the armed services under General George Patton because of its similarity to North Africa, lost three of its sons. Seaman First Class Louis Edward Cremeens and Fireman First Class Roy Eugene Wood were residents of Yuma. Harold "Pat" Patterson had arrived in Yuma from Texas with the Civilian Conservation Corps (CCC) and had completed his third year of high school there. His family urged him to return to Texas, but he was unable to find work there so he joined the navy and the *Arizona*.

THE ROBINSON FAMILY lived in a trailer court in Benson, where Rhea's husband, Reed, worked for the U.S. Border Patrol. Reed Robinson checked buses and vehicles coming into the United States from Mexico. Rumors abounded in the early days that Japan might attack the United States by invading California or coming up through Mexico. Moreover, the military thought that enemy bombers might be attracted by the Southern Pacific Railroad lines, the highway through Tucson, Davis-Monthan air base, Fort Huachuca, the Phelps Dodge copper mines, and the Apache Powder Company's plant near Benson.

RHEA ROBINSON

Rhea Robinson looks over her husband's (Reed's) photographs of the Japanese internees at Triangle T Ranch.

Rhea Robinson's memory remains crystal clear about that fateful day in December. In a personal interview, she tells how she had given birth the previous Friday to Robert Robinson and was recuperating at St. Mary's hospital in Tucson. She remembers that within a very short time, St. Mary's was short of medical help.

Rhea also remembers one day in February 1942, when a U. S. Border Patrol Agent told her husband to be ready to go on assignment in thirty minutes. Weeks later she received a letter from Reed, postmarked El Paso. She hadn't known that he had been on a special detail at the Triangle T "just twenty minutes down the road" from their home in Benson.

For many years the federal government denied rumors that high-ranking Japanese had been detained at the remote Triangle T Guest Ranch, near the town of Dragoon in southern Arizona, during World War II. But Rhea Robinson's husband, Reed, had guarded these Japanese prisoners, and she had the photographs and his logbook to prove it.

On a February 1942 morning, a Border Patrol officer appeared at the Robinson home in Benson. Rhea recalls, "He told my husband, Reed, to be ready to go on assignment in thirty minutes. Reed packed a dress suit, a uniform, and work clothes. Weeks later I received a letter from him, postmarked El Paso. I did not know that he was actually on a special detail at the Triangle T Guest Ranch just twenty minutes down the road."

The Triangle T Guest Ranch has a long and romantic history of its own. In 1913 George Brown received a patent on the land, signed by President Woodrow Wilson. He called the place Three Oaks; several large live oaks are still on the premises. A few years later the Seabring family acquired the land and a fruit ranch. In 1929 it came into the hands of Katherine Tutt, as a result of a suit for breach of contract to marry. Tutt, who built the cabins and provided them with artistic furniture, modern electric lights, and running water, suc-

Nagao Kita, Japanese consul general at Honolulu. Kita played an important role in planning the Pearl Harbor attack.

cessfully ran the property as Triangle T Guest Ranch. The ranch hosted many prominent visitors, including John D. Rockefeller, Jr., and General Jack Pershing. Later, it provided settings for the TV series *Young Guns*. Western films featuring John Wayne in *West of the Divide* and Glen Ford in *310 to Yuma* were filmed on location at the Triangle T.

For several years, rumors that high-ranking Japanese had been imprisoned at the Triangle T during World War II received one response from the federal government: "No such records exist." Ultimately, the National Archives found and declassified the Triangle T World War II records. The incredible boulder outcroppings of Texas Canyon, which surround the ranch, had been a deciding factor in its selection as a place to imprison the Honolulu diplomats who had played important roles in plotting the Pearl Harbor bombing.

During the first week of December 1941, apprehensive Japanese diplomats at the Honolulu consulate had huddled around their shortwave radio to listen to news from Japan. Above the crescendo of exploding bombs and wailing sirens, they had heard three words—"East Wind, Rain" —during an otherwise routine weather report. This code phrase officially informed them that Japan had declared war on the United States.

After the bombing, Consul General Nagao Kita and his staff knew that momentarily they would be arrested and, they believed, very likely killed. Although it was supposed to be a secret, Kita had learned that Emperor Hirohito and high-ranking military officers had agreed to sacrifice the Honolulu consulate for the glory of Japan. Kita knew of the impending war, but he did not know the exact date of the attack.

When the Americans arrived to place Kita, his staff, and their families and servants under house arrest, they found the diplomats burning incriminating documents in a tub. The twenty-six prisoners included Consul General Nagao Kita, Vice Consul General Otojiro Okuda, First Secretary Sainon Tsukikawa,

Japanese internees at the Triangle T Ranch: The Okudas (upper left), Takeo Yoshikawa (standing second from right), Robert Hiroyoshi Sumida (front left), Sainon Tsukikawa (middle front), and Kohichi Seki (right front).

Second Secretary Kyonosuke Yuge, Treasurer Kohichi Seki, Fourth Secretary Takeo Yoshikawa (a.k.a. Tadashi Morimura), and their spouses, children, and servants.

Although the State Department detained many consular Japanese at the elegant Homestead Hotel in Hot Springs, Virginia, FBI Director J. Edgar Hoover wanted the Honolulu Japanese kept apart from the others because of their espionage activities and involvement in the Pearl Harbor bombing. He insisted that the place chosen for their detainment should be one where their activities could be closely monitored. President Roosevelt wanted to keep Kita incommunicado from even his staff. Roosevelt, who viewed Kita as a critical figure in the Pearl

Otojiro Okuda, vice consul general at Honolulu. Okuda preceded Nagao Kita as consul general.

Harbor bombing, requested, "Plenty of food but no communications in or out." However, fear of Japanese reprisal against Americans and Allies precluded such action as banning all communications.

State Department Special Agent Edward W. Bailey had just forty-eight hours to find suitable lodgings for these Japanese. After he chose Arizona for its remote areas, Bailey, with Arizona Postal Inspector Harry H. Smith and Border Patrol District Supervisor Eddie E. Adcock, canvassed the state and selected the Triangle T Guest Ranch. In a patriotic spirit, Smith used his own car and informed the government that he would not charge mileage.

On February 8, 1942, servants at the Japanese consulate in Honolulu packed trunks and the Japanese prepared for a journey, they knew not where. They left Honolulu aboard the USS *President Hayes,* quartered in first-class staterooms. When their ship arrived at San Diego on February 17, Bailey assumed responsibility for them. Under heavy guard, Border Patrol officers transferred the Japanese by bus to the rail-road station, where they boarded air-conditioned Pullman cars. In Los Angeles, these cars were switched to a Southern Pacific train bound for Tucson.

Reed Robinson and Consul General Nagao Kita at the Triangle T Ranch. Robinson, a member of the U.S. Border Patrol, also served as a guard at the ranch.

Two days later, after a detention of several hours in Tucson, the train arrived at Dragoon in the late afternoon. Border Patrol guards drove the Japanese in unmarked Immigration Service cars to the Triangle T. After receiving their cabin assignments, they ate dinner and retired for the night. Except for government officials, no one—including managers Donald Huntington and Marjorie Murfree—knew the full identity of their guests.

The guards fenced off three acres with barbed wire. Anyone touching the fence would cause a panel to light up in the guards' tent. Five "perfectly trust-worthy colored servants" prepared their meals, did their laundry, and cleaned their cabins. Twice a week Bailey took their shopping lists, which he said "read like a Sears Roebuck catalog," to Tucson, where he purchased their toiletries and clothing. Rhea Robinson recalls, "Occasionally the guards grumbled because they lived in tents while their enemies enjoyed comfortable cabins." Within these limits, the Japanese exercised or relaxed. All Triangle T entrances were blocked off except for one guarded gate. Bailey supervised the only telephone in Huntington's office. Reed Robinson later told his wife, "We put fuses on empty boxes along the fence and told the Japanese that their movements were being photographed."

A few days after the Japanese arrival, FBI Agent Fred G. Tillman appeared at the Triangle T to interrogate them. Through barbed wire, Bailey told Tillman that he would not be allowed to question the Japanese until the State Department cleared his request. A disgruntled Tillman returned to Benson to wait three days for a State Department letter of authorization.

For the next couple of weeks Tillman interrogated the male Japanese who spoke English. They all stoically denied committing espionage. Consul General Nagao Kita described his consular duties as routine. When Tillman produced evidence that Kita's

Kokichi Seki, left, and Nagao Kita at the Triangle T Ranch. The Japanese internees were given first-class accommodations and treatment, in part because U.S. authorities wanted American internees to be treated well.

consulate had forwarded information to Tokyo pertaining to the U.S. Fleet movements, Kita shrugged and said, "Such acts might have been performed by my staff."

Otojiro Okuda, who served as consul general until Kita arrived, had failed to notify the U.S. State Department when his duties terminated on June 25, 1941. Okuda squirmed when Tillman pointed out that this oversight deprived him of diplomatic immunity.

Takeo Yoshikawa, trained in espionage, had slipped into Hawaii under the alias Tadashi Morimura. He knew every ship in the American navy and had filed daily diplomatic reports on U.S. Fleet movement. The handsome twenty-nine-year-old spy associated with geishas at the Shuncho-ro Tea House who provided him with information they had gleaned while entertaining American

Takeo Yoshikawa, a.k.a. Tadashi Morimura. The Japanese slipped Yoshikawa past U.S. authorities under his alias, and he sent vital military information to planners of the attack at Pearl Harbor.

sailors. Here Yoshikawa also observed Pearl Harbor and Hickam Field. He noted that the American fleet was brightly lit at night and visible in the early dawn hours. In a 1960 interview with Lieutenant Colonel Norman Stanford, Yoshikawa, still arrogant, contended that "for a brief moment I held history in the palm of my hand."

Tillman noted that Yoshikawa's left ring finger had been amputated at the first joint. Although he denied it, Yoshikawa probably belonged to the Black Dragon Society, whose members mutilated their fingers for identification. This fanatical group hated foreigners and imposed the death penalty on anyone who questioned the emperor's divinity.

After Tillman completed his interrogations, life at the Triangle T settled into a routine while both sides waited for news on the prisoner exchange. The Japanese received censored mail but no newspapers or magazines. The U.S. government paid the Triangle T $900 per week for the prisoners' room and board, $225 for the eight Border Patrol guards, and $35 for tips for the servants. In addition, the State Department remitted $100 from its Confidential Fund to Bailey for transmittal to Kita to pay for incidentals.

Even haircuts required confidentiality. Bailey proposed employing Benson City Councilman and barber Val Kimbrough. He would make his contact through Mayor Vince Gibson, known to be "a man of discretion." The State Department okayed the plan and advised Bailey to tell Kimbrough to cut their hair short so they wouldn't have to go so often. By the time he got approval, however, Bailey had bought clippers and the Japanese did a fair job of cutting their own hair.

A Benson physician, Dr. Alexander Shoun, treated the prisoners' medical problems, which usually involved simple infections or toothaches, except for one night, when a servant, Hanu Kusanobu, cried with severe abdominal pain. Shoun made a preliminary diagnosis of appendicitis. Bailey drove her, Robert Hiroyoshi Sumida, and a Border Patrol guard to the Desert Sanitarium (now Tucson Medical Center). Further examination showed that she had a ruptured tubal pregnancy, and Dr. Victor Gore performed surgery. During Kusanobu's recuperation, seventeen-year-old Robert Sumida served as her translator, and her husband was allowed to visit her. The U.S. government paid for her medical expenses but refused to pay the Triangle T for her room and board while she was in the hospital.

On May 21, 1942, when negotiations between the United States and Japan for the prisoner exchange were complete, the State Department ordered Bailey to prepare the prisoners for repatriation. Ten days later, the prisoners under Border Patrol escort, including Reed Robinson, boarded the train at Dragoon.

On June 7, 450 German and Japanese diplomatic officials who had been stationed in the United States, Canada, and Latin America arrived in New York City with their families. Border Patrol agents and the New York City police guarded all entrances to the top two floors of the Pennsylvania Hotel where the Japanese prisoners were lodged.

After World War II the Triangle T Guest Ranch reopened, and today it hosts guests in the same cabins used by the Japanese during those four months in 1942. Evening sunsets turn the colors of the extraordinary rock formations from soft pink to a deep indigo and recall a time over half a century ago when the lives of foreign enemies who stayed at the Triangle T were shrouded in the diplomatic secrecy of a world war.

MUCH HAS BEEN written in recent years concerning President Franklin D. Roosevelt seeking to provoke Japan's attack on Pearl Harbor. Nothing substantiates this claim; however, it cannot be denied that military awareness at Pearl Harbor was extremely lax. During the 1930s Japan sought to expand its empire, but it remained dependent on the United States for petroleum, iron, and machine goods. The United States, while fighting to survive the Great Depression, imposed high tariffs on its imports. In 1940 Japan entered into the Tripartite Pact with Germany and Italy, thus establishing the Axis Alliance.

When questioned as to the advisability of the Pearl Harbor attack, Admiral Isoroku Yamamoto replied, "If we have Heaven's blessing, there will be no doubt of success." Japan did not have Heaven's blessing, and the United States won the war, but both countries paid a terrible price for that day which has lived on in infamy.

3

ARIZONA DIVIDED

ANDREW B. RUSSELL

PREGNANT WITH HER first child, Susie Sato was living with her husband Carl in the Little Tokyo section of Los Angeles when she learned that Japan had bombed Pearl Harbor. As elsewhere, shock and uncertainty gripped the Japanese community. "We really didn't know what was going on or what was going to happen," Susie remembers. In March 1942 Susie, Carl, and four other members of the Sato family decided to "voluntarily" evacuate from the West Coast to avoid being sent to a concentration camp. They moved to Arizona to live with Susie's parents and siblings on the Ishikawa farm in north Mesa.

The move hardly solved all of the couple's problems. Arizona's Japanese Americans had not—and would not—escape assorted efforts to deal with the wartime "Japanese problem." As in California, the FBI had arrested some leaders of the Arizona Japanese community during the early hours of the war. The government had frozen bank accounts, imposed curfew orders and travel restrictions on Japanese Americans, and ordered "enemy-alien" families to turn in all cameras, radios, maps, firearms, and other types of "contraband." By the time the Satos arrived, military authorities had created a huge zone—Military Area No. 1—that encompassed the western half of Washington, Oregon, and California as well as southern Arizona. From this zone, all Japanese Americans were to be expelled.

This exclusion line cut right through the Phoenix valley, roughly four miles south of the Ishikawa farm. Many of the Japanese families of the valley found themselves on the wrong side of the line, and those in the free zone also had reasons to question their future fate. They soon learned that two massive relocation camps would be built in the Arizona deserts to house tens of thousands of Japanese Americans who were being removed from the West Coast. This news caused more problems for the Arizona Japanese by making the general population more suspicious and hostile.

For Japanese Americans Arizona had become a land divided. Stark differences separated past and present, the free and restricted zones, the camps and the outside world, the "Japs" and everyone else, the "free" Japanese Arizonans and the evacuees from California—who suddenly outnumbered the former group by more than fifty to one. Focusing on Japanese Americans of Arizona, this chapter offers a glimpse of what happened on both sides of these lines that divided Arizona during World War II.

Susie Sato holding her infant daughter, who was born in April 1942. Behind her is the house on her parents' ranch, northeast of Mesa, where she and her husband lived when they arrived from Los Angeles. The ranch sat in the nonmilitary zone, so the Satos were not interned.

THE LINE THAT DIVIDED

The line that drew the boundaries of the military exclusion zone entered Arizona near Needles, California. It zigzagged down various roads and through the town of Wickenburg. Heading south, it entered the Phoenix area on the highway now known as Grand Avenue. At Van Buren, it turned east, then turned south at Mill Avenue and crossed the Salt River. At Apache, it headed east again, through Tempe and Mesa, out to the Miami-Globe area, and on to the Arizona-New Mexico border.

Why were Japanese Americans singled out as a security threat and so mistreated during the war? Slightly different interpretations have been offered over the years, but the best simple explanation may be the one given by a congressional commission that investigated these questions in the 1980s. The commission concluded that the troubles stemmed from "race prejudice, wartime hysteria, and a failure of political leadership."

The West had witnessed a long history of anti-Asian sentiment well before the war started. In the early 1900s the Japanese seemed to inherit the animosity that had been mainly directed at the Chinese in the 1800s. This legacy of hatred led to laws and court rulings that banned Asian immigrants from holding certain jobs, made them ineligible for U.S. citizenship, excluded them (in time) from further immigration, and prevented them from buying land in most western states. The *Issei* (immigrants from Japan) felt the brunt of anti-Japanese discrimination, but the *Nisei* (first American-born generation) could not escape the prejudice that was directed at anyone who looked Asian.

The decision to remove *all* Japanese Americans from the West Coast and southern Arizona developed gradually. After a short period of relative calm, newspapers, politicians, anti-Japanese organizations, and the military authorities in charge of the West Coast region (the Western Defense Command, or WDC) began to agitate for removal. These forces claimed that the "Japs" (immigrant aliens and American-born alike) posed a major threat. A string of startling Japanese victories in the Pacific fueled those irrational fears.

Charges that Japanese Americans were planning or capable of committing acts of espionage and sabotage ran rampant. The FBI launched more raids and made more arrests in January and February of 1942. But the Western Defense Commander, Lieutenant General John L. DeWitt, and several other high-placed figures in the War Department demanded greater authority to remove enemy aliens and all Japanese Americans from the West Coast. On February 19 President Franklin D. Roosevelt bowed to pressure and signed Executive Order 9066, giving the military the authority it sought.

Now authorized to exclude "any and all persons" from the region under his command, as a matter of so-called military necessity, DeWitt began to designate a series of zones as off limits to Japanese Americans. Notices were posted giving Japanese Americans only a few hours or days to move away from the West Coast, where the vast majority lived. A few thousand attempted to relocate voluntarily to eastern California and interior states, but this only caused more problems. Residents and leaders of the interior states announced that they didn't want the "dangerous Japs" to roam at large in their communities. They made their feelings known to DeWitt, and in late March the defense commander froze voluntary evacuation. Thereafter, the policy of exclusion developed into a policy of mass incarceration in relocation centers (concentration camps) that would be built in the interior.

Japanese internees boarding a train en route to relocation centers in Arizona in early 1942. Although most were American citizens, authorities regarded them as enemy aliens and placed them under military guard.

Arizona was, in one sense, swallowed up by these large regional events. DeWitt and his staff at the WDC headquarters in San Francisco drew the line that placed many Japanese Americans of Arizona within the massive exclusion zone. Compelling evidence suggests, however, that homegrown Arizona forces influenced the drawing and redrawing of the exclusion line. In all likelihood, Arizonans—like Californians and other westerners—helped to cause the mass evacuation and incarceration of the Japanese.

Arizona, after all, had not escaped the type of anti-Japanese sentiment that laid the foundation for the evacuation. In 1913, Arizona lawmakers actually passed one of the first alien land laws, specifically designed to prevent the Japanese from buying farms. They passed a similar law in 1921 to prevent long-term leasing by Japanese farmers. Despite the restrictions, Japanese farm families grew and prospered, mainly by growing spring lettuce, fall lettuce, and cantaloupe. The mid-1930s brought new attempts to drive Japanese farmers out of the central valley during an event called the Salt River War. The "war" began with massive anti-Japanese rallies; it evolved into several bombing and shooting incidents and led to the destruction of Japanese crops and irrigation systems. The campaign lasted several months and caused a diplomatic crisis between Japan and the United States before the trouble subsided.

On the eve of World War II about 630 Japanese Americans lived in Arizona. Most were American born, and over 80 percent lived in Phoenix and

During the war Japanese farmers north of the military dividing line in Arizona had to truck their produce to Anglos, who then drove it to Phoenix markets. K. and Paul Ishikawa are shown preparing to take a load to a man named Sharp for transshipment.

the nearby communities of Glendale, Tempe, and Mesa. Farming remained their main occupation. A few families had managed to buy farmland, with the help of non-Japanese friends and by making their American-born children the registered owners. Others leased farms, and a handful operated stores and other small businesses.

The Japanese of central Arizona had built a strong community over the years. They had formed a local chapter of the larger Japanese Association, which fought against discrimination and organized activities to preserve and promote Japanese culture. The community had established Japanese Buddhist and Christian churches, and the Nisei of Arizona had founded one of the first chapters of the Japanese American Citizens League (JACL) to promote better race relations. Despite lingering prejudice, most Issei were accustomed to dealing with white business associates. The Nisei excelled in the classrooms and in various school sports, and they usually counted non-Japanese kids as friends. Both generations could look back with pride on the major contribution they had made to Arizona agriculture, and few would have been anticipating the wartime troubles that were about to descend on them.

A few signs of the problems to come surfaced within hours of the Sunday attack on Pearl Harbor. The Phoenix office of the FBI arrested several "enemy-alien" nationals in Arizona almost immediately. Leaders of the Japanese Association or the Buddhist Church, Japanese language teachers, people who had recently visited or lived in Japan, and those who had once served in the Japanese military or had contributed to nationalistic organizations were subject to arrest. Usually accompanied by local law enforcement, and often at night, the FBI would suddenly appear at the door. Agents would demand to search the homes and businesses of the frightened "suspects," gathering "evidence,"

THE TADANO FAMILY'S
INTERNMENT EXPERIENCES

★ ★ ★

The Takeshi Tadano family gathered for this prewar photo. Members of the family were interned in New Mexico and Texas.

Michiko Tadano remembers how the FBI came to arrest her father-in-law a couple days into the war. Takeshi Tadano, an Issei, had valiantly served in the Japanese army many years before. Apparently, this qualified him for a place on the Phoenix FBI's lists. But agents sent on this raid learned that Takeshi had recently suffered a heart attack and was bedridden. The agents went away—only to return when the old man was healthy enough, with orders that he report to the Lordsburg internment camp in New Mexico.

Takeshi's son, Takeo (called "Frank"), escaped the "long tentacles of the law" for several months. But then authorities apparently learned that Frank had been born in and had grown up in Japan. He had arrived in America several years before on a business visa, but he had not changed his papers since moving to Arizona.

Frank was arrested in early 1942. Strangely enough, Frank spent several months in the Phoenix jail before being transferred to Lordsburg. His sister-in-law remembers, "We used to bring him cartons of cigarettes to pass out to other inmates so they would not be mean to him." Frank was married to Grace Tadano and the couple had two small children, Marian and Thomas. His wife and kids depended on help from the rest of the family until mid-1943. Finally, they decided to join Frank in the camp designed for families of internees at Crystal City, Texas. The oldest Tadano son, Michiko's husband Tadashi, became the head of the family that remained in Arizona.

Ironically, the first arrested (supposedly the most dangerous) was also the first released in this case. Takeshi again fell very ill after being transferred to the internment camp at Santa Fe, New Mexico. The government decided they didn't have the facilities to treat Takeshi, so in 1943 they told the Tadano family to "come and get him." When Takeshi recovered, all he wanted to do was "drive around all day" in the old automobile he had asked the family to buy for him. It would be about another year before Frank, his wife, Grace, and their children would see freedom and the Tadano farm again.

and spiriting the male head of the house off to jail. Within a few weeks, these men would be brought before an enemy-alien hearing board that reviewed evidence and FBI testimony, then recommended whether the men should be interned or released. Most detainees were interned, and their family and friends would not see them again for two or more years.

Bill and Margaret Kajikawa, married shortly before the war, vividly remember the fears that surfaced on December 7. According to Margaret, people were deeply "afraid of what would happen to them in the moments of hysteria, that innocent people, Japanese who were American citizens, would get hurt." Representatives from the Buddhist Church, the Free Methodist Church, and the JACL all wanted to assure other Arizonans that they remained loyal to America. Word of their concerns reached Arizona Governor Sidney P. Osborn, who announced over the public radio airwaves: "Bill Kajikawa, come in to see me." The governor singled out Bill, in part, because he was a leader in the Arizona JACL. More important, he had gained widespread acclaim as an all-state tailback at Phoenix Union High School. A recent graduate of Arizona State Teachers College (ASTC), where he attended on a work-study football scholarship, Bill was the new ASTC freshman football coach (a job "Coach Kaji" would transform into a legacy over the following decades).

On December 9 the *Arizona Republic* reported that Governor Osborn met with Bill and the delegation, which included Tsutomu "Tom" Ikeda, Helen Okabayashi, Harold Takesuye, Shigeru Tanita, Toko Kuroiwa, and Henry Yoshiga. They had come "to offer our services to Uncle Sam." The governor accepted the offer and told them: "I believe in your sincerity, and I sympathize with your position." But he may have revealed some suspicion by also telling them that "the best job they could do for America would be to live as loyal citizens and immediately inform the Federal Bureau of Investigation of any subversive activities among them."

Within a few short weeks this climate of tolerance evaporated. By March of 1942 the southern half of Arizona (including much of Maricopa County) became part of the huge military zone from which all Japanese Americans were to be evacuated. Military planners at the headquarters of the WDC ultimately drew the exclusion line that cut across Arizona, but Arizona forces probably played a significant role in the shaping of evacuation policy within the state. Considering the high levels of anti-Japanese antagonism that had surfaced during the Salt River War, it is not difficult to imagine that some Arizonans would

BILL AND MARGARET KAJIKAWA

Warriors on Two Fronts

★ ★ ★

Bill and Margaret Kajikawa were prominent in the Japanese American community. Bill served in Europe with an all-Nisei army regiment.

Married in the summer of 1941, the Nisei couple Bill and Margaret Kajikawa reacted to news of the bombing of Pearl Harbor with "disbelief," like most Japanese Americans. "I couldn't believe it happened," Bill remembers. Instantly, the popular football coach at Arizona State and his wife became transformed from happy newlyweds into activists fighting for the fragile rights of the Japanese community.

Within hours Bill was summoned to meet with Governor Sidney P. Osborn as an official community spokesman. He answered the call to leadership in many unexpected ways. His greatest desire was to enlist in the military— and he tried. But when he and a Caucasian friend went to enlist, his friend got in, but Bill learned the government had put a ban on any new Nisei recruits. He would have to wait until 1943, when the Nisei were finally allowed to volunteer and became eligible for the draft. Meanwhile Bill and Margaret led a long battle against antidemocratic forces closer to home.

Bill fought mostly for the rights of Nisei students to attend school, but he also joined the army in 1943 and served with the famed all-Nisei 100th Battalion–442nd Regimental Combat Team in Europe. Meanwhile he and Margaret continued to challenge every new order that came down at home. When the Arizona legislature passed a bill stating that Japanese people could not buy anything but food, and Margaret had trouble buying a bar of soap from Sears, she mentioned the problem to Dixie Gammage, wife of the president of Arizona State Teachers College, who thought "that was ridiculous."

The years have not erased all the pain caused by the war, such as the combat deaths of two of Margaret's brothers in Europe. But these activists also haven't forgotten the allies who aided their struggles for basic civil rights in Arizona. Bill, Margaret, and others who fought these battles remember that "the Gammages were terrific," that attorney Simpson Cox helped her and other Japanese Americans challenge and win lawsuits against unjust restrictions, and that other Arizonans demonstrated crucial support and trust during these uncertain times.

have jumped at an excuse to finally rid the valley of Japanese farmers. Governor Osborn's collected papers and state newspapers bear witness to the steady growth of anti-Japanese sentiment in wartime Arizona.

For instance, the Osborn papers contain a December 18, 1941, telegram from the Northern Arizona Defense Council that vented fury on the "dastardly, cowardly Japs" who had attacked Hawaii. It warned the governor about the presence of more "fifth columnists" (enemy saboteurs lying in wait) in Arizona than at Pearl Harbor. In early January 1942, the Arizona Civilian Defense Coordinating Council submitted a call for the internment of all Japanese nationals in the United States and the surrender of all property and businesses to a "property custodian." Mid-February brought an intriguing letter from Arizona congressman John R. Murdock, showing that the mood of Arizona's leaders had deteriorated further. This letter reported that the governor's hopes of excluding aliens and Japanese Americans from the Far West had been relayed to the proper officials in Washington. Murdock noted how difficult it was "for these Easterners to realize" the gravity of the situation out West, but he seemed hopeful they would realize it "before it is too late."

The army originally decided that the zone of exclusion would cover only a strip of land near the Arizona-Mexico border. Scores of other restricted zones were to be designated around military bases, public utilities, and other sensitive areas in Arizona—but few Japanese families would have had to move under this original plan. Some people felt this did not go far enough, arguing that canal systems, telephone lines, and other infrastructure in and around Phoenix were also susceptible to acts of sabotage. The Arizona military maps were redrawn. The new exclusion line would cut through the middle of the urban center, trapping many of the Arizona Japanese on the wrong side of the dividing line.

Most of the Japanese farms, homes, and businesses of Glendale and Phoenix and some in Tempe and Mesa sat to the south of the exclusion line. Some families sold off belongings, packed up necessities, and dutifully moved to the north of the line. Why more did not escape is not hard to understand, considering the circumstances. Moving would mean abandoning the crops they had in the ground. Few had the money to plant again, and few white people were willing to rent homes—much less farms—to the Japanese by early 1942.

Besides, the government might issue new orders at any time. Hiro Nomura, who had just graduated from Phoenix Union High in 1941, remembers how he and his family tried to get information from the FBI and the district attorney's office. "They couldn't give us any answers. It was just confusion after confusion. Nobody could promise us that if we moved across the line we could stay out of the camp permanently." Then, with no warning, DeWitt ordered a freeze on voluntary evacuation in late March. Those who had not moved by then had to wait until May. That month, the army issued orders giving them only a couple of days to sell or dispose of their property and prepare for forced removal from the evacuation zone.

Those Japanese Americans fortunate enough to be living to the north of the line also worried about the future. Susie Sato often wondered, "What if they eventually declared all of Arizona a military zone? That didn't happen, fortunately, *but it was on our minds.*" Moreover, the imaginary line offered no protection for some in the free zone, like Kay and Henry Takemori and their two small children. The Takemoris owned a small grocery store in Phoenix on the north side of the Van Buren section of the line. "We were in the free zone but they made exceptions." The army told them that they were "a quarter of a mile too close to the airport," so they too would have to be evacuated. They sold their fifteen thousand–dollar property for eight hundred dollars in advance of the move.

Everyone on the north side faced other kinds of hardships and violations of their civil rights for months to come. Organized religious worship ceased because the Japanese Buddhist and Christian Churches were located in Glendale, south of the line. Susie Sato recalls how Japanese Americans could no longer shop at stores or visit banks in the restricted zone without a permit. When she was ready to give birth, the Mesa police had to contact the FBI and get permission before she could be admitted to Southside Hospital. Also, some grammar and high school students were effectively expelled, because their schools were in the restricted zone. Susie Sato sees that as "one of the most ridiculous things."

Fittingly, the fight to get the Nisei students back into high school became the special project of Bill Kajikawa. That July he contacted Bob Ashe, the principal of Peoria High School, and asked if the school could enroll about thirty Nisei students from around the valley that fall. Ashe recalled years later in a high school commencement address, "I was sympathetic to his request so I introduced him to my superintendent [Mr. Janzen]." The three men launched a secret plan to convince the Peoria School District Board to enroll the Asian students and introduced the idea at the next school board meeting. "The board members," said Ashe, "asked the [essential] question: 'Are these boys and girls citizens of the U.S.?'"

After careful thought, the board decided that the Nisei had "every right to an education," and admitted them. The board members agreed to give no publicity to their decision. Ashe proudly noted that "we didn't have a single ugly situation at school that year," thanks to skillful planning.

The line that divided the state caused more serious problems for those trapped in the exclusion zone and slated for mass incarceration. Moving day for the most unlucky Arizonans arrived in early May 1942. The army ordered Japanese Americans of the Phoenix area and southern Arizona to meet at various assembly points. Rules dictated that they could bring only one suitcase each and as much bedding as they could carry.

Most Japanese Americans cooperated fully with mass relocation. The immigrant generation frequently stated the old Japanese saying *Shakata ga nai* (It can't be helped) during these ordeals. Many Nisei tried to believe that they were serving their country by cooperating, as the government told them. But the cooperation and the forced smiles masked many negative emotions and great financial losses caused by the evacuation orders.

The next stop for the Arizona evacuees was the Mayer Assembly Center, located near the town of Prescott. By most accounts, Mayer "wasn't such a bad place." It had been a Civilian Conservation Corps (CCC) camp before being converted into an assembly center. Holding the roughly 250 persons evacuated from Arizona, Mayer was the smallest of many temporary assembly centers. While some West Coast evacuees had to live in converted horse and livestock stalls, surrounded by barbed wire and guard towers, the Arizona families were housed in four fifty-person barracks. The compound included a recreation hall, two bath houses, and a school. A local paper noted that the camp residents had organized recreational activities and planted many gardens by June. Soon thereafter, however, the government transferred the uprooted Arizonans from Mayer to a much more depressing temporary home—the Colorado River War Relocation Center.

Better known as Poston, this facility was located about twenty miles south of the town of Parker, Arizona, on land belonging to the Colorado River Indian tribes. Poston became one of two massive Japanese American relocation camps constructed in the Arizona deserts. It would eventually house almost eighteen thousand Japanese Americans, mostly from southern and central California.

Hastily constructed Butte Camp, which was part of the Gila camp on the Gila River Indian Reservation, is shown after it was opened in 1942.

The Rivers War Relocation Camp (Gila River), built on land belonging to the Gila River Indian community near the town of Casa Grande, eventually housed thirteen thousand evacuees from California. These were the only relocation camps built on Indian reservations and, for a time, they became the third and fourth largest "cities" in Arizona.

After this move, the fate of the evacuated Arizonans became intertwined with that of roughly 120,000 Japanese Americans from the West Coast who were incarcerated in ten relocation camps built in the interior West. Imaginary lines and barbed wire fences created more divisions and more varieties of experiences in the camps than can be adequately covered in this chapter. Briefly stated, the camps caused tensions between generations, between camp administrators and prisoners, and between those who remained pro-American and those who protested every new restriction the government imposed. Fences and army checkpoints, row after row of crudely constructed pine and tar-paper barracks, the scorching desert heat, blinding dust storms, snakes, scorpions, and other creatures that occupied the region and occasionally invaded homes—all this added to the surreal nature of life in the camps.

Demoralizing conditions existed at Poston and Gila, but the latter was at least located in a more scenic Arizona desert, peopled with saguaro and cholla cactus. The exteriors of the Gila barracks were painted white, making them appear more like modular homes. Still, Gila residents likewise dealt with rattlesnakes and scorpions, extreme temperatures, and dust storms that contributed to outbreaks of tuberculosis and valley fever.

Gila River offered particularly good soil and climatic conditions, unlike Poston. The Japanese applied their famous farming know-how and soon made Gila "the vegetable capital of the ten relocation centers." They converted hundreds of acres of raw desert and alfalfa fields into a garden oasis. In time, Gila and Poston also raised beef cattle and hogs. They shipped their excess produce and canned meats to other camps, helping to make them nearly self-sufficient so far as food needs. Gila River also sported an experimental flower nursery that produced a steady supply of blooms for funerals, hospital rooms, and camp celebrations.

These two little girls seemed to find moments of happiness even in a relocation camp.

One of the most fascinating aspects of the camps involved the many ways that the Japanese Americans battled against boredom and made the best out of the cards dealt to them. Besides activities already noted, the Nisei organized chapters of the YMCA, YWCA, the Boy Scouts and Girl Scouts, and the Young Buddhist Association. In time, the Issei organized many groups that taught traditional arts and crafts, dance, judo, and sumo wrestling and put on exhibitions. The residents produced weekly newspapers, newsletters, and school yearbooks (though all of these were subject to censorship).

Occasionally, tensions boiled over into resistance inside both camps. The most serious single incident in the Arizona camps became the Poston Strike of November 1942. The arrest of two men accused of beating a so-called *inu* (Japanese for dog), or suspected informer, triggered this protest.

★ ★

ELEANOR ROOSEVELT VISITS GILA

In 1943 Eleanor Roosevelt visited the Gila River camp—partly to investigate charges that the government was "coddling the Japs" while most Americans faced rationing and other wartime hardships. The First Lady witnessed the harsher realities of camp life and recorded her impressions of the Gila camp.

First Lady Eleanor Roosevelt being welcomed to the Gila camp during an inspection tour of the relocation centers.

America had not granted citizenship to the Japanese, she noted. "So now we have a group of people, some of whom have been here as long as fifty years, who have not been able to become citizens under our laws. Long before the war, an old Japanese man told me that he had great-grandchildren born in this country and that . . . all he cared about was here on the soil of the United States, and yet he could not become a citizen."

Following the attack on Pearl Harbor, "there was no time to investigate families, or to adhere strictly to the American rule that a man is innocent until he is proven guilty." Reflecting the excuses offered by military authorities, Mrs. Roosevelt explained that Japanese Americans had been sent to the camps "both for their own safety and for the safety of the country."

The Japanese were not being coddled. "The early situation in the camps was difficult, . . . sufficient water was not available, food was slow in arriving." During this period, "the Japanese proved to be patient, adaptable, and courageous for the most part."

"I can well understand the bitterness of people who have lost loved ones at the hands of the Japanese military," she continued. "These understandable feelings are aggravated by old time economic fear on the West Coast and the unreasoning racial feeling which certain people, through ignorance, have always had wherever they came in contact with people who are different from themselves." But hatred and fear "leads nowhere and solves nothing," she concluded, and "we cannot progress if we look down upon any group of people amongst us because of race or religion."

★ ★

THAT DAMNED FENCE

An anonymous poem circulated at the Poston Camp

They've sunk the posts deep into the ground
They've strung out wires all the way around.
With machine gun nests just over there,
And sentries and soldiers everywhere.

We're trapped like rats in a wired cage,
To fret and fume with impotent rage;
Yonder whispers the lure of the night,
But that DAMNED FENCE assails our sight.

We seek the softness of the midnight air,
But that DAMNED FENCE in the floodlight glare
Awakens unrest in our nocturnal quest,
And mockingly laughs with vicious jest.

With nowhere to go and nothing to do,
We feel terrible, lonesome, and blue:
That DAMNED FENCE is driving us crazy,
Destroying our youth and making us lazy.

Imprisoned in here for a long, long time,
We know we're punished—though
      we've committed no crime,
Our thoughts are gloomy and enthusiasm damp,
To be locked up in a concentration camp.

Loyalty we know, and patriotism we feel,
To sacrifice our utmost was our ideal,
To fight for our country, and die, perhaps;
But we're here because we happen to be Japs.

We all love life, and our country best,
Our misfortune to be here in the west,
To keep us penned behind that DAMNED FENCE,
Is someone's notion of NATIONAL DEFENCE!

The story of how the Japanese Americans resisted within the camps has only started to come to light in recent years. This is changing our understanding of camp experiences, but it is not likely to overshadow all that we know—and continue to learn—about the many ways that the camp residents made the best of their situations and contributed to the war effort in the process. These contributions ranged from cooperating with government orders, helping make the camps as self-sufficient as possible, and working in war-related industries established within the camps to joining the armed services and women's auxiliary corps when that became a possibility for the Nisei.

The camps employed some people from the reservations and the nearby towns, but most Arizonans were oblivious to the daily workings of the camps. Newspaper coverage, when it did occur, tended to be negative. Between 1943 and 1945, story captions like the following occasionally appeared: "Rivers Japs Take 600 Jobs," "River Center Ousts 27 [Disloyal] Japs," "Resettlement of Japs in Arizona Protested," and "[Officials] Forbid Japs to Leave Camps Lest Hostile Acts Occur."

Additional negative articles appeared when the public learned that the prisoners at Gila River had established a profit-making operation called Gila River Cooperative Enterprises, Inc. The cooperative began by marketing soft drinks and sundry items through small stores or canteens. It eventually financed various small shops and businesses, such as barber and beauty shops, laundries, and radio repair shops. More negative publicity and political fallout stemmed from the War Relocation Authority (WRA) policy of letting people leave the camps to accept temporary jobs or resettle permanently outside the military zone. In 1943 when the government opened a Japanese employment office in Phoenix, Arizona's leaders quickly forced federal officials to close it down. Senator Carl Hayden, in a letter to one newspaper editor around this time, wrote, "If the Japanese insisted on colonizing the Intermountain states, their future is sure to be full of trouble."

The free Japanese Americans of Arizona didn't know it, but the flames of prejudice licked again at their heels in midsummer 1943. A team of army investigators from the WDC had to travel to Phoenix that summer because some Arizonans had blamed "Japanese sabotage" for fires that consumed two produce-packing sheds. Governor Osborn had launched a new fact-finding study into the local "Japanese problem." The Central Arizona Shippers and Growers Association led this latest campaign for removal. According to the army report, one association member was heard to say that they were "not interested in obtaining facts, but their purpose was 'to get rid of the Japs.'"

DeWitt decided not to propose any new Arizona evacuations, and 1943 passed into a less hostile 1944. By January 1945, the federal government had lifted the West Coast exclusion orders and announced that the relocation camps would soon close. Not surprisingly, some California newspapers, politicians, and pressure groups made it known that the Japanese were not welcome back in that state, regardless of the government's new position. Some people who left the camps wrote back to report that they were encountering hostility and economic problems as they tried to resettle on the West Coast. All of this caused renewed concerns that the camp populations might try to settle in Arizona.

This grandfather at the Gila camp was delighted to welcome his two visiting granddaughters.

Even when the Arizona evacuees got permission to leave the camps, they received no warmer reception. Hiro Nomura, for example, managed to leave the camp after about a year "because they needed us for manpower on the cotton fields and produce fields." When he could finally return to his family's property, he found that someone had broken into their bolted and boarded-up garage. The intruder had stripped their car of the battery and tires and had stolen a radio and some expensive farming equipment. "We knew who did it, but you couldn't prove a thing."

Considering the major losses, hardships, and financial setbacks experienced by Japanese Americans on both sides of "the lines that divided," postwar recovery happened quickly. In central Arizona, Japanese American families reestablished themselves as some of the most successful farmers in the valley. In the 1950s, flower horticulture became the main occupation of some, and the Japanese flower gardens on Baseline Road became a popular attraction for tourists and locals alike. Some of the Nisei, and most of their offspring (the *Sansei*), attended college and pursued professional careers. They helped to eliminate the anti-Japanese laws on the Arizona books, and most of the social barriers and prejudices also faded over time.

Japanese Arizonans can recount few if any pleasant memories of World War II, but most have not dwelled on these bad times and the hardships and challenges they endured. Nor have they boasted about their many and varied contributions to the war effort. Nonetheless, the record shows that they fought heroically against fascism on two fronts—and from both sides of the imaginary lines that divided Arizona and the West.

4

WOMEN AND THE WAR EFFORT

DIANE BURKE FESSLER

FEW PEOPLE EVER ask Arizona women what they did during World War II, but the interesting responses may range from piloting military aircraft to preparing mining towns for air raids. The women of Arizona welded metal for airplanes; managed Red Cross clubs in far-off India; nursed patients in Europe and the Pacific theater of war; served in the Women's Army Corps (WACs), Women Accepted for Volunteer Emergency Service (WAVES), members of Semper Paratus—Always Ready (SPARs), and marines; and did whatever else was necessary to win the war.

Talk of war had been spreading to every city and town in Arizona before Pearl Harbor was bombed, but individual participation in the form of enlistments and readiness increased immediately after that December day in 1941. As their brothers and husbands were called to join the military in the next months and years, women across the state found themselves involved, answering the call to support the war effort.

Nurse, teacher, secretary, or housewife were almost exclusively the career choices available to most women of the 1930s. Soon Arizona women of all backgrounds and ages began doing what their mothers never dreamed could happen. Having lived through a dreadful depression, they were drawn to the mainstream of military and industrial life as the need for their talent and involvement became apparent.

Those who graduated from nursing schools were in much demand when the war sped into full gear. Military nurses had to be already trained as registered nurses (RNs) in order to join the army or navy.

"My parents took me to the train when I joined the army and left for my first assignment on December 1, 1942," recalls Dorothy Wood. "I remember Mom saying, 'You might accept sending your son to war, but not your daughter.'" Her mother's words still come to mind as Dorothy tells of her experiences with the Army Nurse Corps.

"Our troop train stopped in the middle of nowhere at a station in Arizona, and we were ordered to get off with all of our gear. A sign at the station said Hyder but there were no other buildings." Thus Lieutenant Wood began her life as a U.S. Army nurse in the vast and barren desert at the western edge of Arizona.

Gas mask drill did not deter this secretary from her work at Marana Army Air Field.

"Someone took us by truck out into the desert, where we lived in tents, and it was so darn hot. For three months we were subjected to desert training, ten-mile hikes, crawling under barbed wire with bullets whizzing over us, gas mask drills, and all sorts of things. General George Patton's troops were in our desert to prepare for fighting in the desert of North Africa. We expected to go there, but when we finally boarded another troop train, my next assignment

Army nurse training in the Arizona desert included crawling under barbed wire with bullets whizzing overhead.

was to the jungles of New Guinea, with the Fifty-eighth Evacuation Hospital. Our desert training was all but forgotten in the Pacific."

Laura Celaya also remembers the long, long hikes in the desert, and then the army's surprising her by sending her to Milne Bay, New Guinea, far from

any desert. Born in Tempe, Laura graduated from Tucson High School in 1928, and next, St. Joseph's Hospital School of Nursing in Phoenix. She volunteered for the Army Nurse Corps in 1942. "I was only four feet, nine inches tall, and they added an inch so I could meet the minimum height requirement. Once in the army, size didn't make any difference."

After a few months in the desert, Laura was assigned to the South Pacific with the Thirty-sixth Evacuation Hospital. "We moved with the troops, right behind them. We set up a tent hospital, and when the fighting moved forward or to another area, we closed up that hospital and set up another one. We got the wounded and dying fresh from battles, and sent them back to their outfit, or on to other hospitals as soon as they could be moved. They weren't with us

Laura Celaya was a member of the Army Nurse Corps in the Pacific theater.

very long, except for the ones who were dying. Then we got very close to them, and stayed with them at their bedside, just as though their family was there."

"One of the boys had a silk parachute," Laura remembers, "and had me bring it to his bed. He wanted me to have it, the only thing he had to give me. He died, and I'll never forget him. When I was in the Philippines towards the end of the war, I had a beautiful nightgown made out of it. I wore that gown for many years."

Laura's unit moved to Finschafen, then to Hollandia in New Guinea, and finally to Leyte in the Philippines, just after the Americans invaded in October 1944. Manila was her final assignment, where she joined the 120th General Hospital. "We arrived in Manila on a hospital ship that had all the Red Cross markings it was supposed to have, denoting it wasn't armed, and across the bay I saw a plane that looked like it was sitting on the water, only it came closer. It swooped up in front of our ship and dropped a bomb, but missed us somehow. I was frozen in place, but that plane was so close, I could see the Japanese pilot's face."

Charlotte Sherwood was born in Hunt, Arizona, attended school in Holbrook, and graduated from St. Joseph's Hospital School of Nursing in 1937. A third-generation Arizonan and member of the pioneer Udall family, she went to work as a surgical nurse in Miami, Arizona, where Anaconda Copper operated the mines. "In 1940 I married Paul Hendricks, who died in an accident shortly before war was declared. In January 1942 I went to Luke Field and volunteered to join the Army Air Corps.

"I discovered that a new program to train military nurses in air evacuation was just beginning. I was accepted, went through the training at Bowman Field, Kentucky, and became one of the first flight nurses, graduating in December 1943. I received secret orders to join the 807th Medical Air Evacuation Squadron in Catania, Sicily, to replace one of thirteen flight nurses who were missing on a plane that crash-landed in Albania. I'd met Leonard Wiehrdt, a fighter pilot, at Luke Field and we were married in Virginia where he was stationed. He was soon assigned to the same area in Europe, and we were able to see each other occasionally."

The 1940s hold vivid memories for Charlotte. "The 807th flew wounded patients out of war zones in Italy to military hospitals in Algiers, North Africa. One flight in particular I'll never forget. The plane was loaded with men with head wounds, and then lost an engine. The pilot asked us to place parachutes on the wounded, preparing for a crash. The medical sergeant and I got the parachutes out of the rear of the plane, and found that someone had removed the nylon and substituted GI blankets in the packs. We were concerned that the injured men wouldn't have survived a parachute fall anyway, but were greatly relieved when the plane landed safely." Charlotte Wiehrdt later raised six daughters and lives in Mesa, Arizona.

Charlotte Wiehrdt, one of the first military flight nurses, served in North Africa, Sicily, and mainland Italy.

During World War II the number of African American nurses in the army was limited by quota, and black nurses could only be assigned to treat black soldiers in the segregated army of the 1940s. Fort Huachuca, Arizona, was one of the major training bases for these troops and had a large medical detachment

These African American army nurses served troops at Fort Huachuca, near the Mexican border.

at the all-black hospital. As many as a hundred nurses were stationed at Fort Huachuca at one time, but many went overseas from there to Liberia, England, Burma, and New Guinea.

Lillie Emory Skinner worked at the hospital for a year, when she met and married her husband, an army dentist, before they were each assigned to separate parts of the world. "I was ordered to England and he was sent to the Pacific. We didn't see each other for two years, until the war was over. I was at the 168th Station Hospital and cared for all nationalities, except Americans, including German prisoners. Some were Nazis and even the other Germans were afraid of them. We weren't allowed on their ward without an armed guard."

Not all military nurses met such excitement. Dorothy Payne Cady, a graduate of Yuma Union High School, was enrolled at the Good Samaritan Hospital School of Nursing in Phoenix when she heard that Pearl Harbor had been bombed. A senior student, she and several classmates decided they would join the army or navy when they graduated. Dorothy chose the Navy Nurse Corps and was assigned to duty in Southern California, first at Camp Pendleton and then San Diego. Dorothy recalls with a laugh, "I didn't get far from home, though I wanted to join the navy and see the world."

FOR THE FIRST time, manufacturing plants pleaded for women to join the assembly lines "to get the job done." Work in the Arizona defense plants at Goodyear Aircraft Corporation, AiResearch, and Aluminum Company of America (ALCOA) rapidly increased production of aircraft parts and other war-related products. The nickname "Rosie the Riveter" was soon applied to women working in manufacturing jobs.

Edna Gleim graduated from Phoenix Union High School and Arizona State Teachers College at Tempe, then taught school in the Goldroad mining district in Mohave County for a year. The mine closed when the war began because gold was not considered a necessary metal, so Edna returned to Phoenix to take a job at Goodyear Aircraft. "I worked as a riveter on the grave-yard shift for three-and-a-half years, making airplane parts. I liked that shift because it gave me time to go horseback riding and do other things in the day-time," she explained.

Edna's life took another career change in January 1945 when a government scholarship offer was posted on the bulletin board at Goodyear for training as an occupational therapist. "After being selected," Edna recalls, "I went to the University of Southern California for training, then worked for Civil Service and in the army active reserve, from which I retired."

Elizabeth Groom was at the Fox Theater in Phoenix with her fiancé, Lee Blanton, on December 7, 1941. Lee was in the Army Air Corps, stationed at Luke Field, and he returned to the base as soon as they heard the war news. Elizabeth goes on to tell, "We got married in January 1942. I was living with my parents in 1944 while my husband

A civilian woman rigging parachutes at Marana Army Air Field. Women served at most Arizona bases.

was overseas, and I heard about the defense work, making metal for airplanes at ALCOA Aluminum. The plant was at Thirty-fifth Avenue and Van Buren Street. There were three furnaces in the remelt room where metals were poured into molds for ingots. I was a pit boss, pouring metal into the molds. I had to wear gloves with gauntlets, a hat with a scarf on my neck, long-sleeve shirts, pants, and steel-toed shoes for protection. There was a possibility of burns from the hot metal, so my father and husband asked me to quit, and I did."

Agnes Begay and her husband and children moved from Many Farms on the Navajo reservation in October 1943 to work and live at the Navajo Ordnance Depot, west of Flagstaff. In an oral history in the book *Navajos and World War II,* Agnes tells of being hired by the Bellemont Corporation to work in the personnel office, and as a security guard, a position requiring her to wear a uniform and carry a pistol. "We were assigned nice two-bedroom quarters, and education and child care was provided for our children. There were all different tribes, mostly Navajos.

"When the war ended in Europe, bells started ringing and we all thought the Japanese had attacked us. Everyone started running here and there." After working at the ordnance depot two years, they were ready to return home. Continuing the oral history, Agnes proudly goes on to relate, "My brother had been taken prisoner in the Philippines, and when he was released, we all returned to Many Farms together, where a medicine man performed the ceremony to welcome him home."

SOME WOMEN TOOK to the air to aid the war effort.

"I was going to do it or pop! I knew I would regret it my whole life if I didn't go," cries Evelyn Jackson, at her home in Apache Junction. Selected to be in the second class of the Civilian Pilot Training Program in Globe, she loved every aspect of flying from the first moment.

The U.S. government began pilot training in 1939 all over the country because there weren't enough pilots to go to war, if it was necessary. This program was in response to Hitler's troops invading European countries and the warnings of a major conflict that loomed in the future. To keep anyone from thinking that the United States was making plans for war, a sort of smoke screen was arranged that allowed women to join the flying classes, in very small numbers. For every ten men, one woman was admitted to the program. Hundreds of women applied as soon as it was announced.

Evelyn Hicks Stewart Jackson married right after graduating from Globe High School, and she had always wanted to fly. "My husband didn't like the idea, but when I passed the physical test, and was in the ground school, I couldn't stop. I got my license in 1940. It cost too much to fly very often, so I was slow at building up many hours."

When the war did start, a program to have women pilots work for the military, but as civilians, was implemented by Jacqueline Cochran, one of the early woman pilot pioneers. Evelyn tells of meeting this outstanding aviator: "She came to Phoenix to interview women for the WASP [Women Airforce Service Pilots], and though it took all day to get there from Globe, I went. She told me I didn't have enough flying hours to qualify, but since the program was just beginning, I should wait a few weeks, and they would lower the requirements. Three weeks later I got a letter to report to Sweetwater, Texas, for training with the WASP. My husband and I were separated and nothing held me back from fulfilling my dream. It didn't take me long to pack and head for the train to Texas."

The Women Airforce Service Pilots were assigned to fill flying jobs that would release male military pilots from routine flying and allow them to go into combat. More than a thousand women qualified as WASPs. Their job was to ferry airplanes from factories to bases across the continental United States. They also towed targets for male gunnery students to shoot at, towed gliders, flew repaired planes as test pilots, and became bombing instructors.

"I received my wings in October 1943, and my mother came to the graduation, though she wasn't thrilled about the whole idea. I was stationed in Enid, Oklahoma, where I flew basic trainers. We all loved what we were doing," exclaims Evelyn, "and were so crazy about flying. Once I heard someone comment as I was walking across a runway with some others, 'There go the luckiest girls in the world.'"

Ina Petsch flew with the Women Airforce Service Pilots (WASPs).

Ina Barkley became a WASP after taking flying lessons at Arizona State Teachers College at Tempe, where she majored in physical education. A graduate of Tucson High School, she received her WASP wings in May 1944 and flew twin engine planes based at Coffeyville, Kansas. Ina met Roy Petsch when she landed at Perrin Field, Texas. He was the duty officer, whose job was to meet all the planes. When she and the other WASP pilot got out, he asked

RUTH REINHOLD

★ ★ ★

Ruth Reinhold served as a wartime flight instructor, as a captain in the Arizona Civil Air Patrol, and later as Senator Barry Goldwater's personal pilot.

The Civilian Pilot Training Program that taught Evelyn Jackson, Ina Petsch, and Byrd Granger to fly included a prominent Arizona aviator and author as instructor at Sky Harbor Airport. Ruth Reinhold came to Arizona from Los Angeles in 1933 and moved into the rapidly emerging world of flying. In 1942 she won her multi-engine license. She taught civilian and military pilots the primary training segment of their course and taught instrument flying to pilots who were ferrying four-engine B-24s overseas. When Ruth (who was just about five feet tall) flew, her plane was often referred to as pilotless because the tower operator could hardly see her in the cockpit. She also participated in search-and-rescue operations as a member of the Arizona wing of the Civil Air Patrol with the rank of captain.

Her postwar achievements included induction into the Arizona Women's Hall of Fame, becoming personal pilot for Senator Barry Goldwater during his presidential campaign and flying with him for twenty years, and receiving many important aviation awards. After retiring from commercial flying, Ruth Reinhold authored *Sky Pioneering: Arizona in Aviation History,* published by the University of Arizona Press.

---

where the pilot was. Not believing that it was a woman, he climbed up in the plane to check. They kept in touch, married, and eventually moved to Phoenix to raise a family.

Arizona became one of the premier flight training areas during the war, with military air fields throughout the state. The WASPs flew in and out of them all, and were based at Douglas, Kingman, Luke, Marana, Williams, and Yuma air fields. Over the years, many of these women returned to live permanently in Arizona, including Byrd Howell Granger, who thoroughly documented the story of the WASPs in her book *On Final Approach.* Dr. Granger became a professor at the University of Arizona, where she received numerous awards for her work about Arizona and its history.

Years later Ina Petsch and Byrd Granger became active in the effort to obtain official government recognition for the WASPs, who had never received any benefits despite their having worked exclusively with the military. Even before they were disbanded in December 1944, when one of them died on duty, her family was responsible for the cost of shipping the body back home. There were thirty-eight WASP fatalities recorded, two of them in Arizona.

Evelyn Jackson recalls, "When the WASP program ended before the war was over, we were all so mad because we would have flown for nothing. I just packed up my things and took the train to Phoenix and returned to Globe. I never piloted again, but married, and lived happily on a ranch."

THE WOMEN'S SERVICES that were established in 1942 set quotas for each state, and two hundred WAVES were expected from Arizona. Among the local inductees was Ensign Marjorie Osborn, daughter of Governor Sidney P. Osborn.

When the U.S. Navy and U.S. Coast Guard sent recruiters every month to the YWCA on Adams Street in Phoenix to interview women for the WAVES and SPARs, Gertrude "Skeeter" Williams was there to join either group. "I showed up for two years, until I was twenty years old, and finally old enough to enlist. My fourth-grade teacher, Martha Jane Oliver, had become Director of the Y, and told me the navy was the best choice."

Many Arizonans know that William Garland, founder of Garland's Oak Creek Lodge, is a World War II veteran and was a prisoner of war in Germany. When Bill married Georgiana Isham in 1946, few knew she had been overseas for almost two years.

At the start of the war Georgiana, who had grown up in Flagstaff, was teaching at a grammar school in Phoenix. A friend told her about the Red Cross workers who had gone overseas to almost every station where the United States was involved in the war. She joined the Red Cross in June 1944 and went through their training in Washington, D.C. The next nineteen months were beyond the imagination of a girl from Flagstaff, as she worked and traveled throughout the China-Burma-India (CBI) theater of war.

"We sailed from the East Coast on the USS *President Wilson,* a troop ship," Georgiana recalls, "and fifty-three days later landed in Bombay, India. Then we went by troop train to Calcutta and from there, my first airplane ride, to Karachi."

GERTRUDE "SKEETER" WILLIAMS

★   ★   ★

Gertrude Williams was a member of the navy's WAVES.

Skeeter Williams was a senior at Phoenix Union High School on December 7, 1941, when she heard about the bombing in Hawaii. "We were at a church outing and the boys were all concerned whether they would get to graduate, and some wanted to enlist right away. After graduation I went to work for Mountain States Telephone & Telegraph Company for two years, while waiting to be old enough to enlist. We all were affected by the rationing coupons, and mostly I remember having to wait in line at Korricks department store to buy silk hose.

"Another girl from the phone company, Pat McIntosh, left for boot camp along with me and when we were leaving a big crowd was at the train station in Phoenix to see us off. Besides our families, office workers and telephone linemen took time off to say goodbye. Along the way two other Arizona girls, Anne Mihelich from Douglas and Herminia 'Minnie' Morales from Morenci, joined us on the train. When we got off in Chicago, the Shore Patrol directed us to a troop train full of hundreds of women, all going to Hunter College in the Bronx, New York. From the train station in New York, we walked to subways to get to Hunter, where the navy held six weeks of boot camp for WAVES.

"I chose to attend Storekeepers School, which was held at Georgia State College for Women in Milledgeville. It lasted for three months, and then I was assigned to Oakland, California.

"When we were at home on leave the phone company took portrait photos of all former employees. They put up a billboard with the names of all navy women from Arizona.

"I really enjoyed the two years I was a WAVE, and would have stayed longer if asked," Skeeter remembers. "But when the war was over, everyone was discharged, sort of automatically. I returned to the phone company, served four years in the Naval Reserve, and retired from work after forty years."

Georgiana worked in the entertainment division, setting up recreation centers for GIs to come to when they had time off. Georgiana continues, "They played cards and games. We fed them and provided tours all over India. My second post was in Subatu, north of New Delhi." Exotic experiences opened up, such as being entertained by a maharaja and touring leper colonies. At the end of the war in August 1945, she was working in Madras, and from there went back to Calcutta. "While the GIs were waiting for transportation to return home," Georgiana Garland remembers, "I set up a Red Cross club for them in a former jute mill. I came back on a troop ship and returned eventually to Arizona from halfway around the world."

Rose Cahall, a member of the army's Women's Army Auxiliary Corps (WAACs), is shown wearing her first dress hat, called a "Hobby" in honor of the first WAAC director, Oveta Culp Hobby.

Rose Bisirri Cahall arrived in Arizona by train in May 1943, assigned to Luke Field. Rose owned a beauty shop in West Virginia but sold it to join the Women's Army Auxiliary Corps (WAAC). It didn't take long for her to begin to enjoy her new life, working in the post office at the base. She stayed in Arizona after the war, as did thousands of other veterans.

"I remember how barren the land was around the base, and took advantage of the three-day passes we got to Prescott, where we stayed at the Hassayampa Hotel. It reminded me of home in West Virginia. Every six months I was able to go back on furlough, but looked forward to returning to Arizona. The San Carlos Hotel in Phoenix was another popular place to go on a pass, and their dinners were a great treat from food on the base."

In July 1943 the WAAC dropped the word "Auxiliary" and became known as the WAC. Women were in all the services, but nurses and WACs were the only military women to go overseas during the war.

"I was listening to a football game on the radio with my family when an announcer broke in with news of the bombing of Pearl Harbor," states Fran Griffin McClendon. As soon as the army formed the WAAC, she enlisted. Leaving her home in New York by troop train, Fran found herself stationed at Fort Huachuca, where she spent the next year. "I was a supply specialist, working in the warehouse. I enjoyed the work, but also took as many passes to Tucson and Phoenix as I could. I had relatives in Phoenix, and would take the train up there to visit. You can imagine how interesting it was to a girl from New York to see something like South Mountain Park."

"When we became WACs," explains Fran, "I was offered the chance to attend Officer Candidate School [OCS], and left Arizona. After graduating from OCS, the army sent me to Europe as an officer with the 6888th Central Postal Battalion. I stayed in the army and retired after twenty-six years, but returned to Arizona with my husband." Fran McClendon became well known in the antique business in Arizona as owner of The Glass Urn in Mesa.

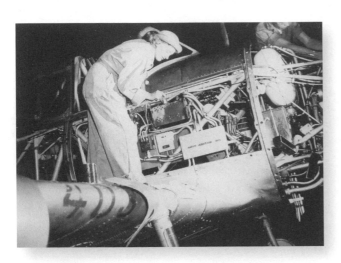

Trained as aircraft mechanics "to get the job done," women and men worked side by side at Marana Air Field, as well as at other air bases in the United States.

Janette Arkie enlisted in the WAC in 1943, hoping to join her husband, who was already in the army. A graduate of Tucson High School, she arrived in Daytona Beach, Florida, for basic training to find the nearby Atlantic Ocean not to her liking. A member of the Papago tribe, Janette and several others from desert areas did not like any part of the training that took them near or in the water. Eventually she was assigned to Victorville, California. "I worked with the pilot training program and, using charts, I evaluated the men as they went through training.

"When I heard my brother was killed just three months before the war ended, I cried. But I realized that you have to take what comes and just keep going. My husband and I were never stationed together, so I got out of the army as soon as the war was over."

Polly Rosenbaum was working in her garden on December 7, 1941. "It was a beautiful sunny day, and my husband called from work and said, 'Did you hear the news? We're at war.' We lived in Hayden, at the mining camp run by Kennecott Copper Company. I was stunned, and turned on the radio.

"The whole town was stunned. Some of the men were World War I veterans and were soon called back. My husband was a veteran, but wasn't called. High school students all joined as soon as school was finished. Women went to work to fill in as men left for war, mostly in offices. I taught high school and then grammar school. In Globe and Miami the women had to take on big jobs, and did whatever was needed in the mines, including driving big huge trucks."

William George Rosenbaum had been trained as a pharmacist and opened the town's first drug store. "But the hours were too long, so he sold it and became a foreman at the mill," Polly explains. "He was in the legislature, which met every two years, and we would stay at the Adams Hotel when we went to Phoenix.

"During the war years there was a feeling of cooperation among everyone. The mine, mill, and smelter never stopped running. Everyone in the town learned first aid, and took it seriously because we felt that if the bombers ever came over the U.S., they would try to hit the mines. We had good instructors from the Red Cross, with classes in the church basement.

"Once we put together a program to help with morale. We used to have dances and parties to keep everyone in good spirits. This time we were all gathered in a big hall, and everyone was seated. Mary, a woman who worked at the bank, started towards the front, and seemed to faint halfway there. We rushed to revive her, and bandaged her and splinted her, and did whatever we knew how, then carried her up front on a litter. At first there was concern, but then they realized we were just demonstrating our skills. The men all said, 'The women did a darn good job.' That was the entertainment that night.

"I'll never forget when we heard about the first casualty in Hayden," Polly says with sadness. "It was a flyer. The man who ran the depot called the family's house and wanted to talk to the husband. The wife told him to tell her the news, because she knew why he was calling. In the next few days, the whole town, absolutely everyone, came to the house to offer sympathy."

Women shared coupons with each other, helped with clothes or whatever was hard to get, Polly remembers. "Food and supplies came by train, so it always seemed to take a long time. Food rationing meant no sugar or flour. Gas was rationed too, and we only had unpaved roads to either Tucson or Phoenix. But sometimes if we got enough gas coupons to go to Nogales, we would pick up some Mexican sugar. It made good desserts, which everyone missed. We had to use margarine instead of butter.

"Once my husband won some kind of bet with a man who owned a dairy, and when he was offered the ten dollars, which was a lot of money in those days, he said he wanted butter instead."

Polly recalls, "When the war ended, we heard the news on the radio, and I remember being afraid to believe it."

Polly Rosenbaum (her given first name is Edwynne), took over her husband's seat in the Arizona legislature when he died in 1949, and was elected continuously until 1995, when she retired at age ninety-six.

IT WAS THE custom during the war for families throughout the United States to display a service flag in the window, showing that at least one member of the family was in the military. The flag, approximately nine inches wide by eleven inches long, had one or more blue stars centered on a white background with a red border. Some were store-bought, and others were lovingly stitched by hand. When a military family member died, a gold star replaced a blue one.

Maria Petra Yanez de Soza, who was born in Benson, was among those in Arizona who hung a service flag with multiple stars in the window of her home, showing that six sons served in the military during the 1940s. Maria might have covered a window with these flags as she also had three brothers and one sister on active duty during World War II.

After Maria's oldest son was killed in action aboard the USS *Chicago* in January 1943, a gold star was centered on her flag, surrounded by five blue stars.

Beginning when eight Arizona men were entombed in the USS *Arizona*, after it sank in Pearl Harbor, gold stars appeared in windows throughout the state, bringing sorrow to the mothers and families of servicemen and servicewomen. The symbol of what the war meant to thousands might be summed up in the meaning of the gold star.

5

AMERICAN INDIANS
AND THE WAR EFFORT

SHARON S. MAGEE

THE COLD STEEL of a rifle pressed into William McCabe's back. Since all he was doing was searching for orange juice, he thought one of his buddies was joking around. "I kept digging," he says years later when relating the incident.

"Come on, you dumb Jap, let's go!" the soldier wielding the rifle ordered. McCabe froze.

As a Navajo Indian, his genes, the ones he had inherited from his Athabaskan ancestors who crossed the land bridge from Asia many centuries before, gave him a slightly Asian look. That, he knew, along with his brown skin, raven-black hair, and short stature, could cause military personnel to mistake him for a Japanese soldier. They were known to infiltrate American military camps. McCabe also knew a firing squad awaited those who were caught.

One of the Navajo code talkers who used their native tongue to send coded messages during World War II, McCabe and his fellow marines had won a bitterly contested victory over Japanese forces on Guadalcanal and were packing up to leave. Simultaneously, U.S. Army personnel poured onto the beach, preparing to mop up the vestiges of the Japanese occupation. Chow dumps sprouted like errant anthills as the army transported food supplies ashore. McCabe's craving for orange juice had pulled him toward those chow dumps.

The soldier took him to the provost marshal. McCabe's marine uniform, dog tags, and fluent English carried little weight. "There's a lot of Japanese that go to Ohio State, you know," the provost marshal said, and, because they had no facilities to hold prisoners, ended the interview with, "I don't want the Jap. Go shoot him."

Fifteen soldiers surrounded McCabe, some with machine guns, and the sergeant of the guard held a cocked .45 against his back. They marched him away. "I didn't know whether to run, or cry, or do anything," McCabe remembers. "I had my hands up. I kept them up high all the way and didn't move them at all."

Desperate, he told them, "My outfit's down there," but he wasn't quite sure where; sweat poured down his face, making it difficult to see. Someone believed him, or possibly thought it a good idea to check out his story before shooting him.

When at last they found McCabe's fellow marines, their lackadaisical, "Yeah, he's one of ours," didn't cut it with the sergeant of the guard. He wanted proof positive, and he wasn't getting it. As he turned to go, ready to carry out the provost marshal's command, a lieutenant appeared.

"We caught this man over there in our yard," the sergeant told him. "We think he's a Jap. If you guys don't identify him, we're gonna go back and shoot him."

Not only did the lieutenant identify McCabe to the army's satisfaction, but the marines assigned him "a real tall white guy" as a bodyguard who followed him everywhere, even to the shower and the head.

Samuel Holiday, also a code talker, had a similar experience on Saipan. When he was the last man out of a water hole after skinny-dipping with his buddies, a military policeman spotted him and saw only a short brown-skinned man with black hair, who was most definitely out of uniform. "I turned around and they had the bayonet right between my eyes," Holiday recalls. As with McCabe, his unit vouched for him.

McCabe's and Holiday's stories are not unique. Because of this inclination to misidentification, the marines commonly assigned bodyguards to code talkers.

Earlier, when the Japanese threw down the gauntlet at Pearl Harbor on December 7, 1941, America's native sons were among the first to answer the call to arms. This threat to their native land evoked their warrior spirit.

In Arizona, as elsewhere, the need and desire to defend their homeland was so great that Arizona's Indians traveled by horse, wagon, or their own two feet to enlist. The day after the bombing of Pearl Harbor, James M. Stewart, super-intendent of the Navajo reservation, looked out his window and saw dozens of pony-tailed men in faded jeans and dusty boots, old muskets or hunting rifles in hand, and personal items wrapped in red bandanas, ready to fight. Many stood for hours in the snow and cold at Fort Defiance, Arizona, to sign their draft cards. Boys of fifteen and sixteen left classrooms or family sheep herds and, claiming to be eighteen, enlisted. Navajo Sidney Bedoni hitchhiked sixty miles, thirty-four in pouring rain, to get his parents' permission to join the marines, and then hitchhiked back to the recruiting station.

Writer Estelle Webb Thomas wrote of this eagerness to serve, "They are itching to fight 'He-Who-Smells-His-Moustache' [Hitler] and 'Man-With-Gourd-Chin' [Mussolini], and most of all do they long for a crack at the Slit-Eye People."

For many, practical reasons entered into the equation. Code talker Wilson Keedah, Sr., says, "I went to war because there were no jobs on the reservation."

But patriotism was the most often mentioned reason for joining up. "When I was inducted into the service," Navajo David Patterson recalls, "one of the commitments I made was that I was willing to die for my country—the U.S.—the Navajo Nation, and my family."

The navy attracted many of Arizona's American Indians. This Navajo sailor on leave visited his family at their hogan.

This patriotism by Arizona's Indians is remarkable. The U.S. government had usurped their lands and freedom. Fewer than eighty years before, in 1864, Kit Carson's scorched-earth policy had forced the Navajos off their land and on the Long Walk that saw thousands of Navajos die. Additionally, at the time of the United States' entry into World War II, the government was slaughtering four hundred thousand head of Navajo livestock under the auspices of the Stock Reduction Program. In a further insult, Indians in Arizona did not yet have voting rights.

The swastika, symbol of Nazi Germany but also a good-luck symbol to many Indian tribes, was banned by the Apaches, Hopis, Navajos, and Papago at the outset of World War II for use in basket and blanket weaving and other crafts.

Adding their own brand of confusion, Nazi sympathizers encouraged native men to resist the registration process.

The Indians would have none of it. They abhorred the Nazis' attitude of racial superiority. A young Indian said of a possible Nazi regime, "We are not Aryans and we [w]ould be used as slaves." In 1940, the Apaches, Papagos (now Tohono O'odham), Navajos, and Hopis formally banned the use of the popular swastika design, an ancient good-luck symbol, from their crafts.

Whatever the reason for joining the fight, no other ethnic group made a greater per capita contribution. In 1940 American Indians in the United States numbered 350,000. More than 44,000 would see service during World War II. In 1942, the selective service reported that 99 percent of all eligible American Indian men had registered. Journalist Richard Neuberger wrote in that same year, "Army officials maintain that if the entire population was enlisting in the same proportion as Indians there would be no need for Selective Service."

The rejection rate for Arizona Indians ran high, however. About 45 percent did not meet military standards. Illiteracy and health were the main culprits, with trachoma and tuberculosis being the major ills. Age also exempted many. A thirty-seven-year-old Pima man said, "I [was] rejected seven times on account of having old."

These rejections infuriated many chompin'-at-the-bit warriors across the country. A Chippewa, when told he was exempted because he had no teeth, said, "I don't want to bite 'em—I want to shoot 'em." Another, from Arizona, given a pass because he was too heavy, said, "Don't want to run; want to fight."

Still, they would not be deterred. In Arizona, Papagos without basic reading and writing skills learned to write their names and memorized enough English phrases to pass muster. On the Navajo reservation, where the illiteracy rate was the highest, leaders established remedial English classes.

American Indian enthusiasm had not been nearly as great when Congress enacted the first peacetime draft law in 1940. Several East Coast tribes either

★ ★

THE THREAT FROM THE SOUTH

During 1940 and 1941 rumors abounded that the Japanese would invade the United States from the south, and that the southern Arizona Indians were eager to join the "yellow peril" on the warpath against white people.

The authorities took these rumors seriously. Elmer Flaccus wrote in the *Journal of Arizona History*, "Inside every Yaqui, Pima or Papago (it was suspected), lurked a fifth columnist who kept his rail cutters handy and waited only for the Japanese arrival to start severing tracks." A note in an air-raid warden's manual outlined plans to evacuate Tucson's citizens to the Skyline Country Club area where "they would never find us."

Former senator and presidential candidate Barry Goldwater, who served as a gunnery instructor during World War II, said, "We had warnings about the Japanese possibly attacking us from the Mexican border. We had to fly an escort ship with every airliner that passed."

Legend has it that a Japanese commando group landed near Libertad, Sonora, but an American battalion wiped them out before they could cross the border. Japanese kamikaze pilots supposedly were shot down as they raced toward a Pacific Coast installation, intent on blowing it up. The government kept these incidents secret, so the legend goes, so as not to cause panic among the American people.

Many Arizona American Indians served in the army. This group undergoes machine gun training at Fort Sill, Oklahoma.

claimed not to be United States citizens, although all Indians had been granted citizenship in 1924, or claimed that as sovereign nations they were not obligated to register to fight in a white man's war. In Arizona a group of Navajos refused to register for fear they would be hauled away in big trucks. A Navajo headman convinced his people they need not register unless Hitler invaded the United States.

The Hopis and the Zunis claimed conscientious objector status; however, the Hopis later agreed that nothing in their religious beliefs forbade them from participating in the war effort. Authorities arrested six Hopis in June 1941 for refusing to register. They belonged to a group known as the Hostiles, who opposed any government interference in their lives. Five of the six served a year and a day in a prison camp. The Hopis would become the only tribe in America prosecuted for draft evasion.

In another case, John Collier, head of the Bureau of Indian Affairs (BIA), requested and received deferment for a young Zuni sun priest when tribal leaders pleaded that they needed him to bring rain not only to the reservation, but "to the whole world."

On a remote part of the Papago reservation in southern Arizona, in a tiny village called Stoa Pitk, a charismatic, aged leader and medicine man named Pia Machita (a.k.a. Chief Grinding Stone) urged his men to dodge the draft. The old chief was arrested, convicted—not for draft evasion, but for assaulting a federal officer—and sent to prison for eighteen months.

Machita proved the exception. Beyond his small, isolated village, the Papagos signed up in record numbers.

When the United States declared war in 1941, members of every one of Arizona's twenty-one tribes, even the pacifist Hopis and Zunis, participated in some way in the war effort.

PIA MACHITA

★ ★ ★

P ia Machita walked from his fields in the early morning hours after watching a plane carrying U. S. Marshal Ben McKinney circle his Papago village of Stoa Pitk. He milked his cows, then ate breakfast. Outside deputies waited patiently for him. Machita knew the running and hiding were over. He stepped outside and held out his wrists for the steel manacles.

It had been a long struggle for this man who, his people said, could "make magic stronger than any modern invention the white man may have."

For years Machita had fought against anything American. Rejecting the Gadsden Purchase that annexed Papago lands to the United States, he flew a Mexican flag over his small village. Machita had counseled Papago parents to ignore census takers and to refuse to send their children to government schools. He opposed inoculation of cattle and opposed white Roman Catholic priests. He did, however, allow Mexican priests, whom he called "little brown brothers," to minister to his people. In 1936, he blocked, for a time, the construction of the El Paso natural gas pipeline.

Many considered Machita a maverick, while others deemed him simply an old man trying to preserve the traditional lifeway of the Papago. Authorities pretty much ignored Machita's antics until 1940, on the eve of World War II, when he took an antidraft stance.

Machita's grandson Carlos Manuel remembers the night the BIA agents came for his grandfather. "He was asleep in his bed and they pulled him out of there," he relates. Machita called for help and a crowd of angry Papago surrounded the BIA agents. They shoved the agents to the ground and kicked them, seriously injuring one. An agent set off a tear-gas bomb. "That's when everybody stopped fighting," Manuel says.

The Papago had won the battle, but not the war. The agents limped back to Tucson but returned several times, only to find that Machita and his men had fled into the hills.

Now, on May 19, 1941, it was ended.

While Machita awaited trial in the Pima County Jail in Tucson, McKinney took him to see an army airplane and for a ride in an elevator to the top of a bank building to view the city. Machita was amazed to see a city in which more than two or three white people lived.

His trial was held in July. Many thought he would get probation, but after Judge A. M. Sanes intoned, "Denying the sovereignty of the United States is an offense far too serious in these times," he sentenced Machita to eighteen months in California's Terminal Island Federal Prison.

Machita began to change while in prison. He sent word to Stoa Pitk that they should send their children to school and insisted the road be improved so the buses could get through.

On his release, he returned to a much-changed Stoa Pitk, where he lived out his days. He is buried there.

As many as forty thousand Indian men and women nationwide went to work in defense industries off the reservations. Approximately 20 percent of the Navajo tribe labored in the industrial segment, most at the Navajo Ordnance Depot near Flagstaff. The San Carlos Apaches counted 136 tribal members in the military—70 percent of whom were volunteers—while another 235 men had jobs away from the reservation. Both Hopis and Apaches worked on railway construction gangs, while Papagos labored in the Phelps Dodge copper mine in Ajo and in the cotton fields. Many Pima worked off-reservation in agriculture and railroad construction.

Some eight hundred native women across the country elected to enlist in the Women's Army Corps (WACs), the Women Accepted for Volunteer Emergency Service (WAVES), and the Women Airforce Service Pilots (WASPs). They did so to further their education and acquire skills, but more important to aid their fighting men. Many attempted, unsuccessfully, to register in the male branches of the military.

American Indians also dug deeply into their pockets. By 1944, they had purchased $50 million in war bonds and donated generously to the Red Cross and the army and navy relief societies. In Arizona, a Navajo man trudged miles on foot to a trading post to contribute thirty cents to the war effort—ten cents each for himself, his wife, and his son. Another contributed his entire life savings of seven cents. Navajo families who had been awarded fifteen thousand dollars in the death of six children in a train-bus accident used five thousand of those dollars to buy war bonds and stamps. The Papagos ranked among the biggest contributors per capita in Arizona. With a tribal population of five thousand, they purchased war bonds in excess of ten thousand dollars. Wealthy rancher and Navajo tribal leader, eighty-three-year-old Henry Chee Dodge purchased thirty thousand dollars' worth of bonds. Following his lead, well-to-do Navajo ranchers and government employees pledged 20 percent of their income for bonds. The Navajos contributed silver jewelry, mutton, rugs, and corn—considered their staff of life—to the Red Cross. Almost everyone planted victory gardens. Only two hundred strong, the Havasupai, living on the floor of the Grand Canyon, plowed and planted a gulch bottom for "the starving people across the sea."

Meanwhile overseas the Japanese controlled the islands of the South Pacific and broke U.S. codes at will. The Japanese captured thousands of American soldiers in the battles of Bataan and Corregidor, in which more than three hundred Indians fought, including a descendant of Apache war-leader Geronimo.

Desperation reigned and this desperation was about to make heroes of some 420 Navajo men.

A civil engineer and World War I veteran named Philip Johnston had a solution for the code problem. He had grown up on the Navajo reservation and spoke the language fluently. Johnston suggested building a code around this language, using Navajos working in pairs to transmit and receive messages. It would be unbreakable, he promised. After rigorous tests, which proved the Navajos could unerringly encode, transmit, and decode a three-line message into English in twenty seconds versus the thirty minutes needed by machine, the marines bought into his plan.

In 1942 the Marine Corps recruited the first twenty-nine code talkers—

COUNTING CADENCE THE NAVAJO WAY

During basic training a competition was held to decide the best-drilled platoon. When a platoon of Chinese Americans counted cadence in their native tongue, the white drill instructor (DI) of a platoon of Navajos determined they would not be outdone. He ordered them to count cadence in Navajo. But the Navajo numbers, lacking the rhythm of "Hup, two, three, four," did not lend themselves well to such an activity.

Code talker William McCabe recalls, "Well, we'd go three or four steps while we were counting 'one.'" They decided to "mix things up, using some bad words," which included names for the DI that were less than flattering. Soon, McCabe says, "We were laughing so hard we couldn't march."

The DI caught on and ordered no more counting cadence except in English.

PHILIP JOHNSTON

★ ★ ★

Marine Technical Sergeant Philip Johnston, a white man raised on the Navajo reservation, played a key role in developing the secret code used by Navajo code talkers in the South Pacific. He is pictured here during a tour of recruiting duty on the Navajo Reservation in 1942.

Philip Johnston sat in his office staring, unseeing, out the window. It was 1942 and his idol, General Jonathan Wainwright, was getting beaten at every turn by the Japanese in the South Pacific. Johnston jumped up and began to pace, pondering a major problem: No code remained unbroken for more than a few hours.

Although born to English-speaking white parents, Johnston spoke Navajo fluently. At the age of four he had traveled with his parents to the Navajo reservation, where his parents served as missionaries. As young Philip grew up, he played with Navajo children, and it was natural he would speak their language. He became so adept at it that at age nine, he was asked to translate for President Theodore Roosevelt on a Navajo visit to the White House.

While he mulled over Pearl Harbor, Bataan, and Corregidor, he remembered the Navajo language and a plan began to form. He contacted Major James E. Jones, Area Signal Officer at Camp Pendleton, California. "What if we could develop a code in the Navajo language?" Johnston asked.

"That's been tried," responded the harried officer.

"Yes, but what I'm proposing," persisted Johnston, "is a code within the Navajo language—one that would be unbreakable." After due deliberation the major asked to see a demonstration.

Two weeks later Johnston appeared at Camp Elliott in San Diego with four English-speaking Navajos. By the end of the demonstration, no one needed further convincing. General Clayton B. Vogel, who had been observing, said, "I've never seen better translations in any language." The Navajo code talkers were born.

Johnston, a veteran of World War I and a civil engineer, chafed at not being a part of the program. He asked Jones if any way existed for him to participate. Within days, the marines issued waivers, and he became Staff Sergeant Philip Johnston in the USMC Reserve, responsible for the training and directing of the Navajo code talkers.

When the recruiting of Navajos as talkers dwindled to nothing, Johnston left the service, taking up civilian life, again working as a civil engineer.

some as young as fifteen and sixteen—from the Navajo reservation and Indian boarding schools. They traveled to Camp Elliott in San Diego for basic training. Here in the world of Semper Fi they proved themselves without peer, recording unprecedented high scores. "No strenuous drill or forced march [was] too tough," an officer remarked.

After basic training and then training in communications at Camp Pendleton, these twenty-nine Navajo boys and men, now the 382nd Platoon, United States Marine Corp (USMC), devised the code.

The code was brilliant in its simplicity. They assigned Navajo names to what would eventually be 450 military terms. For instance, a battleship was a *lo-tso* (whale), while a bomber was a *jay-sho* (buzzard), and a howitzer was a *be-el-don-ts-quodi* (short big gun). In those cases when they needed to spell out a word, they assigned Navajo words for each letter of the English alphabet: *Tkin* (ice), *yeh-hes* (itch), *and* a-chi (intestine), for example, all represented the letter "I."

An officer who spent his entire military career in cryptography remembers, "It sounded like gibberish. We couldn't even transcribe it, much less crack it." A Navajo, unfamiliar with the code, called it "crazy Navajo." And a San Diego newspaper reported it resembled "the call of a Tibetan monk and the sound of a hot water bottle being emptied."

Because the code was classified as top secret, they wrote nothing down. To add to the complexity, they continually updated it. McCabe explains, "In Navajo everything is in memory. From the

Navajo code talkers Private First Class John Goodluck of Lukachukai, right, and Private First Class George H. Kirk of Leupp are shown on a hillside in Guam. Both had combat experience against the Japanese. (Marine Corps photograph, courtesy of the National Archives; no. 94236)

songs, prayers, everything, it's all in memory. So we didn't have no trouble."

Between 1942 and 1945, they made no error on any message, no matter how dire the situation. A code talker remembers, "Sometimes we had to crawl, had to run, had to lie partly submerged in a swamp or in a lagoon, or in the dead of heat, pinned under fire. But there was no problem. We transmitted our messages under any and all conditions."

He recalls one terrifying occasion: "I had a cord tied around my wrist and to my buddy's hand. If I pulled the string and he pulled back there in the dark, I knew he was still alive. One night a screaming Japanese soldier leaped into the trench and killed my partner with a samurai sword before other marines could shoot him. I had to stay there sending messages with my friend's blood gushing over me. They tell me that in spite of what happened, every syllable of my message came through."

Because the government felt they might use the code talkers in future wars, they were sworn to secrecy. Many never told their families what they did in the war. "I was a radioman" was a typical response. Others divulged their roles only after the government declassified the code in 1968. "They said we'd go to the firing squad if we told about it," one code talker explains.

The code was so secret that Navajos untrained in its use could not decode it. When the Japanese captured army Sergeant Joe Kieyoomia at Bataan and discovered he was Navajo, they tried to torture the secret from him. He could translate the strange sounding words into English, but could not say how they related to the code. Finally, at Nagasaki prison on the Japanese mainland, they stripped him and left him in twenty-seven degree weather on an icy parade ground covered in six inches of snow. "The guard said if I moved, he would shoot me," Kieyoomia recalls. When they finally granted him permission to return to his cell, his feet were frozen to the ground. The guard pushed him, and the skin tore from the bottom of his feet. "I left my soles on that parade ground," he says.

Only once did word of the code leak out. James Stewart, the Navajo reservation superintendent, reported on the project in the June 1943 *Arizona Highways* article "Navajo Indians at War." While this upset the War Department, nothing came of it, and they chalked it up to an innocent mistake.

The code talkers would take part in every marine assault in the Pacific. They debuted on Guadalcanal. At first, the brass was reluctant to test the Navajos' coding skills, as yet unproven in battle. Instead the Navajos served as foot soldiers, fighting the Japanese and acting as runners. They proved to be natural guerrilla fighters and adept night scouts. Their ability to spot a snake by smell or sound astounded their comrades. And, says an officer, "They could crawl through the jungle without a sound and hide where there wasn't anywhere to hide." As the battle heated to its climax, the military called more and more on the Navajos' coding talents.

CARL NELSON GORMAN

★ ★ ★

Marine Private First Class Carl Gorman manned an observation post on a hill while Marines consolidated their positions on the island of Saipan in the Marianas.

Carl Gorman lied.

He had just lost his job, and while he was gambling with friends one day, a boy told him that the marines were recruiting Navajos who spoke both Navajo and English. At thirty-five, Gorman knew he was too old to enlist, so he lied about his age. Considering himself a complete failure, he told his friends, "If I get killed, that's all right with me."

Born in 1907 in Chinle, Arizona, to the Black Sheep Clan, Gorman loved to do two things as a boy—ride horses and draw them.

At ten, his parents sent him to the Rehoboth Mission boarding school, where the missionaries required him to speak English. When Gorman refused, they beat him repeatedly and finally chained him in a corner of the cold, damp basement for a week.

Now, in 1942, that same government was asking him to speak the Navajo language to thwart the Japanese's code-breaking efforts.

When asked why he chose to serve a government that had badly used him, he said, "Before the white man came to this country, this whole land was Indian country and we still think it's our land, so we fight for it. I was very proud to serve my country."

As one of the original twenty-nine Navajo code talkers, Gorman helped develop the code. After training, he and his fellow code talkers headed for Guadalcanal, and then on to the other South Pacific islands where they served with distinction. He missed Iwo Jima and Okinawa; malaria confined him to the hospital.

In the midst of this nightmare war, Gorman's sense of self returned. "The marines made a man out of me," he would say years later. "They also made a proud Navajo out of me."

After the war, he remembered the horses he had drawn as a child and enrolled in the Otis Art Institute in Los Angeles. He became one of America's outstanding Indian artists.

Carl Gorman died on the Navajo reservation in January 1998.

Arizonans Corporal Henry Bahe, Jr., of Fort Defiance (right), and Private First Class George H. Kirk of Leupp relayed orders in Navajo code on portable radios in the jungles of Bougainville.

The Saipan campaign proved their worth. The U.S. troops had penetrated farther than anticipated and friendly fire bombarded their position. Desperate messages to "Hold your fire" proved useless; all day the Japanese had imitated American broadcasts. Finally, the call went out: "Do you have a Navajo?" followed by cries of "Arizona," battlefield shorthand for code talker. A code talker got on the radio, sent an encoded message to a code talker on the other end, and the firing stopped immediately.

Their shining moment came early in 1945 on the tiny island of Iwo Jima. In the initial battle, which raged for two days, six networks of code talkers sent eight hundred flawless messages while mortar and artillery exploded all around them. When the United States finally raised the Stars and Stripes on Mount Suribachi a month later, the talkers announced the feat in code as "mouse-turkey-sheep-uncle-ram-ice-bear-ant-cat-horse-itch" (Mt. Suribachi). Major Howard Connor, fifth Marine Division signal officer, says, "Were it not for the Navajos, the marines would never have taken Iwo Jima."

The irony of their mission was not lost on the Navajos. Teddy Draper, Sr., says, "When I was going to boarding school, the U.S. government told us not to speak Navajo, but during the war, they wanted us to speak it!"

While the Navajos are the best known of the code talkers, the Comanches, Sioux, Chippewas, Seminoles, and Choctaws also sent code talkers into battle. In Arizona, eleven members of the Hopi tribe served as code talkers in the South Pacific.

The code talkers were not the only Arizona Indian heroes to come out of World War II. Ira Hayes, the reluctant hero from the Pima Reservation, could not hide from fame even on Iwo Jima. On the summit of Mount Suribachi, he helped raise a pipe with an American flag tied to it. An Associated Press photographer snapped a picture that would win a Pulitzer Prize and thrust Hayes into unwanted celebrity. This celebrity would haunt him until his death on the Pima reservation at thirty-two years of age.

Then there was Sam Russell, an Apache, who garnered full credit for rescuing his platoon, which had no communications and was surrounded by Japanese. A comrade says, "You should have seen him. He took a reel of communication wire and went forward, looking for A Company as unconcerned as if he had been strolling down a street in his hometown." E. R. McCrary, superintendent of the San Carlos Apache Indian Reservation, says that Russell was simply "running true to his traditions."

Company F of the 158th Infantry Regiment, 40th Division, of the Arizona National Guard consisted of students and alumni of the Phoenix Indian School. The rest of the regiment consisted of members of twenty Indian tribes, Mexican Americans from the barrios of Phoenix and Tucson, and some Anglo Americans. Begun in the 1860s with a ragtag lot of Mexican Americans and Pima Indians whose mission it was to defend Arizona Territory against marauding Apaches, it now operated as an elite fighting machine.

These Bushmasters captured a Japanese soldier at Toem-Arare in the South Pacific in June 1944. The man to the prisoner's left is Amos Kane of Whiteriver, Arizona, a member of Indian F Company.

Trained in the jungles of Panama in hand-to-hand combat, knives, and assault weapons, they adopted the nickname Bushmasters from the pit viper that inhabited the Panamanian jungles. Their insignia depicts a snake coiled around a machete; their motto: "cuidado" (take care). The regular soldiers disliked them intensely and called them "blanket-asses" and "spics." Many considered them weekend warriors. Tokyo Rose, the bewitching Japanese propaganda voice, dubbed them "Butchers of the Pacific." But General Douglas MacArthur understood their true worth and requested their help in his island-hopping campaign in the South Pacific. He said of them, "No greater fighting combat team has ever deployed for battle."

Although American Indians fought primarily in the South Pacific, they also served on all fronts from Alaska to Australia, North Africa to Normandy, and Bataan to Berlin. They served in all branches of the military; many desert-dwelling Navajos opted for service in the navy. While Indians are most often associated with the marines, only 574 American Indians served in the marines, while 19,284 served in the army.

By the time the war ended with the surrender of Japan in September 1945, American Indians had garnered seventy-one air medals, fifty-one silver stars, and forty-seven bronze stars for valor on the battlefield. Two received the Congressional Medal of Honor. Many had died. The Navajos sent thirty-six hundred boys and men into battle. Three hundred, including seven code talkers, were killed.

The war-weary warriors returned home. No other event, other than the establishment of the reservation system, had altered Indian life as much as had this war. A lot had changed. No longer sheltered, unworldly individuals, most had earned a consistent, decent living for the first time in their lives. They had gained status, respect, and worldliness, creating in some a determination to emulate their white brothers and sisters. Some decided to live in the cities. The traditionalists' fear that this assimilation into the white American culture would weaken family ties and lead to the deterioration of the traditional ways often proved true.

Others returned to the reservations. Those who had left at fifteen and six-

★ ★

BLOOD BROTHERS

Lieutenant Hal Braun's heart beat wildly. Navajos from his Bushmaster company had tied him to a post and were brandishing razor-edged machetes. *Why,* he wondered. He had always been friendly with them, and though they tended to keep to themselves, he thought they liked him. One grabbed his wrist and drew his machete lightly across it. The Navajos then pressed Hal's bleeding wrist to his own, which had also been cut, mingling their blood. The other Navajos followed suit and, grinning, released him.

They were now blood brothers.

teen returned to high school. Many wanted to help their reservations move into the twentieth century. Still others longed to return to the reservation's quiet, simple world and heal their minds and bodies among their people and their beliefs.

Homecomings for the veterans varied. The Navajos welcomed the white influence the soldiers brought with them. Several code talkers won seats on the tribal council, and another was appointed a tribal court judge. On the Papago reservation, whose members in the service numbered more than five hundred, elders voluntarily gave up their leadership positions to the returning vets, believing their experience in the white world better suited them to govern in the twentieth century; Thomas Segundo, a twenty-eight-year-old army veteran, was elected tribal chairman in 1947. The Zunis, on the other hand, forced their 213 veterans to go through rites of purification to eliminate all traces of the white world. A Zuni mother, who greeted her son at the train station, refused to touch him until he had done so. Because of this treatment, almost all of the Zuni veterans had left the reservation by 1947.

The ancient healing ceremonies helped most returning warriors rid themselves of the horrors of war. On the Navajo reservation medicine men held three-day Enemy Way ceremonials to exorcise the painful memories and the ghosts of the dead. After one poured out his story to a medicine man, the healer told him, "Now my son, don't tell it no more to nobody, anywhere. That way you won't be bothered in the future." Code talker Deswood Johnson, Sr., said in 1990, "My family had two-day and two-night healing ceremonies to help me get well, but I am still sick."

Threats to their country continued to evoke the warrior spirit in the country's first citizens. American Indians not only fought in both world wars, but in the Korean and Vietnam wars, and more recently in the Grenada, Panama, Somalia, Persian Gulf, and Afghanistan conflicts. Again, their numbers ranked the highest per capita of any ethnic group. In 1994, in honor of these patriotic Americans, Congress authorized the installation of the Native American Veterans' Memorial on the Washington, D.C. mall. In 2000, President Bill Clinton signed a bill granting congressional gold medals to the original twenty-nine code talkers and congressional silver medals to the other approximately four hundred code talkers who followed.

This warrior spirit, this willingness to engage the enemy in battle, continues to serve our native peoples, our state, and our nation well.

6

MILITARY BASES EVERYWHERE

DEAN SMITH

ADOLF HITLER GRABBED half of central Europe in the late 1930s, started the wholesale murder of Jews, built the world's most powerful military force—and America did nothing.

Hitler's legions invaded Poland in September 1939, with screaming Stuka bombers terrorizing endless columns of helpless refugees, and launched World War II. Still America waited on the sidelines.

But when the cream of the British army narrowly escaped annihilation at Dunkirk, and Hitler's legions goose-stepped through the Arch of Triumph in Paris in the spring of 1940, America began to make feverish preparations for possible entry into the war.

In May 1940 President Roosevelt urged Congress to beef up America's military capability. Soon National Guard units were federalized, and the first peacetime draft started converting America's young men into combat-ready soldiers. Thousands of Arizonans were among those who donned GI khaki or olive drab, and many others enlisted in the navy or marines. Among them was a nineteen-year-old Phoenix Union High School graduate named Bill Mauldin, who had joined the Arizona National Guard only to make some extra spending money. He served with the ground forces in Europe, and his "Willie and

Bill Mauldin, who attended Phoenix Union High School, became the most celebrated cartoonist of World War II.

Bill Mauldin's cartoons depicted the combat life of enlisted men.

Joe" cartoons depicting the misery of the American combat infantryman made him probably the best-known GI of them all.

Arizona was about to be converted into an armed camp, and military installations sprouted like dandelions on a green lawn from Douglas to Kingman, from Yuma to Bellemont, and at many points in between. For years it seemed that the entire state might be covered by aircraft runways and makeshift barracks.

Washington soon became aware that Arizona had just what the army ground forces, the air corps, and even the navy coveted so passionately: desert for north African combat training, unlimited sunshine and plenty of flat land for flying instruction, and wide open spaces for artillery and tank warfare exercises.

Tucson sent one of its most prominent citizens, Monte Mansfield, to the nation's capital with a delegation of business leaders in early 1940 to lobby for a major flight-training base in their hometown, and they won out over spirited competition from other Sunbelt cities. Venerable Senator Carl Hayden used his considerable political clout to establish Davis-Monthan Army Air Field at

Tucson. With Arizona's junior senator, Ernest W. McFarland, Hayden lobbied his influential friends and assorted military bigwigs to bring many more installations to the state.

Still clawing its way out of the Great Depression in 1940, Arizona gloried in this newfound economic bonanza. For building contractors, and especially the Del E. Webb Corporation, which landed several of the juicier contracts, it was a dream come true. In that era of frenzied effort to rebuild America's military capability, the sky was the limit, and cost was of little concern. "Cost plus" deals, which encouraged builders and suppliers to spend as much as possible to maximize their profits, created a new class of millionaires.

Senator Carl Hayden, right, shown at Davis-Monthan air base in Tucson with Col. John A. Des Portes, the base commander, was instrumental in persuading military leaders to establish air corps and army bases in Arizona.

Davis-Monthan was the first of Arizona's new Army Air Corps training bases, and for a very good reason: The core facilities were already there. The field, named for two Tucson boys who lost their lives flying for the army, was Tucson's municipal airport. Starting in late 1940, the air corps pumped millions of dollars into enlarging the base from three hundred to sixteen hundred acres, lengthening runways, and building housing and other facilities to accommodate three thousand men. Every Tucsonan (with the possible exception of municipal airport personnel) took pride in "D-M," as the base was popularly known. Civilian aviation had to share the base with the army for many months, and it was eventually necessary to find a new site for the municipal airport.

Davis-Monthan soon became one of America's largest pilot-training bases. The antiquated B-18 was the first aircraft employed. Later came B-24 bombers, and finally B-29s. Airmen from twenty-nine countries were trained here during the war, and some 17,500 pilots received advanced instruction at the base.

Those who trained the youthful flying cadets took their lives in their own hands, trying to keep their students from killing themselves along with their instructors. "An instructor pilot learned to keep one foot about 1/100th of an inch above the pedal (shifting control of the plane to the instructor)," declares one who survived the harrowing experience of flying with neophytes, "and sometimes it was only 1/1,000th of an inch!"

Ryan Field was opened twelve miles west of Tucson in 1942 by a privately owned San Diego firm, Ryan School of Aeronautics, and operated during the

★ ★

INSTANT INSTRUCTORS
AND FAST-HEALING PILOTS

So great was the need for pilots early in the war that cadets were often trained by young instructors who had been students themselves only weeks before.

"I had just recently earned my wings at Luke Field," recalls Jack Kennedy, "when I was one of twenty-one graduates chosen to be instructors at Williams. We were given some instruction manuals to read and were checked out in an AT-9 trainer—a total of an hour and a half in the air. We learned that the plane took off at ninety miles per hour and landed at ninety miles per hour, and a few other details about its performance.

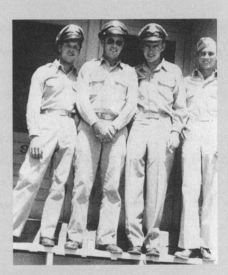

Four pilot instructors relax at their barracks. Instructors treasured their rare off-duty time. They spent many long, tense hours in the air each day.

"When that brief training was over, they blessed us, christened us twin-engine flight instructors, and sent us up in the air to train student pilots."

Charlie Falletta, who was shot down seven times in the South Pacific but blasted fifteen Japanese planes from the skies, was sent back to the States to give inspirational speeches to cadets at various training bases. He then spent eight months at Williams Field before becoming base commander at Ajo.

Falletta remembers how urgent was the need for pilots in the Pacific. "After one of my forced landings," he says, "I spent thirty-four days making my way through the jungle to my base and lost thirty-four pounds in the ordeal. When I got there, a doctor examined me, gave me two aspirins, and told me I was ready to fly."

war as a pilot-training base supervised by the army. Its PT-22 planes were so rugged that they went through their first seventy-two hundred air hours with only one engine failure. More than six thousand pilots received training here before the field was closed in 1944. Ryan Field is now a general aviation facility controlled by the Tucson Airport Authority.

At the end of the war, Davis-Monthan was selected as a storage site for decommissioned military aircraft. The famous *Enola Gay* B-29, which dropped the first atomic bomb on Hiroshima, briefly found a home there but was soon moved to a museum in the east. Some five thousand aircraft are now stored at the base. Davis-Monthan Air Force Base (as it was renamed after the war) escaped the many closures of the 1990s and today has six thousand military personnel and seventeen hundred civilian employees. It is one of the key installations in the U.S. Air Combat Command.

MARANA ARMY AIR Field, thirty miles northwest of Tucson, was carved out of the Aguirre Ranch and occupied more than three square miles of what was essentially desert land. It was opened in April 1942 as a basic flight-training facility, and it became the largest of the air corps' basic training schools in the entire nation. Cadets came to Marana from primary training bases and sharpened their flying, aerial acrobatics, and navigational skills in BT-13 airplanes before going on to advanced flight bases. More than ten thousand cadets, members of thirty classes, went through the rigorous training.

Evan Mecham, later to become governor of Arizona, went through the Marana program. He remembers the hastily constructed base as a sea of tar-paper–roofed barracks and instructional buildings. It must have seemed a rude comedown for cadets who had taken their primary instruction at privately owned "country club" schools such as Wickenburg's Claiborne Flight Academy and the two Thunderbird Fields near Phoenix, which had permanent buildings and served meals in a style worthy of good restaurants.

A few weeks after the Japanese surrender in 1945, the Marana base was closed down. Everything movable was hauled out and the structures and runways were left to decay in the desert sun and wind. But Marana was revived from its deep sleep in August 1951 when the air force decided it needed more pilots for the Korean conflict. Pumice stone barracks were built, along with a theater, chapel, dining hall, and cadet club. In 1958 Marana was closed again

WAR BROUGHT MECHAM TO ARIZONA

★ ★ ★

Evan Mecham took Army Air Corps pilot training in Arizona and flew fighter planes in combat in Europe. In 1986 he was elected governor of Arizona.

His disabled P-51 was spiraling earthward in flames over eastern Germany on a March day in 1945, and Lieutenant Evan Mecham was praying as he struggled desperately to extricate himself. One last mighty effort freed him from the doomed craft, and he parachuted into a waiting contingent of German soldiers.

Thus the burning desire to fly that had brought him to air corps training fields in Arizona came perilously close to ending the life of a future governor of the state.

"My first visit to Arizona was in a troop train crossing the desert on an unbelievably hot July day in 1943," he recalls, "and I said to myself, 'how could anybody possibly live in a place this hot?' Little did I know that I would be spending most of the rest of my life here, and loving it."

Mecham, a Utah native, was attending Utah State College when his call to active Army Air Corps duty came in early 1943. He took preflight training at Santa Ana (California) Army Air Field and was sent for primary instruction to Claiborne Flight Academy near Wickenburg. Then came basic flight training, in BT-13s, at Marana Army Air Field north of Tucson. Flying came as easy as breathing to him, and he led his Marana squadron in aerial acrobatics.

He took advanced training in AT-6s at Williams Army Air Field near Chandler. There he earned his wings, his gold bars, and a chance to realize his dream of flying P-38s. That came as a member of a photo reconnaissance squadron in England.

On March 7, 1945, Mecham was flying one of four P-51s as fighter escort for a P-38 on an aerial photo mission over east Germany when a Luftwaffe jet fighter attacked from below and destroyed his plane. He returned to Arizona after his liberation from a German POW camp and was sent to Luke Field.

When the war ended, he enrolled in what is now Arizona State University. Before he had completed his studies, however, an opportunity arose for him to obtain a Pontiac franchise in Ajo. Mecham became one of Arizona's most successful automobile dealers, a member of the Arizona legislature, and, in 1986, governor of the state.

and remained so until 1962, when it was reactivated by Intermountain Aviation, a regional freight carrier and airplane maintenance company. Today Pinal Air Park, as the area is known, houses civilian aircraft maintenance operations and several federal agencies.

FORT HUACHUCA, AT Sierra Vista near the Mexican border, has by far the most colorful history of all present Arizona military bases. It was established in 1877 during the height of the Apache wars and served as headquarters for U.S. cavalry operations against Geronimo's elusive warriors. The storied Buffalo Soldiers, courageous black troops who proved their mettle on the Arizona frontier, were stationed at Fort Huachuca. In 1916 the fort served as a base for General Jack Pershing's campaign against Mexican rebels under Pancho Villa.

Fort Huachuca, in southeastern Arizona, was a major army training base for African American soldiers during both world wars. The trainees shown here are receiving instruction in firing mortars, a skill that they were to use in combat on several fronts.

In 1940, when America started preparing for war, the fort was Arizona's only major military installation. Arizona's National Guard had been kept in readiness, largely through the efforts of the state adjutant general, General A. M. Tuthill. Weekend warriors from a dozen Arizona cities trained at their hometown armories and took summer training at a site called Fort Tuthill, near Flagstaff, and at other locations. But Arizona had no other army posts, no air corps fields, no navy or marine facilities.

It was in the fall of 1940 that the army activated the First Battalion of the Twenty-fifth Infantry, raising the troop strength at Fort Huachuca to a full regiment.

Today Fort Huachuca, long since racially desegregated, is still a major post, with the Army Intelligence Center as the principal command on the base. The

Fort Huachuca Historical Museum, opened in 1960, attracts visitors by the thousands. The adjoining city of Sierra Vista is the largest in Cochise County, and the area has become a haven for army retirees.

THE ARMY GROUND forces' World War II presence in Arizona is best remembered by most Americans for General George Patton's Desert Training Center, activated early in April 1942 to train soldiers for combat duty in the deserts of North Africa. That sprawling installation covered a vast area extending from Indio, California, to Aguila, Arizona, and from the Mexican border to

★ ★

ARIZONA DUST SAVES THE DAY

When American tanks roared into the north African campaign against Germany's canny General Erwin Rommel, they soon realized that the Sahara Desert was as formidable a foe as the famed "Desert Fox." Sand so infiltrated tank engines that their combat life was little over half an hour.

What to do? Historian Don Dedera tells of the decision of General Motors (GM) engineers to set up a test area where the dust was worse than anywhere else in the nation: the Gila River Indian Reservation south of Phoenix. There they sent tanks around a quarter-mile circle, kicking up a mountainous dust cloud. Other tanks followed, submitting their air

This M-5 light tank was used in training soldiers for combat in North Africa at the Desert Training Center, which had four camps in Arizona.

filters to the harshest possible punishment. Grains as fine as talc made their way into the best filters available, so the engineers developed filters that were up to the task—99.6 percent efficient. And our tanks won the Sahara campaign.

So penetrating was this Arizona dust ("Wonderful, awful stuff," GM engineer Joseph Prophet called it) that it later was sold to test facilities around the world.

Searchlight, Nevada—an expanse of 350 by 250 miles. Amazingly, more than a million men trained here during its relatively brief life.

Patton considered that sparsely populated wasteland, where daytime temperatures often reached 120 degrees, an ideal place to conduct tank and artillery warfare maneuvers and to toughen soft young Americans into battle-ready soldiers. It was not a school for sissies. Some of the troops had wooden floors in their tents, but more did not. A widely repeated story was that of the young soldier who complained to his company commander that he had found two rattlesnakes in his tent. The commander apologized, explaining that "each of us is supposed to be issued only one rattlesnake, so you'll have to give one back!"

Camp Young, Patton's command post, was located thirty miles east of Indio, but much of the training was conducted in three Arizona desert installations east of Yuma: Camp Hyder, Camp Horn, and Camp Laguna.

★ ★

MYSTERIOUS CAMP BOUSE

There was no mystery surrounding the activities at Camps Hyder, Horn, and Laguna in the Desert Training Center. There the routine was simple: Sweat, strain, and swear as you learned the fine art of killing Germans in the north African deserts.

But farther to the north, in western Arizona's Butler Valley, Camp Bouse kept such tight security on its mission that nobody could learn what was going on up there, even after the other Desert Training Center camps were closed down. If anyone had the temerity to try to find out, he immediately found himself surrounded by gun-pointing military police who ushered the intruder out in a hurry.

It was not until 1982 that some military history buffs, members of the Council on America's Military Past (CAMP), finally pried the answers out of British sources. Historian James E. Cook interviewed several veterans of the Camp Bouse experiments and obtained additional information. The Camp Bouse effort, it was revealed, was conducted primarily by the British army. In their experiments, tanks were mounted with shuttered and filtered arc lights that were supposed to confuse the enemy and make the tanks elusive targets. But the idea proved impractical, and the venture was eventually abandoned.

Mysterious Camp Bouse, located in Butler Valley to the north of the others, conducted super-secret tank warfare experiments.

The Third, Sixth, and Ninth Armored Divisions trained in the Arizona camps, as did the Seventy-ninth Infantry Division. The army closed down the Desert Training Center in April 1944, after the North Africa campaign was won. Except for some still-visible tank tracks in the desert, the few relics of its epic wartime service to the nation are housed in the George S. Patton Memorial Museum, near Interstate 10 on the site of Camp Young.

THE ARMY MADE a very different use of the western Arizona desert during World War II: a proving ground for military materiel. The Yuma Test Branch, now known as the Yuma Proving Ground, became operational in January 1943, when officers and civilian experts arrived at Imperial Dam on the Colorado River north of Yuma to begin tests on floating bridges to be used in combat. Soon hundreds of engineers and technicians arrived to evaluate design and materials of many bridge components, and their work paid off handsomely during combat operations in Europe and North Africa, enabling Allied armies to cross the many rivers that barred their path to the heart of the enemy's homeland.

The army broadened the scope of testing at the site, bringing in thousands of vehicles, artillery pieces, and other war materiel for exhaustive tests before permitting them to be used in combat. Allied nations sent their technicians and problems to the Yuma facility. Tens of thousands of troops trained here for desert warfare and tested equipment as they trained.

ARMY GROUND FORCES were much in evidence in Arizona during the war, but the air corps had an even more visible presence in the state. Giant air bases such as Davis-Monthan, Luke, and Williams trained many thousands of pilots and other air-crew members and became permanent installations after the cessation of hostilities. More than a dozen additional air corps training bases, each with several auxiliary air fields, had their years of glory.

The *Glendale News,* a weekly journal that usually featured such earthshaking news as the opening of a new grocery store, trotted out its biggest type on January 10, 1941, to proclaim "Desert Land Cleared at Air School Site." It was the birth notice of Thunderbird Field north of Glendale, a facility to be built by Southwest Airways Corporation. Southwest had a contract with the air corps to train pilots—American, British, and Chinese, and later students from other nations. Among the owners of Southwest Airways were some of the best-known Hollywood headliners of the time: Jimmy Stewart, Henry Fonda, Leland Hayward, Cary Grant, and Hoagy Carmichael. Stewart, in particular, was a rabid aviation enthusiast, and he later earned a general's star in the air force.

Only five weeks after the Thunderbird story broke, the *Glendale News* had another blockbuster announcement: "Airport West of Glendale Assured." This time, the story concerned the Army Air Corps base soon to be named Luke Field after Arizona's Frank Luke, Jr., a Congressional Medal of Honor winner who lost his life in World War I aerial action. The base was destined to dwarf little Thunderbird.

Phoenix community leaders, keenly aware of the economic benefits of such a training field, had purchased the 1,440-acre site for forty thousand dollars and leased it to the Army Air Corps for a dollar a year. The incredible speed with which Luke was built is still a marvel to construction engineers. Underbrush was first cleared from the desert site nine miles west of Glendale on March 24, 1941; on June 6—just eleven weeks later—Luke Field was offi-

★ ★

SAVING A CHINESE CADET

When Major Ira Coles was instructing flying cadets at Luke Field, he was forced to eliminate a young Chinese trainee for lack of progress. In his report he wrote that the student seemed not to be trying to learn.

A Chinese major read the report and asked Coles if he really believed the boy was not trying.

"It seemed that way to me," Coles answered. "Is it important?"

"Yes, it is," explained the major. "If you had reported that he simply lacked aptitude for flying, he would be assigned to some ground duty. But if you say he was not trying, he will face a firing squad!"

Coles grabbed his report and hurriedly made the change that saved the student's life.

cially opened. Instruction started shortly thereafter, in AT-6 trainers and P-40 fighters. The base became so crowded that cadets were often trucked to Phoenix Sky Harbor and several auxiliary fields. But they learned quickly, and on August 15, forty-three members of the first graduating class received their wings. Luke became the nation's largest single-engine advanced pilot-training base, and it remains one of the U.S. Air Force's major bases today.

At the same time Luke was being born, events were moving swiftly on other nearby fronts. Senator McFarland sent a telegram to the *Arizona Republic* announcing that the air corps had selected a site south of Mesa for another major pilot-training base. On July 15, 1941, ground was broken for that base at a desert site ten miles east of Chandler. It was first called Mesa Air Base and then Higley Field before it was officially named Williams Army Air Field in February 1942, after an Arizona-born air corps pilot who was killed in a 1927 crash off the coast of Hawaii. The Del E. Webb Construction Company employed twenty-five hundred men to erect the 160 buildings and build the long runways. The first class of eighty-two students, training in AT-9s and AT-17s, graduated on April 24, 1942.

Aerial gunner trainees flying AT-6 trainers from Kingman Army Air Field and other Arizona fields fired many thousands of rounds at targets like the one shown, a reproduction of the Japanese flag.

The civilian-owned bases were training pilots even before Luke and Williams got into the act. Thunderbird Number 1, near Glendale, put its first students into the air late in March 1941. British cadets began arriving at Falcon Field near Mesa in June of that year, and Thunderbird Number 2, north of Scottsdale, was activated in June 1942.

Almost overnight, Phoenix was inundated by airmen wearing uniforms of many nations. They put severe strains on the Salt River Valley's capacity to house, feed, and entertain them. The many languages spoken by the trainees often caused communication problems. On one occasion, two Chinese airmen

JOHN J. RHODES
Four Years at Williams Field

★ ★ ★

Major John J. Rhodes, far right, and other senior officers welcome Major General Hodges, second from left, to Williams Army Air Field in 1944. Rhodes later represented Arizona in the U.S. House of Representatives for thirty years.

Fresh out of Harvard Law School and awaiting his first permanent assignment with the Army Air Corps in the fall of 1941, young Lieutenant John J. Rhodes learned that he might be sent either to South America or to a new air base in Arizona, then known as Higley Field.

"I wrote to Betty, whom I was soon to marry, and told her the news," he recalls. "She wrote back that she knew where South America was, but where in the world is Higley, Arizona?"

Rhodes soon found out. The base was east of Chandler, and it was about to receive its official name: Williams Army Air Field. Everybody called it Williams Field or, affectionately, Willie. Rhodes arrived just before the Japanese bombed Pearl Harbor on December 7, 1941.

Colonel B. A. (Bunk) Bridget, Willie's commanding officer, faced the daunting task of providing training facilities, housing, and a thousand other necessities for the flood of trainees arriving every day. In his second meeting with his staff, he charged Rhodes with the responsibility of setting up an officers' mess and added, "I want meals served there three days from today!"

Rhodes had absolutely no experience in food service and had no idea where to find cooks or equipment, but he somehow met that deadline. Several months later he was sent to adjutant general's school at Fort Washington, Maryland, and was appointed Williams Field's post adjutant. Later he served in various administrative capacities there and was elevated to executive officer of the base. He wore the silver leaves of a lieutenant colonel when he completed his tenure at Williams Field and was separated from active duty in 1946.

Rhodes remained in Arizona, ran successfully for a seat in the U. S. House of Representatives in 1952, and served thirty years in the House before his retirement from the political wars. He became one of the most respected members of Congress, and served as minority leader of the House. He and his wife now live in Mesa.

"Williams Field will always hold a special place in my memory," he declares. "I brought my bride there in May of 1942, and our eldest son, Jay, was born while I was serving at Williams in September 1943. It was my assignment to the base that introduced me to Arizona and made me an Arizonan for the rest of my life."

were conversing in Chinese while on a training flight and forgot that they were not on the intercom but were broadcasting to the world. Down below, panicky radiomen listened in, and, thinking they were hearing the conversations of incoming Japanese raiders, commanders put bases on high alert for miles around.

British cadets who trained at the Phoenix-area bases never forgot their experiences in Arizona. They were the first to train at Thunderbird Number 1, and those who worked there remember how soon their pale cheeks became sunburned and leathery under the relentless sun. One Royal Air Force (RAF) cadet, Jack May, came to Falcon in the winter of 1942, fresh from the terror and privations of the London bombing.

"Suddenly we left all that horror behind," he later declared, "and there was plenty of food, sunshine, and citrus." Like so many others, May returned to Arizona after the war, married a Phoenix girl, and settled down.

The British cadets loved to party, especially to celebrate the completion of their training. On the night of their graduation, one group flew very low down Central Avenue in Phoenix, raining toilet paper on the astonished citizens below.

Fatal accidents were fairly common at all the bases. Twenty-three cadets are buried in a Mesa cemetery. There were more lighthearted mishaps, too. On one occasion, two nine-plane formations flew right through each other and some actually scraped wing tips. Amazingly, nobody was hurt.

Another time, two pilots were in a Stearman primary training plane that was dipping and soaring erratically, much to the consternation of spectators below. When it landed, the two airmen pointed at each other and admitted with red faces that "I thought he was flying the plane!"

All the Phoenix-area air bases live on today in various forms. Thunderbird Number 1 was closed at the end of the war, and the property was obtained from the government by Lieutenant General Barton K. Yount and several associates, who converted the buildings into an institute dedicated to training students for positions in foreign trade. Its present name is the American Graduate School for International Management. Thunderbird Number 2 has become the Scottsdale Municipal Airport, and Falcon Field is now Mesa's city airport. Williams Field was for years one of the most important advanced flight-training facilities of the U.S. Air Force. After its closure in 1993 it became the Williams Gateway Airport and now is the home of Arizona State University East and a Chandler-Gilbert Community College facility.

AERIAL GUNNERY WAS an important facet of advanced pilot training at the Arizona bases, and the air corps soon found that the state had plenty of open space in which trainees could practice that art. Barry Goldwater, who had wangled his way into a flying job despite substandard eyesight, became a gunnery instructor at Luke Field and helped plan the vast gunnery range in southwestern Arizona that bears his name today. Some stubborn ranchers in the area refused to sell their land to the government for the gunnery range and their ranches had to be obtained by presidential order.

Yuma Army Air Field had its beginnings in June 1942, when a group of air corps personnel arrived at Benjamin Fly Field near Yuma and took down a sign reading "Johnnie's Flying Service, $1.00 per ride." They painted over it the words "Yuma Army Air Base, Army Air Forces Advanced Flying School," and re-hung it. Construction of runways, operations buildings, and barracks began immediately. The base was officially activated on July 3, 1942, while construction was still in progress. Its mission was to train pilots, radio operators, and aerial gunners in a variety of military aircraft. AT-6 single-engine training planes, T-17 multi-engine trainers, B-17 Flying Fortress bombers, and both P-39 and P-40 fighters were among the planes trainees flew.

The Marine Corps Air Station (MCAS) was established on the site of Yuma Army Air Field in 1959. Some four thousand marines and navy personnel and several hundred civilian employees carry on flight training operations at MCAS today. It is the fourth most active air station in the navy department.

DOUGLAS ARMY AIR Field began training pilots in 1942 and became one of the busiest of all the Arizona fields. It was six miles north of Douglas, a city on the Mexican border in Cochise County, and occupied twenty-eight hundred

BARRY GOLDWATER
Determined to Fly for His Country

★ ★ ★

Major Barry Goldwater flew airplanes and trained aerial gunners at Luke and Yuma air bases before flying in the China-Burma-India theater of operations. He later became a major general in the Air Force Reserve and was the Republican candidate for president in 1964.

Barry Goldwater learned to fly at the Phoenix airport in 1930; he tried to enlist in the air corps flying cadet program in 1932 but was turned down because of poor eyesight. He never gave up trying to earn the silver wings of an air corps pilot.

The future U. S. senator and presidential candidate saw his golden opportunity when Luke Army Air Field was activated in 1941. Although he was thirty-two years old, married, and a father, he managed to plead his case with the base commander, Colonel Ennis Whitehead.

"Colonel," he said, "I have an Army Reserve commission as a first lieutenant and I've been flying for more than ten years. Can't you find a place for me here?" Whitehead, who later became one of Barry's best friends, sat him down with an application blank, and two weeks later Goldwater was assigned to Luke with a nonflying status.

Fate offered Goldwater one more chance to fly for the air corps: Desperate for pilots, the air corps created a new rating, service pilot, for veteran civilian flyers, and he was accepted.

With the help of commissioned pilot friends at Luke, he was soon able to learn flying the army way and won his air corps pilot's wings. He instructed in gunnery for a time at Luke, and then he was assigned to Yuma Army Air Field as head of aerial gunnery training. It was there that he and others developed the gunnery range in southwestern Arizona that now bears Goldwater's name.

He spent the remaining years of active duty flying airplanes in the China-Burma-India theater for the U. S. Ferry Command. He had one last burning desire—to fly B-29 bombers in the final campaign against Japan—but that wish was never to come true.

Back in civilian clothes again, but still as eager an airman as ever, he was asked by Governor Sidney P. Osborn to organize the Arizona Air National Guard. This he did and remained its top commander until his election to the U. S. Senate in 1952. He remained active in the Air Force Reserve and rose to the rank of major general.

acres. Six runways handled the heavy traffic, and the huge base at one time had 418 buildings. It was a twin-engine advanced flying school charged with preparing bomber pilots for duty in many theaters of World War II. At the end of the war the field was decommissioned and later became the site of the Douglas municipal airport.

The Douglas base played a special role in World War II history: It was one of only four army air fields in the United States to have black soldiers and the second to receive black members of the Women's Army Corps (WAC).

Lieutenant Anna Mac Clarke, one of the first WACs to be commissioned, led the first cadre of women onto the base in February 1944. Lieutenant Clarke refused to have her charges relegated to the "Negro corner" of the base theater. She confronted the base commander, Colonel Harvey Dyer, and persuaded him to issue an order stating in part that "These colored WACs are citizens of the United States, imbued with a spirit of patriotism . . . and deserve our greatest respect. They are to be extended the same courtesies and privileges extended to white officers and enlisted men." It was a significant victory in the long battle to desegregate America's military forces. Courageous Rosa Parks later refused to sit in the back of an Alabama bus, but Anna Clarke struck a blow for racial equality at Douglas more than a decade earlier.

AJO ARMY AIR Field was first an aerial gunnery training site for Luke Field, and later for Williams Field. Tucked away on the southern Arizona desert between the Mexican border and Gila Bend (site of another gunnery training base), Ajo was not only far from the amenities of a big city, but the facilities on the base were spartan, to say the least.

"Ajo was a former Civilian Conservation Corps camp," says Jack Kennedy, a former instructor at the base, "and the barracks were just plaster board and two-by-fours, without much air conditioning. We soaked our sheets in the shower at night and hoped we could go to sleep before they dried out. The temperature inside the cockpit of our planes got up to 150 degrees and higher." At one time the Ajo base had some eight hundred officers and enlisted personnel. They developed a spirit of camaraderie and a desire for excellence that enabled them to rank high in many gunnery competitions.

At an April ll, 1942, meeting of a board of air corps officers in Kingman, it was decided to construct an air field five miles west of the town. It was to have three sixty-five-hundred–foot runways, cost some $9 million, and be patterned after the new Las Vegas Gunnery School. The Kingman Army Flying School was activated in August 1942, with the primary purpose of training B-17 gunners. The name was changed to Kingman Army Air Field in May 1943.

More than thirty-five thousand students trained at Kingman during the war. Among the trainees and support troops were female personnel, both WACs and Women Airforce Service Pilots (WASPs). Students from China and other Allied nations underwent gunnery training here. At its peak, Kingman was home base to seventeen thousand personnel.

After the Japanese surrender, the Kingman base was chosen as a storage center for surplus military aircraft. By December 31, 1945, there were 4,693 airplanes stored on the field, and the total reached 7,000 before they were moved to Davis-Monthan Air Force Base for permanent storage. Some aircraft were offered for sale at bargain prices: B-17 bombers, $13,750; B-25 bombers, $8,250; and P-40 fighters, $1,250.

Air corps installations big and small were built at many other locations. Those who served there will never forget them: Coolidge, Dateland, Prescott, Hereford, Yucca, Winslow, Safford—all these and others are part of the World War II story in Arizona.

NOT TO BE left out of the Arizona military picture, the navy in 1943 ordered a portion of the Goodyear Aircraft plant near Litchfield Park to be used for aircraft modification. An area adjoining the plant was established as the U.S. Naval Air Facility, the mission of which was to test-fly the modified aircraft and deliver them where needed.

Because large navy bombers were being modified at the Goodyear plant, the navy constructed a huge hangar and a six thousand-foot runway (later lengthened to eighty-five hundred feet). By the end of World War II, more than six hundred aircraft had been modified and then tested at the Naval Air Facility (NAF). The navy's PB4Y-1 version of the army's B-24 bomber was the principal plane modified at Litchfield NAF to meet navy specifications.

The City of Phoenix bought the property in 1968 and converted it into a satellite municipal airport, now known as Phoenix-Goodyear Airport.

FOR THE FIRST and only time in its long history, the U.S. Army built a Navajo village in 1943, complete with hogans and a trading post, at one of its installations, the Navajo Ordnance Depot, a dozen miles west of Flagstaff. Sheep were brought in for food and wool, as were weaving looms for the Navajo women. Why? Because the army needed Navajo workmen at the post, and they would not stay at the depot when they found that the necessities of their culture were not available.

The Navajo Ordnance Depot was established on some thirty thousand acres around the tiny village of Bellemont in February 1942 as a facility for receiving and storing ammunition and explosives for shipment to the Pacific theater of operations. The depot was located along the main line of the Santa Fe Railroad. Proximity to the railroad was vital because most of the artillery shells and smaller ammunition were shipped in and out by rail. Construction was rushed to completion, including some eight hundred concrete storage igloos built in the first year of operation. The igloos were located some distance apart from each other so that an accidental explosion would not blow up the entire munitions depot.

Senator Hayden, who was influential in persuading the army to choose the Bellemont location, was on hand for the opening of the depot and personally loaded the first case of ammunition into a waiting railroad car. "I'm happy to send this bundle of calling cards on its way to the battlefields," he declared.

For many years the depot remained an important storage facility for army ordnance. Now known as Camp Navajo, it is a training base for the Arizona National Guard.

ALL ARIZONA BECAME an armed camp between 1940 and 1946. Papago Park northwest of Tempe was the site of a German prisoner-of-war camp. National Guard armories at towns throughout the state were used for a variety of military functions. Campuses of the state university and colleges echoed to the thunder of marching feet and the bellowing of commands. The University of Arizona's Reserve Officers' Training Corps (ROTC) cavalry unit produced combat officers, and its navy programs did the same. Arizona State at Tempe was headquarters for an air corps preflight school, and Arizona State at Flagstaff devoted its resources to naval training units.

The army built hogans at the Navajo Ordnance Depot at Bellemont to entice Navajos to remain and work at the depot. These workers and their families were urged to buy war bonds by this sign at the entrance to one of the hogans. American Indians did buy bonds, and their enlistment rate for military service was the highest of any ethnic group.

Many thousands of the young men and women who were stationed at Arizona military bases during World War II returned after the Japanese surrender to attend schools, find employment, start companies, marry, buy homes, run for office, and become enthusiastic boosters for their adopted state. It could well be said that their experiences at the many Arizona bases provided the biggest impetus for state growth of any event in Arizona's long history.

There was another important benefit: Scores of military installations were rescued from the wrecking ball and, as described earlier, transformed into civilian or military resources that enrich our quality of life to this day.

7

THE WAR ON THE HOME FRONT

MARY MELCHER

IN FEBRUARY 1945 volunteers at Phoenix's Community Servicemen's Center prepared to welcome their millionth visitor. Located in downtown Phoenix, this center provided a place for soldiers to relax when passing through town or on leave from one of the nearby bases and training centers. For their millionth guest, volunteers had prepared a special date with the Citrus Queen, a "young woman chosen for her poise and beauty." If the GI happened to be married, he would receive a baby carriage instead of a date. When Marine Sergeant Lundy walked in, as the lucky millionth soldier, the Luke Field Band, Governor Sidney P. Osborn, Phoenix Mayor J. R. Fleming, and over twelve hundred soldiers were on hand to witness the event. Lundy was married, so he gave his date to his buddy Sergeant Harold Martin.

The millionth man event, like many others throughout Arizona, displayed the commitment and activity of Arizonans who mobilized to support the war and American troops. "It was an effort of the people," explains Phoenician Angela Menetrey when describing her home-front activities. It was a time of intense change as the federal government constructed dozens of new air fields; prisoner-of-war, desert training, and Japanese American detention camps; and defense plants. As millions of men left to fight overseas, a severe labor shortage developed in Arizona and throughout the United States. To meet the need for wartime goods, some women took on new, untraditional roles in manufacturing plants. Others wowed audiences with their athleticism on championship women's softball teams. Some minorities gained improved situations in mines and defense plants, while Phoenix became a center for troops from surrounding areas, with as many as ten thousand soldiers passing through on a weekend. Citizens dealt with these changes daily and adjusted their lives to aid the war effort by recycling, organizing bond drives, and serving soldiers. At the same time, Arizona miners, farmers, and defense workers labored to provide the material goods necessary to win the war.

These changes began immediately after Japanese bombs fell on Pearl Harbor, and communities organized for civil defense. People feared the Japanese would invade the West Coast or drive through Mexico to southern Arizona. In the days following December 7, the Phoenix Civil Defense Council attracted thousands of volunteers, according to Margaret Kober: "We had the city surveyed and mapped out so that we knew exactly how many people you could take care of in your house if we had this mass evacuation from California." Bisbee residents also organized, fearing a Japanese invasion. Daisy Kasun describes their efforts: "Captains were chosen and districts were formed and precautions were taken at night. Our windows were covered; our lights were low after dark. The captains [air-raid wardens] went around searching for anybody who had a light on that shouldn't be on. They watched our border crossings very closely, who was coming in and out."

The civil defense effort extended throughout the state. In Coconino County, Leo Weaver organized "thirty-five completely equipped mounted patrolmen" and had on hand an additional five hundred Navajo men with horses, if needed. George T. Hanley of Sanders wrote of high school boys who were "anxious to do their bit in this great time of peril." Some high school students wanted to enlist immediately following Pearl Harbor's bombing, but he hoped, "Maybe with a [civil defense] program such as you have I can hold them to do patrol duty on [Route] 66 and the railroad."

Eventually, as people's invasion fears became less intense, citizens and companies struggled to produce the materials necessary to fight the war. The Phoenix Chamber of Commerce worked with Arizona's congressional delegation to bring defense industries to the area. Called the "Big Three," Goodyear, ALCOA, and AiResearch set up operations, producing parts for B-29s, pontoon bridges, flight decks, and small aircraft. Tucson also gained new industry when Consolidated-Vultee Aircraft Corporation of San Diego established a division south of the city. The federal government urged defense companies to decentralize production of war materials. Arizona's open spaces and available land made it attractive, along with its proximity to California. Arizona companies helped to meet the federal government's need for defense goods, and several, along with some Arizona mines, received the coveted army/navy "E" banner for reaching production goals. This wartime production would eventually produce long-lasting change in Phoenix and Tucson; manufacturing gained a firm hold in the economy and expanded after the war.

★ ★

A LETTER FROM ULA K. BAIRD

Letters to Governor Osborn demonstrated the commitment of Arizonans to the war effort. Ula K. Baird, living on Van Buren Street in Phoenix, wrote the following on June 3, 1942.

Home guards were needed, and these Tucson women turned out to train for that duty in 1942. They had only brooms, but they hoped to be given guns later.

Your Excellency:

I am a woman fifty-three years old, a little too old to enlist in the WAC, but I am healthy and capable. I am a typist, and have had clerical and office experience, also apartment house management. I want to enlist in the Citizen's Defense Corps. I have no income, but am willing to serve for a private's pay. Why not a Woman's Home Guard? I can shoot a rifle too. . . . I have the same birth date, January 26, as General MacArthur, surely there is some place I can serve.

Awaiting your orders, I am,

Very Sincerely Yours,

Ula K. Baird

SOME DEFENSE OPERATIONS began before the United States entered the war. Goodyear Aircraft Corporation established a plant in Litchfield Park, west of Phoenix, in November 1941, producing flight decks for naval aircraft. In 1943, the navy cooperated with plant operators to build a runway to enable pilots to fly in B-24s from California for modification. Workers altered the B-24s into Privateers, naval aircraft used for coastal patrol. This government-owned-and-operated plant employed seventy-five hundred at its peak.

Federal projects and companies struggled to meet production goals while coping with labor shortages. To meet labor needs, they recruited employees from throughout the United States, while welcoming women into the work-force as the "margin for victory." By 1944, women made up 36 percent of the total labor force in the United States. In Arizona, they worked as welders, riv-eters, heavy machinery operators, and inspectors. In Phoenix, women made up 75 percent of the labor force in certain departments of the larger plants. For the first time, major employers welcomed married women into the labor force. Women also moved in greater numbers into the clerical and professional fields.

The war provided unprecedented opportunities for minority women, like Laura Dungee Harris, who began working for Goodyear in 1943. Like 75 per-cent of the labor force there, she was untrained. "I heard that they were want-ing workers at Goodyear. . . . So in 1943 I applied for a job," says Harris. "At the plant, I helped to make trailing edges for the B-24 plane. It was just a labor shortage. They needed people, so there really wasn't that much of a qualifica-tion. Practically all of the men had gone off to the service, so most of the men [at Goodyear] were either old or weren't qualified to be in the service. There were about eighteen women and three men in our section."

Dora Mendoza Gomez also found new opportunities at Goodyear, leaving a job as a department store clerk. Her salary moved from $35 a week as a clerk to $50 a week working as a riveter on planes. "I was always inside the wings because I was skinny, and I could get in there and back," she says in an inter-view with Jean Reynolds for "The History of Grant Park Neighborhood."

For the first time, large numbers of women worked on railroads. Mexican American women worked for the Southern Pacific in Tucson, cleaning and servicing the trains. Lily Valenzuela Liu describes her improvement in wages: "I went to the Santa Rita Hotel. . . . and started working as a chambermaid. . . . They called me from the S.P. [Southern Pacific] and then I started working. I was very, very happy because at that time they were paying a little more money for a woman. . . . I think it was fifty-some dollars, which was a lot of money for us at that time."

With women moving into nontraditional work roles, fashions changed as many began wearing pants and overalls in public for the first time. But even as they assumed new roles in the workplace, traditional ideals concerning female behavior remained firmly in place. In an advice column entitled "Pattern for Living Suggested for American Women in 1942," an *Arizona Republic* columnist gave the ordinary woman the following instructions: "Regard waste as stupidity. Do all that she can to keep her home a cheerful, happy place. Pay taxes without complaint. Refrain from criticizing the way those in authority are fighting the war—she can't possibly know much about such matters. Manage to be just as much a woman as she ever was—even though she may be called on to do a man's job as efficiently as any man could do it."

While keeping the home fires burning, working in manufacturing jobs, and maintaining families alone, women were also to remain properly feminine, passive, and quiet.

Although the government called for female laborers in the defense industry, it provided little assistance with child care or domestic chores. Many women relied on relatives to care for children or worked night shifts to be home

---

JOE TORRES

★ ★ ★

Minority males also gained new opportunities during World War II. Joe Torres was a teenager working in the fields at the beginning of the war. His single mother needed his financial assistance, so he had been forced to drop out of school. During the war, he found a job at ALCOA making 45 cents an hour. To get to work he rode in a truck, equipped with benches, that transported workers from throughout the Phoenix metropolitan area. He worked there from 1944 to 1945 and used his extra earnings to buy a zoot suit that he wore downtown every Saturday night. In 1945, at the age of 17, he volunteered for the army. As one of many helping to rebuild Germany after the war, he was horrified to discover babies' skeletons in a tile company oven in Munich. The situation in Europe was a complete shock for this young man—he did not know of the holocaust before his trip to Europe.

during the day. Girl Scouts also provided some help, baby-sitting for working mothers. Still, many children lacked adequate supervision. In a letter to Governor Osborn, Mrs. J. B. Dailey discussed children's recreational needs in Phoenix's new defense housing at Alzona Park: "If something isn't done about playgrounds for the more than six hundred children here by summer, Phoenix will find its hands full of adolescent delinquency. . . . For the only people here who have attempted anything for the children's welfare as a group is Mr. Dailey and myself. . . . The children's eagerness for something, anything, to do has rather overwhelmed us."

JUST AS MANUFACTURERS responded to wartime needs, mining companies doubled their efforts, with some government assistance. Early in January 1942 Governor Osborn noted necessary steps to increase mining production. Osborn called for federal subsidies of new production and higher copper prices (at least 15 cents a pound). By February the Metals Reserve Company, a subsidiary of the Reconstruction Finance Corporation, agreed to pay 17 cents a pound for copper, 11 cents a pound for zinc, and 9.5 cents a pound for lead. These increases enabled small mines to make a profit. According to historian Charles Ynfante, within months of the bombing of Pearl Harbor, three hundred Arizona mines were working twenty-four hours a day, seven days a week.

The long-established dual-wage system of paying Mexican and Mexican American miners less than Anglo miners began to break down during the war. In 1942, Anglo miners at Miami's Inspiration Mine earned up to $1.15 more per hour than workers of Mexican descent in similar jobs. Capitalizing on national calls for unity, the International Union of Mine, Mill and Smelter Workers (IUMMSW) won grievances against Phelps Dodge before the War Production Board and Manpower Commission. In 1944 the IUMMSW filed injunctions against the mining and smelter companies in the Miami area, which temporarily ended the dual-wage system and laid foundations for further action to eliminate discrimination.

WHILE UNION LEADERS spoke out against prejudice in order to bring greater unity and improve production, farmers looked to the south to meet labor needs. Arizona farmers had traditionally relied upon Mexicans to work in

DOTTIE WILKINSON

★ ★ ★

When Arizonans weren't working, many enjoyed watching softball, and their championship women's softball team, the Ramblers, took their minds off the war news. Dottie Wilkinson, who hailed from a south Phoenix farm, played on this team from 1933 to 1965, beginning when she was only eleven. The Ramblers played their rivals, the Queens, and also men's teams from Luke Field and Williams Field, as well as teams from outside the state. Softball "was the only game in town," says Wilkinson. "There could be as many as five thousand in attendance." The crowds loved the games that were played at University Park on 10th Avenue and Van Buren, or Phoenix Softball Park at 17th Avenue and Roosevelt.

Working at Goodyear Aircraft Corporation and AiResearch also kept Dottie Wilkinson busy during the war years. She earned more money than she had ever earned before but found the work tedious. "You didn't know what you were making— a part here, a part there." Nevertheless, the work had significance: "At that time we all thought we were doing the right thing, working for a defense plant."

The Phoenix Ramblers won national championships in 1940, 1948, and 1949. With a career batting average above .300, Wilkinson was inducted into the National Softball Hall of Fame in 1970. A true athlete, she later won bowling championships and was inducted into the International Bowling Hall of Fame in 1990.

the fields during boom times, and this also occurred during the war. Early in the war congressional and farm leaders from the Southwest called for an agreement with Mexico to provide farm laborers. The United States and Mexico began negotiations after the latter nation declared war on the Axis in May 1942, but it was months before the needed laborers would arrive. The delay stemmed from controversy over transportation of workers, pay, contracts, and repatriation.

Early in the war lack of labor forced some to limit their production. According to Ernest Douglas, editor of the *Arizona Farmer*, "The Arizona farmer has done his durndest in the war effort, and he is not cutting down because he wants to—it's because he has to."

Farmers suffered desperately during the fall harvest of 1942. Mexican workers had not yet arrived, and other potential workers were employed in war industries or fighting overseas. In Maricopa County, the Phoenix Lions' Club, Club *Latino* American, and *La Sociedad Mutualista Porfirio Diaz* organized volunteers to pick cotton needed for parachutes, blimps, and gliders.

In Pinal County, near Florence, convicts provided needed labor during the trying fall harvest of 1942. Warden A. G. Walker supervised about a hundred convicts who harvested seven hundred thousand pounds of long-staple cotton between November and January. According to Amos Hankins, supervisor of the crew, patriotism and the presence of their sons and relatives in the armed services motivated the prisoners. "There are men in my crew who quit easier jobs inside the wall to pick cotton when they found out about cotton being needed for parachutes and things like that," said Hankins. "I never wear a gun. I don't carry a gun because I don't need one."

Using convicts, volunteers, and even high school students, farmers struggled through the fall harvest of 1942, while waiting for Mexican laborers. The first *braceros,* Mexican nationals who came to work in the U.S., arrived in Arizona in February 1943. During the war years, over 200,000 braceros entered the United States to work in the fields. An additional 130,000 worked in the railroad industry. Approximately 6,000 braceros labored in Arizona fields from 1943 to 1947, but in 1943, they numbered only about 2,000. Still, they picked approximately 60 percent of Maricopa County's cotton crop that year.

Arizona Republic cartoonist Reg Manning expressed the plight of Arizona farmers who were asked to increase production but who had no farm hands to help them. They had all gone into military service.

While dealing with difficulties securing labor, farmers faced other problems during the war, such as the rationing of gasoline. J. J. Jones, of Coolidge, appealed to Governor Osborn in November 1942: "In many instances they [farmers] have been cut down from 1000 gallons regular necessary use, to as low as 53 gallons for three months. This is absurd, as they can not get their equipment from the gin to their ranches on 53 gallons of gas. It is absolutely necessary to keep the farmers going if they are to produce sufficient long staple cotton, alfalfa and grains, in sufficient quantities to supply the war needs." Jones also explained that he had contacted the state director of rationing, who promised to provide some assistance.

In spite of labor shortages and rationing difficulties, Arizona agribusiness grew during World War II. With the demand for goods at an all-time high, farmers expanded their production to sell crops, cotton, and beef to the U.S. government. Drawing on labor provided by volunteers, Mexicans, and even convicts, they continued producing, supplying food and cotton to Americans at home and overseas.

WHILE MINERS, DEFENSE WORKERS, and farmers supplied goods needed to win the war, others contributed their time as volunteers on the home front. By raising funds for bond drives, rationing, recycling, and serving soldiers, they aided the war effort.

Early in the war, the federal government began to ration goods and services to prevent shortages in the military and on the home front. To supply the

★ ★

LABOR SHORTAGES

Shortages of labor affected all areas of the economy and the service arena, including hospitals. Training as a nurse at Phoenix's Saint Joseph's Hospital from 1940 to 1943, Eleanor Curran gained valuable experience because many nurses had enlisted in the armed services. "Students ran the hospital with the nuns," she says. "There was only one obstetrician left in town." Many of the men serving at nearby air fields and bases lived with their wives, who were having babies despite the shortage of medical personnel. Curran explains that the obstetrician's nurse gave medicine to women in labor to slow the labor, so the physician would be there when they delivered. "The babies were born blue," says Curran. "Then they performed circumcisions [on the boys] to wake them up." The hospital was so crowded that some of the newborns slept in dresser drawers. After completing her training, Eleanor Curran became a navy nurse and served in Sun Valley, Idaho, and San Diego, California.

military with needed goods, such as rubber, meat, leather, and gas, civilians often had to do without. Governor Osborn issued a 1942 proclamation urging Arizonans to ration and recycle: "The luxuries and even many of the necessities to which we have become accustomed through long years of comfortable living may have to be sacrificed to the military effort necessary to bring victory. Things which yesterday we easily discarded as being of no value today have assumed tremendous importance. Among the articles that our war machine requires in vast quantities and of which there is a critical shortage at the moment are all sorts of metals, rubber, hemp, and fats. Our people are called upon by the military authorities to gather and conserve these essential materials and to make them immediately available for use."

To conserve meat, the governor created Meatless Thursdays. Housewives devised new recipes or consulted victory cookbooks to learn to substitute other ingredients for sugar and eggs. People grew victory gardens to conserve vegetables. By the end of the war, more than one-third of the food consumed in the United States came from these gardens. But despite government encouragement and assistance, families encountered difficulties.

In an interview for the Arizona Women's Lives Project, Elsie McAlister describes her rationing experiences: "Rationing was rather a hard thing, particularly with growing children who wear out shoes so quickly, because we had stamps for [shoes] . . . Stamps for sugar. That was a very hard thing for my family to do without. And the gasoline. In fact, we had to discontinue going to the doctor in Miami, the company doctor over there because most of the time we just did not have enough gas to make runs like that. We were issued a liberty cookbook [and] I tried my best to substitute. We used honey a great deal

YOU CAN HELP **WIN** THE **WAR** IN YOUR **KITCHEN!**

★ Of course you homemakers can't stage a direct attack against the enemy with your kitchen equipment, but you can play an important part in making America strong by serving your family the right foods, properly cooked!

Get nutrition conscious! Select nutritious foods and prepare them correctly to preserve their vitamin content. Take full advantage of your gas and electrical appliances to save time . . . save work . . . and save money!

HEAR Ruth Kruger, Home Economist, Discuss

The Importance of "FOOD FOR VICTORY"

In Another Broadcast of "Home Service Of The Air" TOMORROW

KOY ★ **KTAR**
10:30 A. M. 3:30 P. M.

Sponsored by the

CENTRAL ARIZONA LIGHT and POWER • COMPANY •

Newspapers and radio programs called on women to "help win the war" by rationing and substituting for some foods, such as meat, sugar, eggs, and butter.

instead of sugar. And I did make some muffins with honey that my family liked, but most things we had to substitute they didn't care for. We missed the meat terribly."

Housewives saved kitchen fats, including bacon grease, meat drippings, and vegetable shortening, which could be used to make glycerin for explosives. Cooks were instructed to strain these fats into clean wide-mouthed cans. After collecting a pound, citizens took the fat to a meat dealer, who would in turn give it to a war industry.

To gather necessary war materials that were in short supply, citizens organized recycling drives for copper, brass, and bronze items. Major Phoenix intersections became metal collection points. War industries melted donated metal to use in other goods. In November 1942 parishioners of St. Mary's Church donated the church bell for use in armaments. Organizers of the Phoenix salvage drive quipped in an ad, "I've praised the Lord. Now I go to make some ammunition!" People in Flagstaff also contributed, recycling twenty-five tons of scrap metal, including the iron courthouse fence, dating from the 1890s.

Children often aided in these efforts by recycling paper and scrap metals. As part of a national campaign begun in June 1942, the Standard Oil Company organized a contest among Phoenix children to collect scrap rubber. A group of Mexican American children from the Marcos de Niza public housing project, led by administrator Roy Yanez, won the contest by collecting twenty-two hundred pounds of rubber. This amount represented 29 percent of the total collected in Arizona for the month-long salvage drive.

Flagstaff teenagers also became involved, forming a Victory Club in 1943 after hearing news reports about the war on the radio. Their records, contained in Special Collections at Northern Arizona University, demonstrate that they were "a group boiling over with energy and [a] deep and abiding desire to aid in the war effort." They raised funds for war bonds and recycled tin cans and paper until 1945, all the while holding weekly meetings and recording minutes.

Throughout the state, children's organizations worked on the home front. Boy Scouts conducted recycling drives while Girl Scouts baby-sat for working mothers, collected silk stockings, and made scrapbooks of magazine stories for soldiers. Campfire Girls learned flag etiquette and first aid, while also promoting a national nutrition program. Girls volunteered as minute maids to sell war stamps and bonds.

To support the troops serving overseas, citizens became involved in war bond drives. The huge effort of financing the war required participation from nearly everyone. People received encouragement to buy war bonds through community organizations and places of employment. "You bought war bonds at work," says Annie Garcia Redondo of Phoenix. "They'd take so much out of your paycheck every week, when you got paid, and when, you completed twenty-five dollars they'd give you a bond for that. . . . If you wanted to do that, it would help the country. And so if it helped the country you couldn't do anything else but buy a war bond! I bought lots of them."

Fundraising was one of many tasks undertaken by Red Cross volunteers during the war. Red Cross women also worked at hospitals, served in the motor corps and as ambulance drivers, drove during blackouts, rolled bandages, staffed health clinics, and ran United Service Organizations (USOs). Other tasks included assisting servicemen's relatives and recruiting women to serve as nurses in the armed services or as nurses' aides in local hospitals. Connie

Tucson residents gave their all for the war effort, especially in collecting for scrap drives. This impressive pile was collected in 1942.

Women volunteered for many kinds of duty during the war. This group of Red Cross canteen volunteers posed in front of the Phoenix Union Station. The women met military trains and provided refreshments for the servicemen.

McConnell interviewed soldiers stationed in Tucson and aided families of soldiers "who had problems and needed to contact their people who were overseas."

Bertha Palmer, volunteering for the Red Cross canteen at Phoenix's Union Station, made hundreds of doughnuts, her arms aching sometimes from the effort. Providing snacks to soldiers passing through, she saw sick and injured soldiers. "[S]o many invalids were on the train," she recounts in an oral history interview. "We had to carry the food out to them."

The Red Cross also provided recreation and food for soldiers traveling through Sky Harbor Canteen. Volunteers kept a logbook and recorded events on March 26, 1945: "Had a hospital flight. Served four boys on the plane. One was quite ill. We gave him three oranges we had brought for our own lunch. Peeled one for him. He was so pleased. Great tears rolled down his cheeks. He just couldn't talk, he was sort of choked."

To meet these vital needs, the existing women's clubs doubled their efforts. Over seventy-six different organizations provided a thousand volunteers in the

Servicemen's Center on Fourth Avenue and Washington Street. Representing the Business and Professional Women's Club, Garden Club, and Junior League, as well as numerous church auxiliaries and other organizations, they staffed the center every day.

These centers were segregated, as was all of Phoenix in the 1940s. Black soldiers were welcome at the Center for Colored Soldiers in downtown Phoenix. Laura Harris discusses her mother, Blanche Dungee, and her work during World War II: "My mother ran the [black] canteen. It was down on Fourteenth and Washington. They had dances and music. Where my mom worked they had different supplies . . . that they could buy. But mostly it was a place to come and relax, sit around and talk and dance. There were quite a few [troops] coming through."

This announcement for a servicemen's recreation center in Phoenix included information at the bottom of the sign on a "Recreation Center for Colored." These centers were kept separate.

WARTIME EVENTS PUSHED racial contradictions into view and led to increased discussion and agitation for equal rights among the African American population. Roy Wilkins, assistant secretary of the National Association for the Advancement of Colored People, spoke to three hundred people in Phoenix on December 2, 1942. Roy A. Lee, the principal of the Phoenix Colored High School, introduced Wilkins, a national speaker who asked Americans to practice democracy at home by "giving unlimited opportunities to colored people in both war industries and the armed forces." This speech and the large audience present for it illustrated the desire of many black Phoenicians to consider the issue of segregation. An article in the *Arizona Sun*, an African American newspaper, demonstrates the same concern. In

LEW DAVIS

★ ★ ★

Lew Davis, later to become one of Arizona's foremost artists, painted many wartime posters that were reproduced by the military as training aids.

Lew Davis, a European American artist, was born in Jerome, Arizona, in 1910. Known for his paintings of miners and mining towns, he was also a muralist and one of the founding members of Arizona's first art school under the Works Progress Act. Davis became troubled by racial inequality when he accepted a commission to paint a mural in the white officers' mess hall at Fort Huachuca in 1943. This segregated base was the training ground of the Ninety-second Division, composed of African American troops who would eventually fight in Europe. While working at Fort Huachuca, Davis discovered that black soldiers, suffering from poor morale, had torn posters depicting white soldiers from their walls. Davis decided to create new artwork portraying the participation of black soldiers in the war.

With the aid of African American soldiers, he set up a silk-screen shop and created nine posters that were distributed nationally. The posters represented common themes such as the need to contain military secrets, buy war bonds, care for military equipment, and not waste food. Two of the posters reminded soldiers that syphilis could cause blindness, and gonorrhea could be crippling. While at Fort Huachuca Davis created a mural entitled "Negro Participation in America's Wars" for the black officers' mess. This mural, now on display in the Howard University Gallery of Art, contains five panels depicting African American participation in wars from the American Revolution to World War I. Lew Davis bridged racial barriers in order to build greater unity in support of the war effort. Following the war, he went on to become one of Arizona's most prominent artists.

One of Lew Davis's most widely distributed posters was a morale booster for black servicemen.

"Education and Understanding Will Solve the Race Problem," Mrs. S. M. White argued that segregation damaged the war effort. She also stated that Americans with racist attitudes were Nazi sympathizers, and in reality, traitors. According to Mrs. White, black Americans did not want to marry into other races or be in the same social circles; they simply wanted "to be given equal consideration and opportunities to earn a living the same as any other American."

Although racial issues received some attention during the war, segregation remained firmly in place. Sometimes racial divisions led to lack of recreational outlets and poor living conditions—two concerns affecting the African American 364th Infantry, stationed at Papago Park in Phoenix. Another black division, also stationed in the Phoenix area, was the 733rd Military Police Battalion. Rivalry existed between these two divisions, and eventually conflicts between the divisions erupted into violence, according to Jason Gart, author of *Papago Park*.

On November 26, 1942, soldiers at a Phoenix African American café began to fight. A black military policeman tried to control a soldier from the 364th Infantry. Tension had been building for these soldiers due to poor living facilities and lack of recreation in segregated Phoenix. Soldiers from the 364th Infantry rallied to support their friend in opposition to the black military police from the 733rd Military Police Battalion. The police had nearly subdued them when additional armed members of the 364th arrived from Papago Park. Members of the 364th exchanged gunfire with the 733rd Battalion, and civil police also became involved. This riot resulted in the deaths of two people and the injury of twelve others.

Three days after the riot, on November 30, 1942, military officers declared Phoenix out of bounds for soldiers. "Prostitution and gambling were wide open as people came out here in the service," says Frank Snell, a Phoenix attorney. He and other business leaders worked through the chamber of commerce to undercut economic losses caused by the out-of-bounds order. They pressured the city government to clean up the city. But officials were slow to respond, and the chamber of commerce board convinced Mayor Stewart to replace the police chief, city clerk, and city magistrate in December 1942. Military leaders then removed the out-of-bounds order. Eventually, similar problems in Phoenix city government led to the formation of the Charter Government Committee in 1949.

THE NATIONAL EMERGENCY of World War II led to multifaceted changes on the home front. The presence of thousands of troops in Arizona's towns, deserts, and mountains changed the land and the fabric of daily life, sometimes even leading to political shifts. Racial issues came into sharp focus as those from minority ethnic groups proved their loyalty to the United States, contributing time, money, and even their lives to win the war—they gained a powerful means to push for equality. Citizens from every ethnic group altered their work, food, and gas consumption along with their daily activities. The service of loved ones in the armed forces and one's buying habits became public affairs—little was left to the private realm.

When the war ended, Arizonans celebrated their victory with parades and parties. The public war had defined their private lives for nearly four years, and they were ready to regain their equilibrium.

8

PRISONERS OF WAR

LLOYD CLARK

"STRANGE DAT VE should haf to kill each other before becoming such goot friends."

That philosophical epilogue was uttered by a former German U-boat officer as he rode in a convoy with erstwhile enemies. Jürgen Wattenberg, ex-commander of the U-162, had been dozing as the vehicles carrying him and eight fellow ex–prisoners of war journeyed westward across Arizona toward the Colorado River.

They had been invited "to renew in friendship an association commenced in anguish." In a ceremony at the site of their former incarceration at Papago Park, an observance had been conducted on January 5, 1985—four decades after they had been hunted fugitives in the land where now they were welcome.

Kapitän Wattenberg, Wilhelm Günther—a former coast artillery officer who had been captured in North Africa—and Johann Kremer, one of Wattenberg's crewmen, who was taken prisoner when their submarine was sunk in the Caribbean, were three of the twenty-five German POWs who had fled the camp on the outskirts of Phoenix in 1944. With five other former Papago POWs, they were being taken on a motor tour by some Arizona history buffs who had become fascinated with their World War II escapades.

Most notable among these activities was the flight from the Papago Park camp via a 178-foot tunnel dug under their compound. It exited on the west bank of the Arizona Cross Cut Canal, now a part of Scottsdale. As they emerged during the hours of darkness, December 23 and 24, 1944, they initiated what has become known as "the greatest escape by Axis prisoners from a U.S. compound during World War II."

The December 1944 escape of German prisoners of war from the Papago camp was made through this tunnel. A ladder brought twenty-five Germans from fourteen feet below to the surface. The photograph is from the collection of Mrs. Lawrence C. Jorgensen, whose husband was a guard at the time of the escape.

While that event has been described in books, articles, and news features, and on radio and television programs, it was but a blip on the screen of prisoner-of-war experiences in Arizona during 1943–46.

Germans, Italians, and Austrians were detained in barbed wire enclosures in state locales, with the major installations being at Florence and Papago Park. As of June 1, 1945, the head count in eighteen POW facilities in Arizona was 16,844.

Enemy captives were employed at the rate of eighty cents per day in jobs throughout the United States due to the civilian manpower shortage caused by most able-bodied males being in the armed services. In Arizona, crops harvested by POWs included citrus, cotton, corn, and melons. They also cut timber, maintained irrigation canals, did laundry in quartermaster depots, applied their skills as electricians and masons, hauled and stored supplies, and salvaged non-munition items.

The Geneva Convention prohibited the use of prisoners "for manufacturing and transporting arms or munitions of any kind, or for transporting material intended for combatant units." This proviso may not have been strictly adhered to at times. For example, on Sunday, May 15, 1945—a week after victory in Europe (V-E Day)—thirty-nine railroad cars containing 2,082 tons of explosives and ammunition arrived at the Navajo Ordnance Depot at Bellemont, west of Flagstaff. The post commander issued an emergency call for stevedore-type labor. It is likely that some of the 250 Austrians interned there answered the call.

According to historian John Westerlund, civilian foremen who supervised the crews spoke favorably of the POWs' performance and commended "the eagerness and willingness of the prisoners to do a good job on any assigned labor."

Westerlund also found that the Austrians "had disavowed the Nazi party and willingly supported the U.S. No escapes were made or even plotted" at Bellemont. They were content to bide their time in the alpine clime "because

Officers' quarters at the Papago Park camp were a bit more commodious than those housing men of lower ranks.

Construction of this stockade, "the prison within the prison," was underway in December 1944 and January 1945 at the Papago Park Prisoner-of-War Camp. The arrow points to the guard tower that overlooked the camp.

it reminded them of home." Their willingness to assist their captors was demonstrated on May 18, 1945. On that Friday, the U.S. Forest Service supervisor asked Colonel John Huling, Jr., the depot commandant, to provide men to fight a fire in Shultz Pass. Eighty-two prisoners joined 120 local firefighters in quelling the blaze.

ON THE FIRST Sunday in January 1985, the German visitors drove by Bellemont on Interstate 40, on their way to the Grand Canyon. Wattenberg remembered that he had been aware of the POWs being held there during World War II, but he did not recall them as Austrians. After an overnight stay at the South Rim, the travelers again proceeded west on I-40 and stopped at a café east of Ash Fork.

The waitress inquired about the billed black caps the Germans wore and was told that the men were former prisoners of war and U-boat crewmen. A bearded man in his sixties sat at a nearby table. When the server took his order, she commented on the naval tattoos on his arms.

"Yeah," he responded, "I was in the merchant marine during the war. Our ship was sunk by a German U-boat."

Returning with his coffee, the waitress advised the trucker quietly of the backgrounds of the Germans. He then rose and approached the tallest (Wattenberg) of the group, which was preparing to leave. He raised his burly arm in what the American tour guide mistook as a menacing move. That impression was dispelled immediately, however, as the trucker announced to all:

"I want everyone in here to know that these guys in the caps are former U-boaters," he said with a sweep of his tattooed arms. "I was on a ship in the Mediterranean sunk by a German sub during World War Two. If it hadn't been for men like these, I wouldn't be here today. They gave us a raft, jugs of water, and told us which way to row to shore!"

The waitress-informant was the first to applaud, and then all in the café joined in acknowledging the ex-seaman's gesture, with Wattenberg thanking the man in English.

This was one of the many instances during which wartime enemies recognized the seeming incompatibility of their roles while extending courtesy and consideration to one another. In the years since the prisoners were repatriated, some have returned to the States and renewed associations with former guards or with civilians with whom they came in contact while performing work details.

The five-vehicle convoy of Germans and their Arizona hosts proceeded to Laughlin, Nevada, the gaming community on the Colorado River opposite Bullhead City, Arizona. Wattenberg expressed satisfaction at having finally seen "Arizona's Nile."

When interviewed by a Phoenix writer at an Austrian resort hotel in 1984, Wattenberg had commented on an *Arizona Highways* magazine cover photo showing the stream and captioned "The Colorado River—Arizona's Nile." Grinning, he'd stated: "The last time I vas in your state, I haf not occasion to see dis river."

★ ★

WORK DETAIL

One Wehrmacht veteran, Rolf Koenigs—taken prisoner in Tunisia in February 1943—was among Papago Park POWs sent to Idaho in 1945 to harvest sugar beets. On the farm of Horace Hale at Blackfoot, Koenigs become a trusted worker and a lifelong friend of Hale and his wife, Delta. Returning to the States via Canada in 1963, Koenigs hired on as a truck driver, the assignment he had had in the Afrika Korps. He visited the Hales several times before

German prisoners of war, unaccustomed to the desert heat, stripped to their shorts at the Papago Park camp.

they died. Every Easter and Christmas since, Koenigs orders a wreath to be placed on the Hales's graves in the Blackfoot Cemetery.

Now a resident of Glendale, Arizona, Koenigs is a former employee of the Phoenix Parks and Recreation Department. He worked occasionally at Papago Park, where he had been introduced to Arizona as a prisoner.

"Ich kan mich auf nicht daran erinnern," added Günther, who comprehended some English though he did not speak it. He was, with mock seriousness, seconding Wattenberg's ironically stated regret at not having seen the river in 1945. Günther had been one of the "crazy boatmen." That was how the other escapees referred to him, Wolfgang Clarus, and Friedrich Utzolino. Their ill-fated attempt to float on a homemade raft to Mexico earned them that title.

★ ★

THE CRAZY BOATMEN

Three coast artillery officers—Wilhelm Günther, Wolfgang Clarus, and Friedrich Utzolino—captured in North Africa in May 1942 had contrived to escape their captivity by way of the Gila River, which flowed into the Colorado. The Colorado emptied into the Gulf of California. Using canvas and pitch that Wattenberg had requested from the American lieutenant in charge of their compound—"to repair the leaky roofs of their barracks"—Kapitän Günther and Oberleutnants Clarus and Utzolino had constructed a raft out of scrounged materials.

With considerable difficulty—causing worrisome delay during that getaway period of December 23–24, 1944—the three had maneuvered sections of their raft through the underground tunnel. The day after Christmas they made their way to the Gila River, some twenty miles southwest of their barbed wire enclosure.

"Those stupid Americans!" Clarus exclaimed. "They put blue on the map when there's no water in the river."

Because releases from the upstream dam were limited at that time (winter, when agricultural needs were minimal), the water was too shallow to float their craft. The would-be river-boaters laughed dejectedly as they abandoned the raft and resumed their hike, less burdened, along the river valley.

On January 8, 1945, they hiked undetected to within the sight of the small town of Gila Bend. An irrigation canal east of the river was a good place to wash his underwear, Utzolino decided. Despite Günther's warning that his shorts might draw attention, Utzolino draped them on a desert shrub to dry. Some range riders spotted the fugitives and alerted the military, and by midafternoon that Monday, the "crazy boatmen" were being returned under guard to Papago Park.

The tour group stayed overnight at a Laughlin hotel casino. When leaving, Josef Mohr, a jovial veteran who was fairly fluent in English, observed whimsically: "Ve left our *marks* on der tables at Laughlin."

The Germans and their Arizona hosts drove south to Lake Havasu City, a community catering to retirees and promoted as having a reconstructed London Bridge over an inlet of the Colorado River. Wattenberg posed for a photo beside the structure and remarked with a grin: "I alvays vanted to put my boat up de Thames under dis bridge."

But his U-162 had been disabled in the Caribbean by depth charges from three British destroyers on September 3, 1942. His reflections in January 1985 of that event were amplified by a remark: "But I vas too— how do you say?"

"Ambitious? Careless?" the photographer offered.

"Yah, I vas too ambitious," he replied, explaining that on his three combat forays in the Atlantic, he had sunk only two merchant vessels and tankers—no warships. He described his excitement when the lookout spotted a destroyer as they cruised on the surface about forty miles off the coast of British Guiana. Wattenberg had ordered the sub to periscope depth and into attack

In January 1985 Jürgen Wattenberg, former skipper of the German submarine U-162, stood at London Bridge at Lake Havasu City, Arizona, and remarked, "I alvays vanted to put my boat up de Thames under dis bridge."

speed. A torpedo was fired. It went wide of its target, but its wake alerted the skipper of the *Quentin* to the sub's position.

A swarm of depth charges soon rocked the 750-ton submarine as the *Vimy* and *Pathfinder* joined the attack. The British admiralty's account of the encounter reported ten, six, and fourteen depth charges fired, respectively, by His Majesty's destroyers *Pathfinder, Quentin,* and *Vimy*. It noted also that "the captain remained on the bridge until she sank."

The time was a few minutes before midnight of Thursday, September 3, 1942. The Brits picked up all but two of the fifty-one crew members and put them ashore at Port of Spain on their colonial island of Trinidad. Engineering

Officer Edgar Stierwald was killed while releasing scuttling charges, and Seaman Ernst Dettmer was presumed drowned.

Thus began the almost four years of detention of these U-boaters. They were turned over to the U.S. Navy by the British and eventually became charges of the U.S. Army. Transported by trains to Florida, then to processing centers in Maryland, then to confinement camps at Crossville (about fifty miles west of Knoxville, Tennessee), Stringtown (south of McAlester, Oklahoma), Orchard Park (south of Roswell, New Mexico), and other locales, they were keenly aware of the expanse of the United States by the time they arrived at Papago Park in January 1944.

THE ESCAPE AND search for the twenty-five Germans during December 1944 and January 1945 caused extensive alarm among Arizonans. Their trepidation was stimulated by warnings from lawmen that the fugitives were capable of acts of sabotage and inflicting bodily harm. An article in *American Magazine* by FBI Director J. Edgar Hoover—"Enemies at Large: Here's How Uncle Sam Tracks Down These Dangerous and Desperate Foes When They Escape"—cautioned the populace to be wary of furtive strangers.

So it was on New Year's Day 1945 that Verna Cooper reminded the boy left to care for her children:

"Don't let anyone come in. Those Germans are still on the loose and thought to be headin' for Mexico. So, we're right on that route, and I don't want any strangers in my house—particularly Nazis."

She and her husband, Newton, and two ranch hands then headed for the fields to gather grain sacks to prevent them from being soaked by an approaching storm. Leroy Ashmore, a sixteen-year-old from Coolidge, settled into the routine of entertaining six-year-old twins, Janet and Joan, and Richard, age five.

Within a half hour two men approached the Coopers' backyard, where Richard was playing soldier with a toy rifle he had received for Christmas. The lad took aim at the men, who saw that the boy's "weapon" was harmless.

Hans Werner Kraus, former commander of the U-199 and lately a resident of Compound 1-A, Papago Park, and Helmut Drescher, second watch officer on the sub, were abandoning their flight. Drescher's left foot had become infected from thorns of a cholla cactus he had encountered during their desert trek.

According to historian John Hammond Moore, Kapitänleutnant Kraus, fluent in English, told the youngster that they were thirsty. Richard led them into the house. The startled baby-sitter was put at ease by the twenty-eight-year-old officer explaining that they meant no harm and would wait to give themselves up when the adults returned. In the meantime, he would tell them about their adventures as U-boaters and prisoners.

Seed-grain sacks collected, the Coopers and their helpers stopped at the barn to unload the truck. Verna said she would go prepare supper. Upon entering her home, the two men came to attention, clicking their heels, and gave an open-handed salute. Kraus announced:

"Ve are escaped German officers, and ve vish to surrender."

Mrs. Cooper was aghast. She glanced at the children and Leroy. They appeared to be all right. Then she ran outside and breathlessly informed Newton about their "guests."

"Heil Hitler!" the Germans chorused, giving an open-handed salute. Kraus said they wanted to surrender.

Verna began to take notice of the visitors. Their clothes were neat. They appeared clean and were clean-shaven. The younger man, dark-haired Helmut Drescher, was handsome, reminding her of a movie star. The older man was

★ ★

OTHER ESCAPE ATTEMPTS

The tunnel exit from Papago Park was not the only escape route from that camp during its existence from September 1943 to February 1946. There were numerous minor wanderings away from work details, but the disappearance of five U-boat officers in February 1944 was but a prelude to the intrepid flight ten months later.

Packed tightly under a truckload of plywood, the five officers were driven out the gate by a POW trusty the Americans used to make deliveries. Two were taken into custody in Tucson, but three made their way about forty miles into Mexico before being captured by U. S. and Mexican soldiers.

gentlemanly, balding, and had mannerisms like Dr. Schoen, she thought. (Dr. Schoen was a late Casa Grande physician of German descent.)

Newton drove the escapees in his 1942 Hudson Terraplane the two-and-a-half miles to the POW branch camp at Stanfield, where armed soldiers took them into custody and returned the pair to Papago Park. They were the first two of the eleven officers among the escapees to be brought "home."

When he came home, Newton told his wife that the Germans apparently had walked about ten miles south of their ranch before turning back. "I know they got that far," he stated, "because the captain described that stock tank down there exactly." (Measured as the crow flies from Papago Park, that distance was approximately fifty miles.)

Verna fed the children and put them to bed. She and her husband sat down to dinner and to reflect on the most exciting New Year's Day they had ever experienced.

"The kids enjoyed them," she stated. "They wanted to hear more about those Krauts' escapades." (This was before the advent of TV.) "I'm so glad you got them to the camp without any trouble," she smiled.

"Well," Newton offered pragmatically as water began streaming down the windowpanes, "we got the grain sacks in before the rain."

FORTY YEARS LATER Verna Cooper, widowed, was driving her Cadillac southward from Lake Havasu City in the convoy taking former POWs on tour. Although that Tuesday, January 8, 1985, was sunny and mild, the wind whipping through the open right front window of the sedan was causing discomfort. An electrical connection had malfunctioned, and the glass could not be raised.

Helmut Micha, his wife, Erna, and Gine Hatton were passengers in the Cooper car. Gine—a member of the host group—was a teacher of German at Saguaro High School, Scottsdale. During the drive she thought of an expression she learned when working at a U.S. Air Force base in her native Germany following World War II. She decided to "shoot the breeze" as a means of taking their minds off the air turbulence.

Gine translated for Verna some of the information Helmut recounted about his experiences. He had been a crewman on the U-513. It was sunk in July 1943 off the Brazilian coast by a U.S. Navy plane. In a large shipment of prisoners, he arrived by train at the Tempe depot on January 4, 1944.

At Papago Park he maintained at one time within his compound seventeen doves, eleven rabbits, twenty-four chickens, and five ducks. He also had an Irish setter, which he tearfully left behind when he departed in September 1945 for repatriation.

He was fortunate, Helmut explained through Gine's interpretation, to have been a prisoner in America. "I survived," Micha stated laconically. "My sister did not." Erna explained that her husband's sister died in an Allied bombing raid on their hometown, Essen.

The breezy conversation subsided as the convoy slowed when entering Parker. Soon the five vehicles stopped at an automobile dealership where the inoperative window might be repaired. The tour guide sought out the service manager and explained the problem. Before a technician could be made available, ten minutes elapsed. When the mechanic approached the car, Alfred Dietrich, smiling broadly, stated: "It's okay. I fix it." He activated the lever, and the window raised and lowered.

In the short time it took to seek an American's help, Dietrich, formerly the U-162's electrician, had taken off the panel and repaired the connection. Kapitän Wattenberg commented that his *Elektriker* was always prepared.

The convoy proceeded via Wickenburg and approached the Salt River Valley as a multihued sunset adorned the horizon. That evening the travelers dined at a German restaurant, where Wattenberg offered a toast to their Arizona hosts. He stated that a wonderful trip was ending, but it was the beginning of a beautiful friendship.

ALTHOUGH GERMANY AND Italy had been allied in their effort to conquer Europe and North Africa, their fighting forces had virtually no association once they became prisoners. At times, some of the Germans from Papago Park would be at the Arizona State Fairgrounds in Phoenix when Italians were there, but they did not mingle. POWs worked there for the U.S. Quartermaster Corps, salvaging vehicles and equipment. The Salt River Valley Water Users Association (now the Salt River Project) employed details to keep canals and irrigation ditches free of weeds and debris, and the prisoners' labor supplemented the civilian manpower shortage in agriculture and other enterprises. One fortuitous assignment held by Josef Mohr (the U-boatman who punned in 1985 that the Germans left their marks on the gaming tables in Laughlin) was that of a gardener at the Arizona Biltmore. A few years after being repatriated, he opened his own floral shop in Wuppertal, Germany.

Prisoners of both nationalities generally fared well with the civilian populace. Marjorie Moser was seventeen when the Germans picked cotton on the family farm seven miles west of Buckeye in 1945. They were among some two hundred POWs confined at the Buckeye branch of the Papago Park camp.

Marjorie (Mrs. Al Sroka of Phoenix) remembered in 2001 that Walter Rötzel was one of the prisoners who came to the well behind the farmhouse. A water detail of three or four men would fill the barrels early in the day and then truck them to their comrades at work in the fields.

Ethel Moser, Marjorie's mother, occasionally would give slices of cake to the water bearers. Rötzel remarked that he always enjoyed the tasty *Kuchen* his mother made, and in accented English he said Mrs. Moser's cakes reminded him of home.

The friendly exchange led to the Mosers' learning of Walter's musical talent, and he was invited several times to play the piano in their parlor. One of the popular wartime songs that Rötzel played and sang was suited to his status: "Don't Fence Me In."

Late in 1942 the prisoner-of-war camp at Florence received its first contingent of five hundred Italians who had been captured in North Africa. By spring of 1943, twenty companies of two hundred Italians each were confined there.

MISS RUTH WRIGHT was a postmaster at Valley Farms from 1942 to 1972. The postal facility was in her general store on the road between Florence and Coolidge. Miss Wright, eighty-three, recalled in a 2001 interview at her retirement home in Glendale the many occasions when Italian prisoners would be accompanied by their American guards to purchase cigarettes and sundries in her store.

Fluent in Spanish, she was moderately successful in communicating with the foreigners and told them whenever they might be in the Florence POW Camp hospital to say "hello" to her mother, Stella, working there as a licensed practical nurse.

One POW who remembers patronizing her store is Luigi Moscardi. He and his younger brother, George, were taken prisoners by the British in Tunisia in May 1943. Luigi was in the tank corps, and George was an infantryman. Kept together as prisoners, they arrived at Florence in July 1943 and became cotton pickers and general laborers. That was the role of most of the five thousand Italians who were assigned there and detailed to barbed wire–enclosed branches at Casa Grande, Cortaro, Eleven Mile Corner, Eloy, Safford, and Stanfield.

After Italy's surrender to the Allies on July 20, 1943, that nation's detainees were offered affiliation with a military auxiliary serving the U.S. Army. Luigi enlisted as a baker with the rank of corporal. George became a sergeant as a dental technician. They served at posts in California until repatriated. In 1947 the brothers returned home to Venice, where George died in 1989.

This guard tower at the Florence prisoner-of-war camp was typical of the surveillance structures erected at compounds in Papago Park, Florence, and branch camps.

At a party in Cucamonga, California, Luigi had met Alicia Banetti, an Italian American. She came to Italy, and they were married on September 22, 1947, returning to the United States in 1948. They settled in Los Angeles where Luigi worked at odd jobs until 1956. When they moved to Santa Barbara, Luigi opened his own bakery.

In February 2001, the retired eighty-five-year-old Venetian expressed his good fortune at having begun his Americanization in Arizona. "God bless America!" he exclaimed when interviewed, adding: "We were never mistreated as prisoners, and we have prospered in this great country."

Another Italian-speaking soldier came to the Florence POW camp in the latter part of 1942. Newly commissioned as a second lieutenant in the U.S. Army, Elios Anderlini was assigned to the 411th Military Police Escort Guard (MPEG) Company.

Anderlini, a lawyer, had been called into service for training in military government. His first duty as a military governor—according to Colonel William A. Holden, the camp commander—was to take charge of the initial shipment of five hundred Italian POWs to arrive at Florence.

Fifty-nine years later, aged ninety-two and living in San Francisco, Anderlini remembered his experiences in Florence as pleasant. "The Italians were cooperative and happy to be in America for the duration of the war," he stated. "Eventually there were five thousand Italians held at Florence."

LA VETA KEPPEL (Mrs. R. V. Keppel of Phoenix) remembered being with her first husband at Florence. She and Earl William "Jeep" O'Neal had been married for eight months when he was assigned to one of the MPEG companies there in July 1944.

Corporal O'Neal won the Golden Gloves bantamweight title in 1943 and also was the American Athletic Union champ in his class that year. His boxing skills became known among the small contingent of German POWs at Florence, and the camp's athletic officer arranged for matches with prisoners who sought to take on the 118-pound American. Jeep beat all three of the POW challengers.

Mrs. Keppel was fortunate, she said, to be with her husband during his army service. The married couples' quarters were partitioned barracks with toilet and bath facilities down the hall. A communal kitchen and dining facility was about a quarter of a mile distant. The O'Neals would raise four girls and one boy prior to Earl's death in January 1984.

NO SABOTAGE BY POWs in Arizona was ever reported, nor were there any recorded instances of bodily harm to Americans in the state. Austrians, Germans, and Italians realized that the country in which they were captives was a haven—far from the ravages of war in Europe.

Nonetheless, a group of U-boaters with strong allegiance to their Führer perpetrated a homicide.

On the afternoon of March 12, 1945, Werner Dreschler, twenty-one, was among 350 Germans who detrained at the Tempe railway depot and were convoyed to their barbed wire enclosures at Papago Park. Some six hours after he had entered his quarters, Dreschler's badly beaten body was hanging from a rafter in the shower room of Compound 4.

At approximately six o'clock in the morning on Tuesday the 13th, Corporal O. W. Pedersen responded to a call to the guardhouse to check on some mischief in Compound 4. When he entered the bathhouse he was appalled to see the mangled body, clad in underwear, dangling before him.

The discovery set in motion an extensive investigation, which determined that Dreschler had been identified as a stool pigeon by U-boat crews he associated with at Fort Hunt in Virginia. A seaman on the U-118, which was sunk in the Azores on June 12, 1943, by two U.S. Navy planes, Dreschler was not in sympathy with the Nazi regime. He had willingly became an informant for the military interrogators who staffed the Fort Hunt facility.

After a two-day military court-martial, seven POWs were found guilty in the death of Dreschler and sentenced "to be hanged by the neck until dead."

The verdict of August 16, 1945, was appealed. Major General William H. Shedd, commander of the U.S. Army's Ninth Service Command, headquartered at Fort Douglas, Utah (with jurisdiction over the POW installations in Arizona),reviewed the cases and recommended that the death penalties of the seven be commuted to life imprisonment.

The appeal went through channels to the secretary of war and to the president, but on the night of August 23, 1945, the commandant of the U.S. Disciplinary Barracks read orders signed by the president and issued by the secretary of war that the executions would be carried out. Two days later, "commencing at zero zero zero one hours of that date" (August 25th), the first of the Papago Seven went to the gallows. By 2:48 A. M. that Saturday, the last man had dropped to his death.

When the appeal had reached the White House in July, President Truman was reacting to a wave of revulsion at the disclosure of horrors at Nazi concentration camps, to say nothing of his preoccupation with a decision to employ atomic bombs on Japan. But to this day, the sentencing to death of POWs (after their country was no longer at war with the United States) for killing one of their own, whose acts of treason they had surmised, remains questionable. The inside cover flap of Richard Whittingham's *Martial Justice* contains text expressing that concern: "If a man murdered by the Papago Park Seven was an informant and therefore a traitor, who can blame them—let alone execute them for murdering him? If the U.S. military was aware that his role was known to the German prisoners in Papago Park, why was he sent there?"

The Dreschler affair did not get Papago Park public notoriety to the degree that the twenty-five-man escape did, but it had significant impact on the administration of military justice for POWs in subsequent conflicts.

OVER THE YEARS, Arizonans' wartime anxieties about the presence of enemy personnel in the state have mellowed. Time has tempered the anger, hatred, and suspicion that warring nationalities induce, resulting in accommodations that in the 1940s seemed improbable.

Hans Lammersdorf, a naval anti-aircraft gunner captured by American troops in May 1943 at Bizerte, Tunisia, found the Arizona desert attractive during his incarceration at Papago Park. After repatriation, he applied for an immigrant permit to do logging in Canada and eventually obtained U.S. citizenship. A retired Washington State Highway surveyor residing in Seattle, the seventy-nine-year-old former inhabitant of Compound 2 at Papago Park, claimed Phoenix as his "second home in North America." He stated that he and his wife, Reidunn, "have numerous friends in the Salt River Valley where we enjoyed visiting many times."

Like Helmut Micha, whose sister was killed in an air raid on their home in Essen, most of the POWs felt fortunate to have survived the war behind barbed wire. A few returned by midcentury to take up citizenship in the country that had held them prisoners. During those trying times in Arizona, military personnel on both sides of the fences and civilians with whom they came in contact shared unique experiences that produced some enduring friendships.

9

ARIZONA'S WAR HEROES

MARSHALL TRIMBLE

EVERY CULTURE HAS a basic yearning for heroes. If a nation doesn't have heroes, it will invent them. In a time of national crisis it sometimes becomes necessary to create heroes. During the darkest days of World War II, just after Pearl Harbor, a fighter pilot named Colin Kelly was shot down in the jungles of the South Pacific. Morale was low, and Americans desperately needed a hero, so a story was fabricated about how Colin Kelly crashed his plane into a Japanese battleship. President Franklin D. Roosevelt ceremoniously awarded the Medal of Honor to his widow and appointed his infant son to the United States Military Academy.

More than thirty thousand Arizonans served in the military during World War II, and more than sixteen hundred gave their lives for their country. They represented the army, air corps, Marine Corps, and navy. Among these are Silvestre Herrera, John C. Butler, Grant Turley, and Ira Hayes. Two were officers and two were enlisted men. Ironically, I didn't realize this until I had nearly finished my story. I would like to say I planned it this way but I didn't. I chose these young men as the state's greatest war heroes without giving any thought to branch of service or rank. It couldn't have worked out better.

One was Arizona's only World War II recipient of the Congressional Medal

There were few soldiers more worthy of the designation "hero" than the Bushmasters, Arizona's 158th National Guard regiment. They received jungle-combat training in Panama, as shown here, and fought throughout the war in the South Pacific.

of Honor; another fought at the crucial Battle of Midway; one was the state's first ace in World War II; and another had his image frozen forever in the most famous photograph taken in battle.

SILVESTRE HERRERA:
THE BRAVEST OF THE BRAVE

For conspicuous gallantry and intrepidity at the risk of his life above and beyond the call of duty.
>—Private First Class Silvestre Herrera's Congressional Medal of Honor citation

It was a cold gray March morning in the green-grizzled woods of Alsace-Lorraine in northeast France. A chilly rain fell from an overcast sky, shrouding the rocky labyrinths. The dark forest was deathly quiet, the calm before the storm. Private First Class Silvestre Herrera wiped the droplets of water from his M1 rifle and gazed eastward toward the German lines.

That day his outfit, the 142nd Regiment, approached the French-German border town of Mertzwiller, where German troops were dug in. Minefields protected their gun emplacements. When orders came down to advance on the German positions, Hererra was a scout some four hundred yards ahead of his unit. Suddenly the Germans opened up with a furious artillery barrage. Eighty-eight-millimeter artillery shells screamed overhead and hit with a thunderous roar. The soldiers of the 142nd continued advancing when, from atop a nearby hill, a German machine gun nest opened fire, pinning them down.

Armed with only a hand grenade and his trusty M1 rifle, Herrera fixed his bayonet and mounted a one-man charge, knocking out the machine gun nest. Singlehandedly, he captured eight German soldiers.

He sent the prisoners toward the American lines, then mounted a frontal assault on a second machine gun nest, but in the attack he stepped on an antipersonnel mine. It set off another mine that blew off both his feet.

"I heard two explosions," he says. "I looked down, and my leggings and combat boots were gone. My pants legs were on fire." Despite the intense pain and loss of blood he continued to fight, pinning down the German troops. His rifle fire killed two German soldiers and wounded another, allowing his comrades to mount a frontal attack on the enemy position.

For his heroism that day, Silvestre Herrera would be awarded the Congressional Medal of Honor, given only to the bravest of the brave. Herrera's heroism singled him out among the state's other World War II heroes.

On March 16, 1945, a day after Herrera was wounded, the Americans opened a massive artillery barrage and the 142nd crossed the Zintzel River at Mertzwiller. A week later they crossed into Germany. On May 7 the Germans surrendered and the war in Europe was over.

This memorial to the heroism of Silvestre Herrera stands in front of the Arizona capitol in Phoenix.

Silvestre returned stateside and was sent to an army hospital in Utah. After a few months he returned to Phoenix. One August day in 1945 he was sitting beneath a chinaberry tree eating a piece of watermelon when a telegram arrived summoning him to Washington. "I was getting ready to go back to the hospi-

tal," he says, "when the telegram arrived. At first I was scared. I just wanted to be with my family. "

With his wife, Ramona, and her uncle, he traveled to Washington where, on August 23, President Harry S Truman awarded him the nation's highest honor. Herrera was sitting in a wheelchair when the president leaned over and hung the medal around his neck. "I was kind of scared," Herrera recalls. He was among twenty-seven fighting men honored that day. It was the largest number ever awarded the Medal of Honor at one time in history. "I'd rather win the Medal of Honor," Truman said, "than be President of the United States."

Since then Herrera has met and become friends with all eleven men who've occupied the Oval Office. He liked them all, but his favorites were Harry S Truman, John F. Kennedy, and Ronald Reagan. "My favorite general," he grins, "was, of course, Eisenhower."

Silvestre Herrera receives the Congressional Medal of Honor from President Harry S Truman. Herrera was the only Arizonan to win the nation's highest military decoration during World War II.

In 1956, Phoenix Elementary District Number 1 named a school in his honor. When that school was closed in 1986, a new one bore his name.

Ironically, Arizona's greatest World War II hero didn't have to go off to war. He could have stayed home with his wife and three children. When he was drafted into the army in 1944 his uncle told him, "You don't have to go, you're not a U.S. citizen. You were born in Mexico." But Silvestre loved his adopted country, and what better way could a young man show that love than to serve that nation in a time of need?

Ramona died in 1991, and he made a promise to make sure their grandchildren had an education, a chance he and his wife never had. Now he's fulfilling that promise.

Silvestre doesn't need to brag. "I let others do that if they want to," he says with a warm grin. "What I did didn't take ability or intelligence. It took faith, a positive attitude, and determination."

Those are good words for anyone to live by.

GRANT TURLEY:

ARIZONA'S FLYING COWBOY

A tall, raw-boned ex-cowboy who used to punch cows on a ranch near Snowflake, but who now is "punching" Hitler airmen, shot down four German planes on two successive days during missions to Brunswick and Frankfort.

— *Arizona Republic* (Sunday, March 26, 1944)

War always takes its toll on a nation's best and brightest. In times of crisis they are always the first to step up and volunteer for military service, the first to take on the most dangerous assignments. They go off to fight for their country for the noblest of reasons, and all too often they give their lives in the service of their country while still in the flower of youth.

Among those was Grant Turley of Aripine.

War changed forever the lives and dreams of millions of young people like Grant Turley. A few weeks after Pearl Harbor he was in Phoenix taking flying lessons at Sky Harbor. At the age of twenty he had volunteered for the air corps and had begun training to become a fighter pilot. He and his high school sweetheart, Kitty Ballard, were married just before he shipped out. He went into action in the fall of 1943, and in just ten days of action over the skies of Europe he became Arizona's first World War II ace.

Grant was the son of Fred and Wilma Turley, and the younger brother of Stan Turley, who would later serve in the Arizona legislature as Speaker of the House and president of the senate. The boys grew up on the family's Sundown Ranch at Aripine in Navajo County.

In February 1941 Grant started ground school at Phoenix Sky Harbor in preparation for becoming a pilot. He took to the sky naturally and soon was as comfortable in an airplane as he was riding his horse, Comet. By late March he was flying solo, and when he took his flight test in May, he finished at the top of his class. Orders came in early August to report to the air corps classification center in Nashville the next week. He and Kitty Ballard decided to get married before he left, so on August 4 they were joined in wedlock at Holbrook. The next day he boarded the train for Nashville.

On March 25, 1942, Grant was awarded his wings and the gold bar of a second lieutenant. He also received an expert rating on aerial gunnery. Following graduation he was given a ten-day leave to return to Kitty and Arizona for a brief honeymoon. Most of his leave was spent on a passenger train. While he was home the two traveled to Mesa, where they had their marriage vows sealed in the Mormon Temple.

On May 19 Kitty joined him in Tallahassee, Florida, to stay with him until he shipped out for Europe. She remained until July 23, when orders came for him to pack his gear. Kitty later wrote of the poignant parting: "Just as he was pulling out of the station I looked up and there he was walking down the aisle of the train. The conductor had asked him if he would like to ride as far as the base. Who would have ever thought they were to be the last few minutes of our lives together."

On August 4, 1943, he arrived in Scotland. It was also his and Kitty's first anniversary. On August 5 he wrote from "somewhere in England." He was at Duxford Air Force Base, north of London.

On October 9 he flew his first combat mission over Belgium. It was routine, and he didn't see any action. He

Lieutenant Grant Turley, right, with his P-47 Thunderbolt and crew, prepares for another mission over Europe. The swastikas painted on the side indicate the number of enemy planes shot down.

didn't have his own plane and crew yet, so the missions were infrequent. On November 3 he made his first flight over Germany.

Bad weather kept the fighters grounded much of the time. Still he was able to complete ten combat missions by November 9 to qualify for the Air Medal. A few days later he had his own P-47 Thunderbolt.

Although he'd flown many missions, Grant still hadn't fired his guns at an enemy plane. Then on February 10, he shot down his first. He came upon a flight of ten German fighters and plunged into battle.

"We were hounded at 26,000 feet by these jokers," he wrote Kitty. "Well, yours truly and his wingman got on their tails finally and followed them down. I shot three bursts on the way down, then when their leader leveled off on the deck I got off a second burst from dead astern. He blew up and went into the deck from 300 feet. Looked like one big splash of flames when he hit the ground. I then got on the tail of the second and he crash-landed in flames."

On the way home he encountered another German fighter. Once again Lady Luck smiled on Grant. "Saw one 109 coming out, but he didn't see us. I was out of ammo by this time. Boy was I glad to see England."

Lieutenant Grant Turley had bagged his first two kills.

The next day over France he bagged another. "I bounced a 109 and got a good burst, saw strikes all over the cockpit and wing roots and a lot of smoke." On the way home, and low on gas, he shot down an FW-190 on takeoff. Tracer and flak were all around, but he managed to escape unscathed, arriving home with only seventeen gallons of gas left in his tanks.

The following day they escorted some B-17s over France. The mission was uneventful, and on the way home Turley and seven other pilots strafed a German air field. He opened fire from about 250 yards out, destroying a plane as it was taking off. They also destroyed two other fighter planes on the ground.

By this time the media were getting interested in the tall, rugged Arizonan. When a correspondent from NBC interviewed him, Turley modestly shrugged off the publicity, saying "it was all in a day's work."

On Sunday, March 26, 1944, the headline in an article in the *Arizona Republic* referred to him as the "Snowflake Storm" and described his exploits over a two-day period in Brunswick and Frankfurt. Tragically, a few days before the article appeared, Grant Turley had been reported missing in action. He flew his last mission on March 6, 1944. He was in a flight with three other P-47s, escorting bombers, when German fighter planes attacked. Grant got on the tail of one and shot it down. He turned his attention to another, but a third German had positioned himself behind Grant's plane and opened up with his guns. Grant's wingman last saw him as he dove into some clouds in pursuit of a German fighter plane with another enemy plane on his tail.

Lieutenant Grant Turley became an ace in just ten days. He shot down his first two German planes on February 10. He got two more the next day. His fifth kill, making him an ace, came on February 20. Four days later he got another. He got his last one on March 6, although it wasn't credited to his record because there was no film confirmation.

A few days later, on March 17, Kitty received a telegram informing her that her husband was missing in action. She received another telegram several months later, on September 23, confirming her husband's death on March 6.

After Grant was shot down, the Germans pulled his body from the wreckage and gave him a burial. After the war he was reburied in a military grave in Liege, Belgium. In 1983 Stan Turley visited his brother's grave at the Ardennes Cemetery in Belgium. "We searched over thousands of white crosses," he says, "before finding Grant's. At the very moment we found his grave a flight of NATO aircraft flew over. The timing couldn't have been more symbolic."

JOHN C. BUTLER: HERO OF MIDWAY

For extraordinary and distinguished service as pilot of an airplane of Bombing Squadron Three in action against enemy Japanese forces in the Battle of Midway during the period June 4–6, 1942. Defying the extreme danger from a concentrated barrage of anti-aircraft fire and fierce fighter opposition, Ensign Butler, with utter disregard for his personal safety, participated in persistent and vigorous attacks against the Japanese invasion fleet. His gallant intrepidity and loyal devotion to the accomplishment of a vastly important objective contributed in large measure to the success achieved by our forces and were in keeping with the highest traditions of the United States Naval Service.

—Ensign John C. Butler's Navy Cross Citation

The Japanese attack on Pearl Harbor on December 7, 1941, nearly destroyed the Pacific Fleet. Fortunately, the American carriers were not in port and were spared to fight another day, and fight they did. The following April Colonel James Doolittle's army B-25 bombers launched from a navy carrier in a retaliatory attack on Tokyo. Then during May 4–8, 1942, the American navy fought the Japanese to a standoff at the Battle of the Coral Sea. The Japanese advance on Australia was halted, and their aura of invincibility had been shattered.

Undaunted, Admiral Isoroku Yamamoto, who had conceived and planned the successful attack on Pearl Harbor, planned to lure what was left of the American fleet to their doom and end their hopes of winning the war in the

Pacific. It was a daring gamble; he would send a diversionary force to attack the Aleutian Islands, and while the Americans were focused on Alaska, he would attack Midway, landing five thousand troops to occupy the island. Midway was located just fifteen hundred miles west-northwest of Hawaii, and he knew the Americans would never tolerate a Japanese base so close. They would, he reasoned, rush their warships to the area, where he would annihilate them with his superior naval force. He also knew that, without the navy carriers, the Americans couldn't launch another air raid on Japan.

Success for the Japanese depended on the striking power of their four mighty carriers, the *Hiryu, Akagi, Soryu,* and *Kaga.* All four had participated in the attack on Pearl Harbor. Yamamoto's plan was sound, but it depended on his counterpart, Admiral Chester Nimitz, to react to his diversionary attack by turning his attention to Alaska. It was like a giant chess game—a move by one side called for a countermove by the other. Other events, however, can sometimes alter the best-laid plans. Unknown to Yamamoto, the Americans had broken the Japanese code and Nimitz couldn't have been more privy to their strategy if he'd been sitting in their planning room.

The Battle of Midway would pit a smaller American task force strengthened with superior military intelligence against one of the most potent naval forces ever assembled. The odds were overwhelmingly in favor of the Japanese. Among the brave navy and marine pilots who fought in that crucial battle was John C. Butler of Buckeye, Arizona.

Butler was born in Liberty, Arizona, on February 3, 1921. Following his graduation from high school, Butler attended UCLA for a semester, then transferred to San Diego State. The navy offered naval flight training and a commission

This photograph shows the Douglas SBD Dauntless dive bomber, the type of aircraft Ensign John C. Butler was flying at the battle of Midway.

upon graduation, and he signed on. He earned his gold navy wings at Pensacola, Florida, in June 1941 and was then stationed in San Diego.

That fall Butler was assigned to dive-bomber Squadron Three. He had just completed his five qualifying landings in the new Douglas SBD-3 when the Japanese attacked Pearl Harbor. Within twenty-four hours his squadron shipped out on the carrier *Saratoga*.

During the next few months the pilots of the *Saratoga* flew combat patrols between Wake Island and Hawaii and also saw combat in the Gilbert and Marcus Islands. On January 11, 1942, the ship was hit by a torpedo fired from a Japanese submarine. The crippled carrier returned to Pearl Harbor and then stateside for repairs. Ensign John Butler and the rest of Squadron Three were transferred to the carrier *Yorktown*. During his tour with the *Yorktown*, Ensign Butler played a prominent role in Jimmy Doolittle's daring raid on Tokyo, one of the most spectacular events of the war. It was a payback mission for the sneak attack on Pearl Harbor.

During the mission, Squadron Three bombed and strafed Japanese patrol boats. Butler sank one and damaged another. The bombing raid on Tokyo didn't do a whole lot of damage, but the psychological effects were devastating. The Japanese militarists had declared that the homeland would never come under attack, yet just six months after Pearl Harbor enemy bombs rained down on the capital city. It was a harbinger of what was to come in the years ahead.

On May 30 Ensign Butler and the men of the *Yorktown* set sail to join the *Enterprise* and *Hornet* at a place 325 miles northeast of Midway Island called Point Luck, for a rendezvous with destiny. When Admiral Yamamoto's fleet approached Midway in early June, he had no idea there were any American carriers in the area. Japanese intelligence reported the *Yorktown* and *Lexington* sunk at the Battle of the Coral Sea, and the *Hornet* and *Enterprise* were supposed to be in the Solomon Islands.

Ensign John C. Butler, a navy fighter pilot, was killed at the Battle of Midway in June 1942.

On the morning of June 4 the approaching Japanese carriers were spotted right where American intelligence said they'd be and the planes at Midway took to the air. They shot down three enemy bombers before they were swarmed upon by Japanese Zeros. Losses were heavy; seventeen American planes were downed and seven more were damaged.

Meanwhile, more than a hundred Japanese bombers got through American anti-aircraft fire and unleashed their bombs on Midway. Movie director John Ford was on the island and filmed the action. When the smoke lifted, however, the anti-aircraft guns and the air field were still operable.

While the Japanese bombers were pounding Midway, American planes from the island continued attacking the Japanese fleet. They made five separate runs and their losses were astounding. Seven of ten torpedo planes and eight dive-bombers were shot down without scoring a hit on the Japanese warships. Still, most of the planes survived the withering naval gunfire. This caused Admiral Chuichi Nagumo to call for another air strike to destroy the air field on Midway. Unaware the American navy was so close, he had his planes fitted with bombs instead of torpedoes.

Suddenly, a spotter located American surface ships approaching. One turned out to be a carrier. Nagumo knew his carriers would come under attack from the air, and he ordered his planes to change back to torpedoes. In their haste to reload, the bombs were left on the decks of all the carriers. It turned out to be a fatal error, as they would be detonated later in the day by American dive-bombers.

Ensign Butler's Squadron Three, with Max Leslie in the lead, took off from the carrier *Yorktown*. Each of the seventeen planes carried a thousand-pound bomb. One after another the dive-bombers of Squadron Three screamed toward the carrier *Kaga*. At twenty-five hundred feet each pilot pressed his electrical bomb-release button, then pulled the manual release for good measure. By the time it was Ensign Butler's turn to make a pass, the carrier was in flames. He and the rest of the squadron decided to go after other targets. Butler dove on a battleship. He released his bomb and, looking back, saw smoke and flames rising.

Bent on revenge, Japanese planes rumbled off the carrier *Hiryu*'s deck and headed for the *Yorktown*. They broke through the defense screen and attacked just as Squadron Three was coming in for a landing. Butler and the others were waved off just before the enemy dive-bombers made their run. Squadron Three landed on the *Enterprise* to refuel and resume the battle.

The Japanese attack scored three major hits on the *Yorktown,* and soon after, torpedo planes came and put her out of the fight for good. At three o'clock that afternoon, just before a Japanese torpedo bomber gave the carrier its death knell, word came from one of its patrol planes that the last Japanese carrier, the *Hiryu,* had been located.

Now it was the Americans' turn to seek vengeance. At half past three, Ensign Butler, along with the other refugee pilots from the *Yorktown,* joined the pilots from the *Enterprise* and sped off in pursuit of the fourth Japanese carrier. At about quarter to five, they spotted the *Hiryu.* They maneuvered around so they could make their dive from out of the setting sun when they were jumped by several Zeros desperately trying to save their last carrier. Despite the withering fire, the dive-bombers continued their high-speed run in. Three dive-bombers, including Ensign Butler's, were shot down. Other pilots later reported they'd seen him come under attack from a Zero.

Butler had always said he'd wanted to be a fighter pilot and tangle with a Zero. Unfortunately, his Douglas Dauntless dive-bomber was no match against the speedy, quick-turning Japanese fighter plane.

Other dive-bombers fought through the swarm of Zeros. Four one-thousand-pound bombs found their mark. The planes on deck blew up, spreading flames across a third of her flight deck. The crew fought desperately to put out the fires, but around midnight an explosion ripped through the carrier, and

★ ★

THE USS *JOHN C. BUTLER*

Historically, U. S. Navy battleships are named after states; cruisers are named after cities; and destroyers and destroyer escorts are named after navy and marine heroes. Of the many pilots lost that day, only two pilots, one of them Ensign John C. Butler, were recommended to have destroyers named in their honor.

In San Diego, a monument honors eight navy fighting ships, including the USS *John C. Butler.* The ships won glory for their role in the crucial Battle of Leyte Gulf in 1945. For Ensign Butler's family the monument also serves as his tombstone. They never recovered his body.

Irene Butler, mother of Ensign John C. Butler, is shown at the christening of the destroyer USS *John C. Butler.*

Admiral Tamon Yamaguchi ordered his men to abandon ship. He remained at his post and ordered his screening destroyers to torpedo his vessel.

By dawn on the morning of June 5, all four carriers in the Japanese main striking force, the *Akagi, Kaga, Soryu,* and *Hiryu,* had been sunk. The tide of battle had turned, and faced with devastating losses, Admiral Yamamoto ordered what was left of his fleet to retreat from battle. He was heard to say, "The price is too high."

The stubborn *Yorktown* refused to sink and was being towed home by a destroyer when a Japanese submarine administered the *coup de grace* with torpedoes. On the morning of June 7, the mighty *Yorktown* went down. She sank, according to one report, "like a tired colossus, hurt beyond pain."

The American victory was decisive and complete. The Japanese lost 3,500 men, many irreplaceable pilots, four carriers, one cruiser, and 322 planes. The American losses were one carrier, one destroyer, a cruiser, 150 planes and 307 men.

For his heroism, Butler and six other members of his squadron were awarded the Navy Cross, second only to the Medal of Honor for bravery.

Ira Hayes: The Reluctant Hero

How could I feel like a hero when only five men in my platoon of 45 survived, when only 27 men in my company of 250 managed to escape death or injury?

—Ira Hayes

When F. Scott Fitzgerald wrote: "Show me a hero and I will write you a tragedy," he could have been writing about Ira Hayes, the quiet, rather shy Pima Indian from Arizona. Ira Hayes didn't seek honor and fame—it found him. He had all the ingredients of a hero-maker's dream: he bore a charismatic name; he was a man caught on film during a dramatic, historical moment at the climax of the greatest war of the century; and he was an American Indian.

The Pulitzer Prize–winning photograph taken of Ira Hayes, four other marines, and a navy corpsman atop Mount Suribachi on Iwo Jima on February 23, 1945, became the most reproduced image in history and was the model for the largest bronze statue in the world. The statue of the heroic flag-raising has become the symbol of this nation's fighting spirit.

Ira Hayes never really understood why he was called a hero for the flag-

The most famous photograph of World War II, taken by Joe Rosenthal, shows the American flag being raised over Mount Suribachi on Iwo Jima.

raising on Iwo Jima. He lamented being singled out. Like most other combat veterans, he felt every marine and navy corpsman that stormed ashore on those black sands that day, especially those who died there, were the real heroes. In the photo, Ira is the one on the left, at the end of the line. The one whose hands are extended—symbolically reaching out as if for something just beyond his grasp.

Ira Hamilton Hayes was born on the Pima Indian reservation in the community of Bapchule on January 12, 1923. He was the oldest of six children born to Nancy and Jobe Hayes. Two of his siblings died in infancy, two more died before reaching the age of thirty. Another brother, Kenny, still lives at Bapchule.

In school the young Indian students learned about the war America was engaged in, and nine months after Pearl Harbor, at the age of nineteen, Ira enlisted in the marines. Before he left, the Pima gave him the traditional ceremony that his people had received since the days of their battles with Apache warriors. He enlisted on August 26, 1942, and soon was on a Southern Pacific train bound for the Marine Corps Recruit Depot at San Diego. After shipping out from California, Ira's outfit sailed for New Caledonia, eight hundred miles east of Australia.

When Ira enlisted he stood 5' 7" and weighed less than 140 pounds. Reservation life made it easier for him to adjust to the Spartan life of Marine Corps boot camp compared to the city boys. The drill instructors, or DI's, made it tough physically as well as mentally. If a Marine was going to break, it was better to do it at boot camp than in battle where others might die as a result. Ira loved the rich traditions of the Leathernecks. He was proud to be a Marine and remained so throughout his life.

This photo of Ira Hayes was taken after he earned his wings as a Para-Marine, and after he returned from combat overseas.

After boot camp he volunteered for paratrooper school. After six weeks of grueling training, he was the first Pima to earn his wings as a Para-Marine. After getting over his initial fear of jumping out of an airplane, he came to enjoy the thrill of it all. He wrote his parents: "I'm the happiest one here." At jump school he became known as "Chief Falling Cloud."

Ira was assigned to Company K, Third Parachute Battalion, Third Marine Division, and went through advanced training. The tough training developed an intense loyalty, trust, and respect among Ira and his group. In his letters to his parents he wrote continually of the friendships and brotherhood in his outfit.

As noted above, the Third Marine Division shipped out from California, bound for New Caledonia, where they spent the next six months training for combat. On October 14 they landed on Vella La Vella.

On December 3rd, Ira landed with the Third Marine Division at Bougainville, largest of the Solomon Islands. Within a week they were locked in deadly combat with the Japanese. Ira received his baptism by fire at a place that became known as Hellzapoppin' Ridge. It was the scene of some of the bloodiest fighting on that jungle island. One night during heavy fighting, Ira was sharing a fighting hole with a buddy. They took turns sleeping, and while Ira was on watch, a Japanese infiltrator jumped into the hole hoping to catch a couple of marines asleep. Ira was waiting and the two battled hand to hand momentarily before he ran the infiltrator through with his bayonet.

In one firefight seventeen members of his platoon were killed. The next day when they went to retrieve the bodies, they found the Japanese had horribly mutilated them, driving wooden stakes into their arms, chests, and legs, pinning them to the earth. One of the marines had to retrieve the body of his own brother.

Lady Luck was riding with Ira during the bloody Bougainville campaign. Despite having several close calls he was one of the few in his outfit to come through without a battle wound or jungle sickness.

Ira's unit returned to the United States in January where he and other seasoned combat veterans were chosen to form the nucleus of the new Fifth Marine Division. The old parachute battalion was disbanded and he became a combat infantryman.

Ira Hayes was a member of Second Platoon, Easy Company, Twenty-eighth Regiment, Fifth Marine Division, when the battle for Iwo Jima began. He was one of sixty thousand marines who stormed ashore on the black volcanic sands on February 19, which were defended by twenty-three thousand fanatical Japanese who vowed to fight to the last man. Their strategy was to make the cost in lives so heavy on Iwo Jima that the Americans would offer

★ ★

UNCOMMON VALOR

On March 3, five marines in the Fifth Division earned the Congressional Medal of Honor, a record unmatched to this day. In the words of Fleet Admiral Chester Nimitz, "uncommon valor was a common virtue" on Iwo Jima. Twenty-two marines and five sailors were awarded the nation's highest honor for bravery in the month-long battle, more than in any other in the war.

The next day the first crippled B-29 returning from a bombing run over Japan landed on Iwo. The crew jumped out and kissed the ground. One airman shouted, "Thank God for the marines." Four days later three hundred B-29s made the first fire-bombing raid on Tokyo without coming under attack from the Japanese Zeros on Iwo.

them peace with terms rather than invade the home islands of Japan. Of the 23,000 Japanese defenders, only 216 surrendered; the rest were killed.

The battle for Iwo Jima was, to use a modern phrase, the "mother of all battles." The navy figured Iwo would be taken in four days. It took thirty-six.

The dramatic flag-raising photo taken by Joe Rosenthal on February 23 is a story in itself. Earlier that morning another group of marines had scaled the slope and raised a flag atop Mount Suribachi. Marine photographer Sergeant Lou Lowery accompanied them and took a photograph of several marines placing the flag, while others provided cover with their rifles. It was exactly 10:20 A. M., and for a moment the only sound was the flag snapping in the still breeze atop the old volcano. The event brought a resounding cheer from those who witnessed it. Marines who were there that day always considered it the "real" flag-raising.

Then gunfire erupted as the enraged Japanese soldiers stormed out of their caves. Meanwhile, Secretary of the Navy James Forrestal, who was aboard a ship, saw the flag flying atop Mount Suribachi and decided he wanted it. This infuriated regimental commander Colonel Chandler Johnson, who thought the flag belonged with the marines, so he decided to send up a larger flag, ninety-six by fifty-six inches, to replace the original one that was only fifty-four by twenty-eight inches. A forty-man patrol from Easy Company that included Ira Hayes was chosen to plant the new flag.

The marines were going to work in two groups—one would lower the original flag at the same time as the other was raising the larger one. As three photographers reached the summit, Rosenthal noticed a couple of marines carrying a piece of Japanese pipe to another marine, who was holding a neatly folded American flag.

As the marines began to raise the flag, Sergeant Bill Genaust said to Rosenthal, "I'm not in your way am I?" Rosenthal said he wasn't, and out of the corner of his eye he saw the flag arc its way up. "Hey, Bill, there it goes," he said as he swung his camera around and, at the moment he estimated was the peak of action, snapped it. It was all over in a few seconds. This dramatic scene that is considered the greatest photograph ever taken in war was frozen in time almost by accident.

There is a perception that the flag-raising signaled the end of the battle of Iwo Jima, but the flag went up on Day 4, February 23. The fierce battle raged for another month before Japanese resistance was broken for good. Nine days

Mathew B. Juan–Ira Hayes Veterans Memorial Park is in Sacaton, Arizona. Juan was a hero of World War I.

after the historic flag-raising, Genaust was killed in action. The casualties in Ira Hayes' battalion were shocking. Sixteen hundred eighty-eight marines went into battle. Of those, 1,511 were killed or wounded. Of the 177 who walked off the island at the end of the battle, 91 had been wounded and returned to combat.

After the war Ira returned to America and was discharged. Attempting to escape the fame that now haunted him, Ira drifted onto skid row. It is believed he was arrested more than fifty times for drunkenness.

Tormented by survivor's guilt, he returned to the Pima Indian reservation but still found no inner peace. His Pima neighbors didn't understand the stress he was under, and many believed his public behavior had disgraced the Pima people. "I've had a lot of chances," he said, "but just when things start looking good I get that craving for whiskey and foul up."

A little more than two months after attending the dedication of the sculpture in Washington, Ira Hayes was dead at the age of thirty-two. He died in the early morning hours of January 24, 1955, after an all-night card game. All the participants had been drinking heavily, and Ira got into a scuffle with another Pima. Ira's body was found the next morning near an old abandoned automobile.

On January 26, 1955, an editorial in the *Phoenix Gazette* read: "Ira Hayes was a victim of the war as surely as though he had died on Iwo Jima with his buddies. The peace he fought to win never brought him personal peace. But he is no less a hero for that. Arizona will always honor his memory and the proud symbol he helped create."

Dressed in his marine uniform, Ira's body lay in state in the state capitol rotunda where thousands came to pay their last respects to Arizona's most tragic hero. He was then taken to Arlington National Cemetery, where on a snowy day, he was given a hero's burial.

Ira Hayes was gone but he would never be forgotten. The tragic life of this reluctant hero would become the subject of books, movies, and a song. In the 1961 movie *The Outsider* Tony Curtis stars as Hayes. In another film, *The American,* former World War II marine Lee Marvin plays Hayes. Peter La Farge wrote "The Ballad of Ira Hayes," recorded in 1964 by Johnny Cash.

Ira Hayes had found a home in the Marine Corps. Contrary to popular myth, particularly the myth propagated by the movies, he was not an outsider in the corps. It's worth believing that had he chosen to remain in the marines, his life might have turned out differently.

10

VICTORY AND BEYOND

CAROL OSMAN BROWN

AS 1945 BEGAN, Arizona was a hotbed of military activity. Air bases dotted Arizona's deserts, and planes flew overhead constantly. Troop trains rumbled across the state day and night. During these economic boom years, Arizona's population ballooned as wartime employment soared to meet the needs of military installations and defense plants, which operated several shifts. Arizonans pulled together to help the war effort. Citizens responded to a plea from the Phoenix War Housing Committee to make any spare rooms available to those working for victory on the production lines, "so that war workers will not have to live in the streets and parks."

Paul Griffin worked wartime construction jobs for Del E. Webb, who had landed a number of large federal contracts. Griffin served in the U.S. Navy in the late 1930s and received a medical discharge before seeking employment in Arizona. He recalls, "I worked on the internment camps at Sacaton and Poston. Then we built the Yuma air base for the Army Air Corps from scratch during the summer. I'll never forget wearing a short-sleeve shirt and drinking water and taking salt tablets all day while we worked in the heat. When I went to the rental cabin at night, I'd hang that sweaty shirt over the chair. In the morning it would be dry and could stand straight up by itself, because it was loaded with salt."

He and his wife lived in Phoenix in 1945, when he worked at the Goodyear Aircraft Corporation plant west of Phoenix near Litchfield Park. "We were modifying B-24 planes, making them into long-range bombers," he recalls. "We added gunnery turrets and stretched the fuselage seven feet. It was always dark when I left for work in my 1938 Ford V-8 and then picked up four other guys. It was a forty-five minute drive, so we car pooled to save gas ration cards. I worked six, sometimes seven days a week. We didn't have a telephone, and the newspaper cost too much [five cents for a copy of the *Arizona Republic*], so we got most of our news from the radio. We listened every night and were happy when our guys were winning a battle."

Griffin remembers, "One night I heard screaming next door. My neighbor, Curly Wilson, had been drafted and his wife lived there alone. So I jumped out of bed and ran over there. She'd just got a telegram from the War Department saying that her husband had been killed. It was awful. She just kept screaming and screaming."

Wanda Carlock was a Western Union telegraph operator working at the Adams Hotel in Phoenix during the war years. "I had the job of delivering messages from the War Department regarding injuries and deaths of soldiers," she says. "Few people had telephones, but I would try to reach them by phone first. If someone answered, I'd ask if they had someone in the house with them. Sometimes people would start to cry or scream right then, because they sensed it was bad news. It was a sad thing to have to do." She adds, "We always tried to deliver the telegram in person. I sent high school boys out on their bicycles, but sometimes we just couldn't locate people. It was a very tough time for families."

THEN, ON MAY 8, 1945, blasts from city and plant sirens announced Germany's surrender. It was the long-awaited victory in Europe, V-E Day. In contrast to noisy celebrations reported in New York City and Chicago, Phoenix and Tucson held relatively quiet observances of the Allied victory in Europe. Churches throughout the state opened their doors as families expressed thankfulness for the safety of loved ones and said prayers for sons, husbands, and brothers who had paid the highest price for victory. In Phoenix a simple service that embraced all religious faiths took place at the Encanto Park band shell.

Governor Sidney P. Osborn set the subdued tone for Arizona's observance of V-E Day. The *Arizona Republic* reported the governor's words. "This is a day of thanksgiving and rejoicing," the governor said in a statement to Arizonans. "But our rejoicing is tempered by the knowledge that the road to peace is yet long; that American soldiers are at this moment enduring all of the war's hardships and giving their lives in battle in the Pacific areas."

In Prescott, whistles heralded President Truman's proclamation, and the American Legion sponsored a patriotic program, which took place on the courthouse plaza. In Flagstaff, fire engine sirens blared in celebration and sparked an impromptu parade of autos down the main street. Fire department horns also blew for a few minutes in Nogales. Business was suspended in the state's leading cities, but bars were closed in most communities to discourage any untoward celebration.

Luke Field held a military review. Colonel Davies praised the Army Air Corps for its role in victory. He then declared, "The Command now turns its entire energy toward forging the weapon that will bring about victory in the Pacific." At Davis-Monthan Field, B-29 Superfortress crews continued training as usual, preparing to fight Japan; however, the air base acknowledged victory in Europe with two half-hour ceremonies.

Tucsonans heard sustained blasts from the powerhouse siren at the University of Arizona, signifying the long-awaited victory. Later, university students and staff attended a solemn assembly of thanksgiving and patriotism. Cele Peterson, Tucson businesswoman and fashion designer, recalls, "It was a joyous day. There was a great sense of relief and everybody was walking around and holding their fingers up with the 'V for Victory' sign. Friends hugged each other on the street. We all were thinking, 'Now, we have to finish this war and get the boys home.'"

On August 6, 1945, Colonel Paul W. Tibbets flew the Boeing B-29 *Enola Gay* on a historic twenty-nine hundred–mile flight to Japan and launched a new era by dropping the world's first atomic bomb on Hiroshima. Newspapers and radio stations carried the news around the world, explaining that a single bomb, as powerful as twenty thousand tons of TNT, had wiped out nearly five square miles of Hiroshima. More than seventy-eight thousand people were killed and an estimated fifty-one thousand were injured or missing.

Arizonans crowded around radios and waited anxiously for more news. They hoped to hear the familiar voice of Howard Pyle, veteran Phoenix radio announcer (later, governor of Arizona), broadcasting for KTAR radio and NBC news from the Philippines. Employees at AiResearch, engaged in production of vital parts for the giant B-29s, burst into cheers when they heard of the successful mission.

It wasn't until the next day that John Thoralf and M. Eugene Sundt of Tucson's M. M. Sundt Construction Company realized the role they had played in history. This Arizona company had been selected by the U.S. Army Corps of Engineers to handle a project in New Mexico under a shroud of secrecy. They built a power plant, installed a new water system, and erected thirteen buildings as part of the mysterious assignment. When finished in 1943, they left behind a complete city (Los Alamos, New Mexico) with schools, a hospital, and numerous technical facilities. Now Thoralf and the Sundts fully understood that they had built the Los Alamos laboratory where Dr. J. Robert Oppenheimer developed and

Oh What A Beautiful Morning

Reg Manning's "Peace" cartoon appeared in the *Arizona Republic* on August 15, 1945.

tested the world's first nuclear bomb. However, it wasn't until Major Charles W. Sweeney flew another B-29 over Japan and dropped the second A-bomb, this time on Nagasaki, that the war drew to its long-awaited end.

Arizonans spent several sleepless nights hovered over their radios, waiting for news of Japan's surrender. On August 12, 1945, a false news flash from United Press International wire service stated that Japan had accepted U.S. peace terms. This touched off some premature celebrations of the war's end in some cities. Flagstaff's fire engine siren blared and an impromptu parade started. In Phoenix, shouts of jubilation echoed through downtown as hundreds of moviegoers emptied onto the streets. A shower of newspaper confetti fell from the windows of a downtown hotel. But it all ended quickly as radio stations retracted the story.

When news of victory over Japan finally came two days later, it blew the lid off suppressed emotions. Celebrations erupted spontaneously in Arizona's towns and cities. In Flagstaff, when the fire engine sounded its horn and started a parade through town, people asked, "Are you sure it's true? Is it really V-J Day?" Then they joined the throngs in the street, singing and shouting with joy.

The celebration also started slowly in Phoenix but grew in intensity as citizens became convinced the news was true. War plants tied down their whistles, which blew while office workers streamed into the streets. Phoenix's largest air-raid siren, atop the Arizona Title and Trust building, added its wail to the din of honking car horns, whistles, shouting, and laughter from the jubilant crowd.

As the news spread, all the stores and offices closed. Emma Lou Philabaum recalls, "When I heard about V-J Day, I was riding the bus. It stopped at Seventh Street and McDowell, where a boy was selling newspapers. The front page had a big headline, 'Japan Surrenders.' I was so excited, I jumped off the bus and got a copy of the newspaper. But only the front page had a story. I was really disappointed because I expected the whole paper to be filled with stories about it. I went home to listen to the radio with my mother. My sister's husband was flying in the South Pacific, so we were all very relieved to hear the news. I was happy that we could finally stop saving bacon grease. We used to turn it in to the butcher for credit, and then he sent it to the army for making lubricants for munitions."

Another Phoenician, Louise Brown, was pregnant that summer. Her friends had planned a baby shower for August 14. "But when the V-J Day news came, they all went out to join in the celebrations instead. So nobody showed up to my baby shower," she says with a chuckle. Her husband, Garth Brown, had survived when the USS *Oklahoma* capsized during the Japanese attack on Pearl Harbor. After a few more years of U.S. Navy service, he received a medical discharge and returned to Phoenix a month before V-J Day. He remembers, "I worked at fire station number one, downtown, and when we heard the news about V-J Day, we rang the fire engine bell and siren. People were pretty wound up. Everyone was in the streets, shouting and crying. It was quite a time. Everyone was so happy it was over, but we all thought about our buddies that never came back."

In Tucson, which sent more than 60 percent of its military-age men to war, there was a joyous two-day holiday. People from rural areas flocked to Tucson to take part in the festivities, which included a victory parade and a solemn ceremony, during which crowds quietly paid their respects to the men and women who died in the battle for liberty.

Tucson readers appreciated war news reports from the editor of the *Arizona Daily Star*, William R. Mathews, who was aboard the battleship *Missouri* on September 1, 1945, when General Douglas MacArthur marked the end of World War II with the official surrender ceremony. Mathews reported that he "looked down on the surrender from a front-row seat, gun turret two."

People in Arizona's rural towns also looked forward to better times and celebrated in their own distinctive styles. Polly Rosenbaum, who served forty-six years in the Arizona state legislature, representing Gila County, remembers celebrating the end of the war in the small mining town of Hayden. "We knew something big had happened because all the fire bells and whistles from the mines and trucks hauling ore went on and didn't stop. No one except mining officials had telephones, so we all came out

Polly Rosenbaum, now a centenarian, recalls the celebrations of V-J Day at the mining town of Hayden. Mrs. Rosenbaum served in the Arizona House of Representatives for forty-six years.

of our homes and hollered to our neighbors across the fences as we walked down the hill. Everybody gravitated toward the post office, where someone made an announcement, and we all started hugging and kissing. It was a great relief to know that the war was over and we could start living again. It was as if everything had been put on hold."

Many of the boys only went back for a short visit with families. Due to the GI Bill, they had an opportunity to go to college, and they took it. Thousands of returning servicemen flooded Arizona's college campuses from 1945 to 1950, thanks to federal financial aid for veterans. Co-sponsored by Arizona's Senator Ernest W. McFarland, the GI Bill of Rights was passed by Congress in 1944 to help educate returning veterans. The GI Bill, with an expenditure of $14.5 billion, enabled more than half of all World War II veterans to attend college or technical school.

When the war ended, thousands of U.S. servicemen who had trained in Arizona fondly remembered Arizona's sunshine, clear skies, and open spaces. They headed to desert cities, such as Phoenix and Tucson, for a fresh start and inundated the college campuses.

Emma Lou Philabaum was a student at Phoenix College when they

ERNEST W. McFARLAND

★ ★ ★

Senator Ernest W. McFarland of Arizona, at left, is shown with Hollywood subcommittee chairman D. Worth Clark. McFarland led the fight for passage of legislation that created GI-Bill opportunities for World War II veterans.

Often called the "father of the GI Bill," Ernest W. McFarland co-authored the Serviceman's Re-adjustment Act of 1944, which affected the lives of millions of servicemen and their families. It provided medical and health benefits as well as pension plans and low-interest loans for homes, businesses, and education. McFarland served two terms in the U.S. Senate, working with Senator Carl Hayden to establish a VA hospital in Phoenix and introducing 1947 legislation initiating the Central Arizona Project. As Senate majority leader, Senator McFarland sponsored more than forty additional bills for the benefit of veterans and servicemen. This included extending the GI Bill to veterans of the Korean War.

McFarland was elected governor in 1954 and for four years guided Arizona through a period of industrial expansion and population growth unequaled in the state's history. In 1964 he was elected to the Arizona Supreme Court and was chief justice until his retirement in 1971. He was the only person in the nation to hold top positions in all three branches of state government. Ernest W. McFarland died in 1984 at the age of eighty-nine, but his legacy of legislative work is still helping U. S. veterans.

returned. Enrollment exploded, going from 339 in 1944 to 1,084 in 1946. "PC was a small school, sort of a glorified high school, with strict rules and mostly female students during the war years," she says. "If a student got married while in college, she had to get permission from the school president or risk being expelled. Well, all that changed when those veterans came back! It was kind of funny to watch everything being turned topsy-turvy. These men had seen the world and risked their lives. They questioned everything from rules against marriage and smoking to the high food prices in the cafeteria. Things started changing fast."

Increased population created a need for more community colleges, and by the 1990s, the Maricopa Community College District became the second largest community college district with ten colleges.

Sherman Payne, a native Arizonan, served in the Philippines and returned in 1946 to finish a journalism degree at Arizona State College (now Arizona State University) in Tempe. He later became an advertising executive with Arizona Public Service Company, a large electrical utility company based in Phoenix. "There was a big shortage of housing, so the college quickly assembled some trailers and temporary apartments for married students. They called it Victory Village, and you could hardly walk through there because it was a hodgepodge of bicycles, clotheslines, and baby buggies. It stood on the spot where Grady Gammage Auditorium is today," he recalls.

The influence of veterans returning to the United States (at a rate of one hundred thousand a month) was felt everywhere in the state. The train station was the center of attention in Tucson, as the soldiers came back in small groups.

Cele Peterson says, "Some men went back to school, but others went into banking, law, real estate, and retail sales. Many started new enterprises. There was a wonderful feeling of ambition, energy, and spirit as new businesses sprang up everywhere. Tucson had been a small community, and then it suddenly sprouted in the late forties and early fifties. We were ripe for expansion and those returning veterans made it happen."

But sudden growth also caused problems. Bulging with a 100 percent enrollment increase, the University of Arizona gladly accepted help from the Federal Public Housing Administration to build 114 two-family Quonset huts and five temporary dwelling units on the polo field to house married students. This housing became known as Polo Village.

More than twenty-four hundred veterans jammed U of A classrooms in 1947 and revitalized student government. One of those young upstarts was Morris K. Udall, who became an attorney and later served Arizona for thirty years as a U.S. congressman.

"After serving in the South Pacific, I came back to Flagstaff in 1947 and got an administrative job with the college," says Joseph C. Rolle, a native of Bisbee, who later served as dean of students at Northern Arizona University for thirty-five years. "The college built rock cottages, known as Cottage City, which, at that time, was the largest college housing area for married students in the state. It was meant to be temporary housing, but those cottages were used for almost thirty years," says Rolle.

According to Flagstaff historian and author Richard Mangum, "After the war, Flagstaff benefited from tourism, which increased in Arizona. When gasoline and tire rationing ended, people suddenly wanted to take vacations and travel. Route 66 was their route of choice, and it brought thousands of people through Flagstaff. New cars were selling fast and you had to get on a waiting list. If you slipped a dealer an extra hundred dollars, your name moved higher on the list. I knew a Chevrolet dealer who got rich in one year," he admits.

Some of Arizona's increased tourism should be credited to another returning veteran, Raymond Carlson. He edited *Arizona Highways* before World War II, when it was primarily a road-construction journal. After his military service years, Carlson returned and molded the publication into an internationally known travel magazine that lured many visitors to the state. Under his leadership, the magazine expanded and became a pacesetter in the use of color technology.

Arizona's growing reputation for its healthful climate attracted many people, especially those suffering with respiratory conditions such as tuberculosis and asthma. Dr. Bert Snyder, who arrived in Phoenix in 1942, was one of these people. "It was a small town then, with the city limit at Thomas Road. There were few hospitals or physicians," says Dr. Snyder, who was a company doctor for AiResearch in the 1950s and in the 1960s became a founder of John C. Lincoln Hospital in Phoenix. "When the war ended, the VA [Veterans Administration] hospitals throughout the country were severely overburdened because of the large numbers of returning soldiers," he says. Only Tucson

Today's modern Veterans Hospital in Phoenix is a far cry from the primitive veterans' medical facility first located in crude barracks in Papago Park.

and Prescott had VA hospitals. There were reports that disabled veterans in Phoenix were even sleeping in jails due to the lack of hospital facilities.

Dr. Snyder recalls, "A temporary hospital was desperately needed, but there were no funds to build one, so in 1946 people petitioned to use the hospital and wooden buildings that had served as the German POW camp in Papago Park during the war. Phoenix's first VA hospital was there for many years."

"When I practiced internal medicine in Phoenix, I had privileges at St. Joseph's Hospital and Good Samaritan

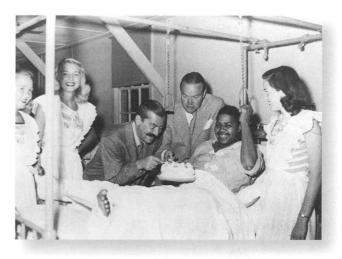

Bob Hope and comic Jerry Colonna came to the Veterans Administration hospital in Phoenix in 1947 to visit its patients.

Hospital," says Dr. Snyder. "As the population grew, more hospitals were built and we began to attract some of the best medical and surgical talent in the nation. Many of these doctors encouraged development of a medical school in this state. The University of Arizona's medical school opened in 1967."

In 1947 the state's economic leaders were still cotton, citrus, copper, and cattle. Tourism followed as Arizona shifted its focus from defending the country to developing the state. In population and industrial growth, Arizona became a pacesetter for the nation; within two decades its plants produced annually $400 million worth of manufactured goods, outpacing both farming and tourism.

Phoenix Sky Harbor Airport became one of the busiest airports in the nation. The Korean conflict and the Cold War kept Luke and Williams Fields (later Luke and Williams Air Force bases) open and added momentum to industrial growth. Daniel E. Noble, an executive with Motorola, a major electronics firm, helped establish a research and electronics center in Phoenix. He realized that Arizona State College in Tempe offered the potential for the development of quality engineering programs. The Motorola operation proved successful and led to the opening of additional plants. Other big employers, including Sperry-Phoenix and General Electric, soon followed.

The only stumbling block in luring workers to Phoenix was the summer heat. Due to the work of Arizona air-conditioning pioneers, including Paul and Mike Johnson, Oscar Palmer, and brothers Adam and Gust Goettl, Phoenix already had a thriving air-conditioning industry. During World War II, many federal and military buildings were cooled by evaporative coolers made in Phoenix. Refrigerated cooling transformed Phoenix into a year-round city of delightful living.

In the postwar years, Phoenix emerged as the metropolitan center of commerce and industry in the Southwest. During the 1950s, the city's population increased more than 300 percent. This astonishing growth could not have occurred if the water and power resources had not been available to serve the Phoenix metropolitan area. Major utility firms such as Arizona Public Service, Mountain States Telephone and Telegraph, and Salt River Project struggled to keep pace with the city's expansion. The Salt River Project's reservoirs on the Verde and Salt Rivers supplied water for agricultural use. In addition, the project's dams had hydroelectric generating equipment to produce electricity for the booming area. During the war years, crops flourished as farmers went into full-scale production of food for the nation's workers and servicemen. However, between 1948 and 1958, thirty-two thousand acres of irrigated land in the Phoenix area were taken out of agricultural production and converted to residential and commercial use. Farms were disappearing from the Arizona landscape.

Karl Abel grew up on a farm north of Glendale. After serving as an ordnance company commander during World War II, he returned to Phoenix in 1945 and started farming with his brother. They ran a large produce-farming operation throughout Maricopa County. "Farming got harder, and many farmers sold their land to developers. As the subdivisions moved farther out into rural areas, people complained because they didn't like the smell of stockyards and they were afraid of pesticides we used to control bugs," says Abel, who served as president of Salt River Project from 1972 to 1982 and witnessed many battles over water issues.

He recalls the bitter controversy surrounding the Central Arizona Project (CAP), a plan to bring Colorado River water to central Arizona. In 1944 Congress approved the Colorado River Compact. In 1946 the Central Arizona Project Association was formed to develop the canal and to lobby for funding. California objected strongly, and in 1952 Arizona went to the U.S. Supreme

Court to defend its right to the Colorado River water. Arizona's Senators Carl Hayden and Ernest McFarland led the fight for federal funding of the project, but the CAP water wars continued for years. Senators Barry Goldwater and Paul Fannin played important roles, as did other World War II veterans, Congressional Representatives John J. Rhodes, Stewart Udall, Morris K. Udall, and Eldon Rudd. In 1965, the U.S. Supreme Court awarded Arizona 2.8 million acre-feet of water annually. Thus continued development in the arid lands was assured.

During the decade following the war, the flood of newcomers created a shortage of housing and office buildings. In the 1950s, John F. Long, a World War II veteran and home builder, created the first large planned community, called Maryvale, to the west of Phoenix to provide affordable housing. Using federal loans, returning veterans could buy a new home for seven thousand dollars and pay less than 5 percent interest. Many of these well-constructed houses are still being used today and selling for more than eighty thousand dollars.

But not all returning veterans enjoyed the economic prosperity of these boom years. Many veterans from racial minorities returned to Arizona in 1945 to face discrimination in employment, housing, and public places. Their military experience had changed their perspective, and they began to question discriminatory practices and to initiate activities that led to social changes.

Ray Flores of Phoenix says, "In the U.S. Army I was regarded as one hundred percent American, but when I came back to Arizona, I was treated as if I was only fifteen percent American. The schools and communities were still segregated. I decided then that it would be my goal to eradicate discrimination in schools, churches, employment, and recreation areas." Flores remembers two veterans, Peter Martinez and Frank "Pipa" Fuentes, who helped form the Thunderbird American Legion Post 41, the first Hispanic American Legion Post established in Arizona. In the spring of 1946 the group became involved in its first race-relations issue when they helped Danny Rodriguez and other Hispanic American veterans in Tempe challenge a policy set by the Tempe Chamber of Commerce. It barred Hispanic American residents from using the Tempe Beach public pool. The post members called on prominent Tempe businessmen and gained support for integration, presenting a unified community effort to change the rule. The chamber members voted for a "limited admission policy" initially, but after another round of discussion, they voted to open the pool to all citizens, with no restrictions.

JOHN F. LONG

★ ★ ★

Actor and future president Ronald Reagan was on hand to congratulate builder John F. Long on the opening of Maryvale, a planned community for returning veterans.

Following his U. S. Army service in Europe during World War II, John F. Long returned to Arizona in late 1945. As a newlywed, this native Arizonan got a GI loan to build his first house in Phoenix in 1947. When the home was nearing completion, he received an offer of purchase at a profit of forty-five hundred dollars—a handsome sum in those days. He accepted and set out to build another house for his wife, Mary, thus launching a stellar career in home-building.

The Longs built and sold about fourteen houses, and it wasn't until three years later that they finally built a home for themselves. "There was a shortage of building materials, so no homes had been built during the war years. Then the GIs came back in droves during the early 1950s and needed affordable housing. New industries were starting up and I figured more workers would come here, so we would need to build houses in volume," says Long, who has built more than thirty thousand homes in Arizona.

An innovator in construction, Long introduced component and modular building, as well as new techniques in energy and water conservation. He demonstrated an ability to build quality features into a reasonably priced home. Long purchased farmland on the outskirts of Phoenix and in 1954 built Arizona's first master-planned community, Maryvale (named for his wife). In addition to a large number of homes, Maryvale included provisions for schools, parks, and community service facilities. "Most people didn't know each other. They came from other states, and by having parks with swimming pools, golf courses, and other recreational facilities, they could socialize and work together to create a community. My concept was to have everything there, so they could shop, live, and work in the same area without having to drive to Phoenix," says Long.

Working closely with city and state governments, he has donated land and buildings to many community projects, including parks, schools, churches, and libraries. He served on the Phoenix City Council for five years and has been active in many land-preservation and water-conservation projects. In 1987, the Department of Veteran

Affairs honored him for his work in helping veterans, and as the builder of the twelve millionth home purchased by a U. S. veteran.

In the 1980s he took a risk by building the world's first solar subdivision, where the electrical needs of the homes were met by solar energy, generated by photovoltaic solar cells. The pilot program attracted worldwide attention from engineers, energy experts, and universities. "It was an experiment on our part and provided research for the future. As energy gets more expensive, builders will have to find an economical way to use solar energy," stresses Long. "I believe that the developer should share the responsibility for helping the community function well, not just be in the business of building houses. Land for schools and parks should be built into the site plan.

"There are times when we have to do something for the future betterment of the whole community, instead of just thinking about our own needs at the moment," he adds.

Buoyed by their success, Mexican American veterans in Phoenix lobbied to create an integrated housing project in the Garfield district rather than accept Phoenix Public Housing Authority plans for an all-Mexican project at the site of an old dump. The case went to the Arizona Supreme Court, which ruled in favor of the integrated project, and Post 41 was given the privilege of naming it. Completed in 1946, it was called the Harry Cordova Housing Project, named for a Phoenix man killed in the battle of Normandy in 1944.

Minorities in Phoenix also faced discrimination from banks and employers. The American Legion post and other veteran and citizen groups helped fight these battles. Meanwhile Flores graduated from the American Institute for Foreign Trade, later to become the American Graduate School of International Management, at the former Thunderbird Field north of Glendale. Flores explains, "I planned to work in Argentina, but then I decided to be a teacher. I got my teaching credentials from Arizona State College in Tempe. Then I faced a tragic situation. In 1949 the Phoenix Union High School District couldn't hire me because I was classified as a Mexican American, yet the school for black students, Carver High, wouldn't hire me because I wasn't black. I kept interviewing for jobs and getting turned down due to my race."

Flores told the principal at Carver High School, "I am an American. I was an American in the army and I happen to have a Mexican heritage. Some people call us Mexican Americans." The school board met four times to decide the issue. In 1950, Flores became the first non–African American teacher hired at Carver High and the first Mexican American teacher ever hired by the Phoenix Union High School District.

Flores taught at Carver High School for three years prior to integration. He joined forces with other outspoken veterans, including African American leaders Lincoln J. Ragsdale and Morrison Warren. H. B. Daniels and Herb Finn filed a suit in 1953 against Wilson Elementary School District in Phoenix, and Maricopa County Superior Court Judge Charles E. Bernstein ruled that segregation in elementary schools was unconstitutional. The Phoenix decisions were taken into consideration by the U.S. Supreme Court when it made its landmark ruling in 1954 that resulted in desegregation of America's schools.

The American Indian population of Arizona also continued to experience discrimination in the postwar years. Although Indians enlisted as U.S. citizens and represented 7.7 percent of Arizona military servicemen, returning veterans could not vote in state or national elections. The performance of Arizona Indians during the war, both in armed services and defense industries, had generated goodwill, and in July 1948, an Arizona Supreme Court decision granted them the right to vote in state elections.

The environmental impact of World War II can be seen throughout Arizona. Thousands of acres of desert land were cleared for use as air fields and training bases in the 1940s. Pieces of spent ammunition still litter the landscape where bombing and gunnery ranges once were active. However, studies show that the most serious impact to the environment was probably caused by more than fifty years of rapid population growth.

In the early 1960s some Phoenix community leaders and government officials launched an ambitious campaign to create the Phoenix Mountain Preserve, setting aside thousands of acres of scenic desert and mountain land around the urban area so that city dwellers could enjoy hiking, horseback riding, bicycling, and other recreational pursuits.

It is ironic that the air bases in the Phoenix area, which were so instrumental in bringing veterans back to Arizona in the postwar years, are being choked out by residential encroachment. Williams Field, later called Williams Air Force Base, closed in 1993. (A community re-use plan is being used to convert it to an air industrial park and educational center.) For several years, there has been citizen pressure to close Luke Field, now Luke Air Force Base, which

LINCOLN J. RAGSDALE

★ ★ ★

Lieutenant Lincoln Ragsdale, one of the Tuskegee Airmen, returned home after the war to become a leader in the fight against racial segregation in Arizona.

Lincoln J. Ragsdale, a noted Phoenix civil rights activist and business leader, was one of the famous Tuskegee Airmen, black fighter pilots who proved their skills in Europe during World War II. In 1945, Ragsdale, a lieutenant, became the first black pilot to set foot on Luke Army Air Field. "They wouldn't salute me at Luke," said Ragsdale, who didn't realize at the time that he was part of President Truman's plan to begin breaking the military color barrier. It wasn't until 1949 that President Truman lifted racial restrictions in the U. S. military.

After the war, Ragsdale returned to Phoenix, where he brashly challenged the status quo regarding racial discrimination in schools, housing, and employment. Working with organizations such as the Arizona Council for Civic Unity and the National Association for the Advancement of Colored People (NAACP), he was at the forefront of the movement to integrate public schools in Phoenix, which succeeded a full year before the U. S. Supreme Court ruling for national desegregation in 1954. During the 1950s and 1960s he advocated "creative confrontation" as he helped orchestrate protest marches and sit-ins to desegregate restaurants, hotels, and other businesses.

Reflecting on those years, he says, "I was a radical for love and integration. I was controversial, but I wanted to make people aware of what was wrong and how we must work together to make things right." He mentored young African American businessmen and for more than a decade served as one of ten advisors to President Ronald Reagan on small and minority businesses.

A staunch supporter of aviation development, Ragsdale served on the Phoenix Aviation Advisory Board in the 1970s. When he died at age sixty-nine in 1995, the Phoenix City Council voted to rename the executive terminal at Sky Harbor Airport in his honor.

pumps an estimated $2 billion into Arizona's economy annually. U.S. Representative Bob Stump, a World War II navy veteran and Arizona cotton farmer, believes the base should remain open. "It is our largest training base for

When some nearby residents complained about the noise of jet planes at Luke Field after the war, *Arizona Republic* cartoonist Reg Manning chastised them with this cartoon.

fighter pilots and I think it is one of our primary assets as far as the military is concerned," says Stump, who, before he retired, was chairman of the House Armed Services Committee, overseeing the nation's $343.3 billion defense budget.

World War II forever changed Arizona. It grew from a population of less than 500,000 in 1940 to become the second fastest-growing state in the nation, with a population of 5,130,632 at the end of the twentieth century. According to the 2000 census report, Arizona's population increased 40 percent in the last decade.

Today, jet fighters from Luke Air Force Base still fly Arizona's skies. Although some residents complain about the noise, U.S. veterans usually look up and grin. They call the noise made by the F-16 jet fighters, "the sound of freedom."

Conclusion

FOUR CRITICAL YEARS

DEAN SMITH

TO THOSE WHO suffered and sacrificed and sorrowed through the World War II years in Arizona, the trials of 1941–45 seemed never to end. But at last those years did end, and after they had passed into history, Arizona would never be the same again.

The monumental changes were not readily discernible at first, but their impact soon made it evident that the state had entered a new and sometimes bewildering epoch in its development. Arizona looked ahead to previously unimaginable growth and change—in its population, in its economy, in its political coloration, in its understanding of alien cultures and people of color, and in its self-esteem.

First came the population explosion. From all over America young men, and more than a few young women, who had trained at Arizona's military bases or worked in its defense industries came flocking back to build careers and raise families. Despite the rigors of their service here, they had seen opportunity awaiting them in this land that had so recently evolved from its Wild West image into national recognition as a state on the move.

Arizona's population soared, with Maricopa and Pima Counties hosting most of the new residents. During the last half of the 1940s Maricopa County's population grew from an estimated one hundred seventy-five thousand to more than three hundred thousand. Tiny Scottsdale became home to luxurious resort hotels and gained a reputation as a haven for millionaires who wanted to spend their money in the winter sunshine. Mesa, Tempe, Chandler, Glendale—and even little Peoria—magically changed from sleepy bedroom communities into cities with burgeoning economies and personalities all their own. Tucson added to its reputation as a magnet for winter visitors while luring many thousands of less affluent permanent residents.

Many small communities around the state enjoyed population increases. Yuma, near where both the army ground forces and air corps had important wartime training facilities, experienced steady postwar growth. Army retirees found a home in Sierra Vista, at the gate of Fort Huachuca. Flagstaff, near the army's Navajo Ordnance Depot, benefited from that installation, from fast-growing Arizona State College, and from the increased tourism that the war helped to spawn. Even Prescott, without a major wartime military base, added to its population because desert dwellers to the south enjoyed its cool weather and forested mountains.

The state's institutions of higher learning found the postwar boom both exhilarating and distressing. War veterans flooded into the University of Arizona at Tucson and the state colleges at Tempe and Flagstaff, crowding classrooms and student housing to the bursting point. Community college enrollments grew just as rapidly.

World War II brought about amazing changes in Arizona's economy, as well. The old pillars—mining, ranching, farming, and lumbering—were rapidly being overtaken by manufacturing, which had received its major impetus from wartime defense plants. Dr. Dan Noble, who had become enthralled with Arizona during a youthful stint as a cowboy on a ranch near Prescott, brought Motorola to central Arizona, and it became the state's leading nongovernment employer. Other high-tech industrial giants soon followed Motorola's lead. Howard Hughes's aircraft plant led the way for Tucson's industrial boom.

The postwar population inundation gave a huge boost to the state's construction industry, too. Del E. Webb, who had made a fortune in building military installations in Arizona during the war years, shifted to residential and business construction. His famed Sun City complex and John F. Long's Maryvale experiment showed the way for many other planned communities around the state.

The importance of women in the scheme of things soared as a result of World War II. Forced by the urgencies of war, women took over jobs previously off limits to them. They proved to the world—and to themselves—that they could perform as well in virtually any capacity as men. Once limited to roles such as teachers, secretaries, and nurses, they threw off those shackles and became skilled in trades and successful executives in hundreds of fields. (And who could have forecast that in a not-so-distant election, women would be voted into all five of Arizona's top governmental offices!)

Just as significant was the improvement in race relations, brought about in part by the mingling of races and cultures in the common striving for victory in war. Arizona was as Jim Crow in character as many Deep South states before, and even during, World War II. Segregation of African Americans and Hispanic Americans in housing, education, entertainment, and many other areas was the accepted norm. But veterans returning from risking their lives for their country were understandably unwilling to return to the old ways of subservience. Led by such firebrands as former air corps pilot Lincoln Ragsdale and many others, they began breaking down the racial barriers. In not too many years, the unimaginable took place: a Mexican American, Raul Castro, was elected governor of the state.

American Indians, previously confined primarily to reservations, got a taste of how others lived and returned from exemplary military service to broaden their horizons. Even the Japanese Americans, vilified after Pearl Harbor and herded into relocation centers, gained new acceptance after the war as Arizonans increasingly embraced the ideal of cultural diversity.

Politics in Arizona would never be the same after the war. A majority of the newcomers to the state were from the Republican Midwest, and they breathed new life into the moribund Arizona Republican Party. Before 1950, it was often declared, Republicans could hold their state convention in a telephone booth. But in that year Republican Howard Pyle shocked the political world by winning the governorship. Two years later, Barry Goldwater upset the veteran Ernest McFarland in the U.S. Senate race, and John Rhodes ousted long-time Democratic incumbent John Murdock from his House seat.

Through the postwar period Tucson and Pima County as a whole continued to elect Democrats, as did some of the rural counties. But populous Maricopa had enough votes to elect Republicans to most of the major state and national offices. A popular escapee from the Republican tide was venerable Democratic Senator Carl Hayden, who never lost an election during fifty-six years of service in the U.S. Congress.

Today Republicans have a slight edge in voter registration, but the two-party system is alive and well. World War II had a lot to do with that.

The remarkably rapid gains in many areas—among them higher education, the fine arts, athletics, entertainment, literature, technology, and transportation—brought about in varying degrees by the World War II years have transformed Arizona. As historian Gerald Nash declared in his book *World War II and the West,* it might have taken forty years of peace to reshape the West as profoundly as did four years of war.

In Arizona, particularly, was that true.

Appendix

A TRAVELER'S GUIDE TO
ARIZONA'S WORLD WAR II SITES

ERIK BERG

DESPITE THEIR IMPACT on the war and on our state, most of Arizona's World War II military bases and historic sites have either disappeared or lost many of their original buildings. Urgency, not permanency, was the motivating factor behind their construction. Although few of Arizona's major wartime sites have survived intact, most still hold some evidence of their World War II history.

At many of the state's municipal airports and local airparks, passenger flights and private aircraft still use runways that once saw cadets in AT-6 trainers or B-17 bombers. Along desert back roads, trails of stone and gravel form the streets and sidewalks of army camps that once felt hundreds of marching feet. Beside our highways and town streets are cracked foundations and concrete rubble where both enemy prisoners and our own citizens spent anxious months wondering when they would see their homes again. In every part of the state forgotten fragments of another era wait like the scattered pieces of a jigsaw puzzle to share their part of the picture with us. Arizona's World War II past is both all gone and all around us.

This section provides the history enthusiast and traveler with a guide to the historic sites and other places of interest associated with Arizona during World War II. When visiting these historic sites, please treat them with the care and respect they deserve. Do not damage or destroy any existing structures, remove any artifacts, or leave any trash. Many of the locations are on private, military, or reservation lands and should not be accessed without proper approval.

NORTHERN ARIZONA

Rough terrain and a colder climate prevented northern Arizona from receiving the large numbers of air fields and prison camps that would cover the southern portion of the state. The few military installations that did locate in the north tended to gather around the major east-west transportation routes formed by Route 66 (now I-40) and the Santa Fe Railroad.

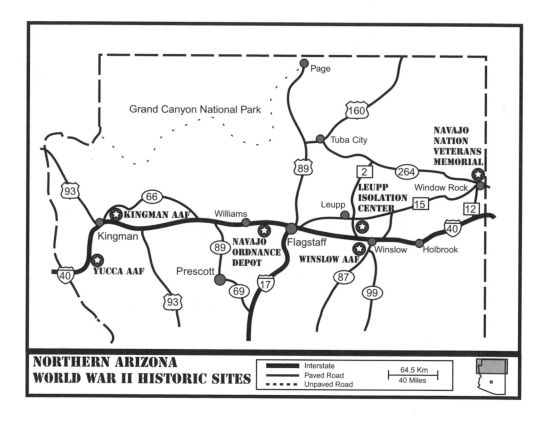

KINGMAN ARMY AIR FIELD
(Kingman Municipal Airport)

Although the army had been using the Kingman airport as an auxiliary field since the spring of 1941, real development did not begin until the founding of the Army Air Force Flexible Gunnery School in August 1942. The large base of more than six hundred buildings became one of the country's top training schools for gunners on the B-17 and other aircraft. Although an industrial park now covers much of the old base, several structures, hangars, a couple of monuments, and numerous foundations serve as reminders of the past. The most striking is the original control tower, located beside the current terminal building.

DIRECTIONS: From I-40, take Andy Devine Avenue (exit 53). Follow Andy Devine Avenue northeast for 4.5 miles and then turn right on Mohave Airport Road into the airport complex. The Kingman Army Air Field Museum is the first hangar south of the terminal. The Mohave County Historical Society is located in Kingman at 400 Beale Street, just east of exit 48 off I-40.

The historic control tower at the former Kingman Army Air Field once watched over rows of B-17 and B-24 bombers. At the base of the tower are plaques dedicated to those airmen who died while training here.

LEUPP ISOLATION CENTER

For much of 1943, a Navajo boarding school at Old Leupp was used as a special Japanese American internment camp designed to hold internees from other camps who were identified as protesters, sympathizers, or troublemakers. The stone school buildings that made up the camp were bulldozed shortly after the war ended, and today virtually nothing remains except for the stone outlines of a few walls and the foundations of a trading post that stood nearby.

DIRECTIONS: From Winslow, take I-40 west to Arizona 99 (exit 245). Follow Arizona 99 north (past where it combines with Route 2) to its intersection with Indian Route 15. Follow Indian Route 15 east over the Little Colorado River, then immediately turn south and follow a dirt road (to Old Leupp) less than two miles to the site of the camp.

NAVAJO ORDNANCE DEPOT
(Camp Navajo; Navajo Army Depot)

The Navajo Ordnance Depot served as an important storage center for receiving military supplies and munitions from manufacturers and then distributing

This building at the Navajo Ordnance Depot has served a variety of functions, including classroom and storage facility. The distinctive skirt-roof above the windows of the first floor was a typical feature of the standardized military designs at the start of the war.

them to ports and military installations on the West Coast. Many of the depot's original 1942 buildings have survived. World War II structures include the post office and PX building, the chapel, the officers' club, a large multistory administration building, the fire department, a two-story classroom building, and several of the motor-pool structures. Approximately 2.5 miles to the west are the streets and faint foundations of the area known as Indian Village, where many of the Navajo workers lived.

DIRECTIONS: Take I-40 11 miles west of Flagstaff to the Bellemont exit (exit 185). The Navajo Army Depot is still an active military base used for training and storage by the Arizona National Guard. Visitors should stop at the visitor center before entering the base.

NAVAJO NATION VETERANS MEMORIAL

Numerous members of the Navajo Nation helped support the war effort as both workers and soldiers. The Navajo Nation has honored the code talkers, as well as the tribe's veterans from other wars, with a serene park and memorials at the base of the town's famous Window Rock.

DIRECTIONS: The Navajo Nation Veterans Memorial is located beside the Navajo government buildings at Window Rock. From Arizona 264 in Window Rock, go north about 0.5 mile on Indian Route 12 and then turn east to reach the council offices.

WINSLOW ARMY AIR FIELD
(Winslow-Lindbergh Regional Airport)

Famous aviator Charles Lindbergh supervised the construction of the Winslow airport in 1929. During the war it became an important refueling stop for military aircraft. Little remains today from the war era, although one of the hangars and part of the terminal building date to the prewar Lindbergh period. In nearby Winslow, the grand La Posada Hotel served a similar refueling function for soldiers on westbound trains. With hundreds of servicemen filling the dining hall daily, the hotel had to add a special addition (nicknamed the "Spam Room" for its limited menu) to continue serving the local civilians.

DIRECTIONS: Winslow-Lindbergh Regional Airport is located along the railroad tracks just southwest of town. From downtown Winslow, take Arizona 87/Arizona 99 south under the railroad tracks and then turn right on Airport Road to reach the terminal building.

YUCCA ARMY AIR FIELD
(Ford Proving Grounds)

The army built this air field in early 1943 as an auxiliary base for the gunnery school at Kingman Army Air Field (AAF), but it quickly grew into a substantial training base of its own, with more than forty-five buildings.

DIRECTIONS: The Ford Proving Grounds is located along I-40, 22 miles southwest of Kingman at Proving Grounds Road (exit 26). The grounds are not open to the public.

CENTRAL ARIZONA

The Salt River Valley was the home of excellent year-round flying weather and plenty of open spaces that were ideal for adjacent air fields. By war's end, the valley was the largest flight-training center in the United States, with several major air bases and numerous war-related industries that would help transform the region into one of the country's largest and fastest growing metropolitan areas.

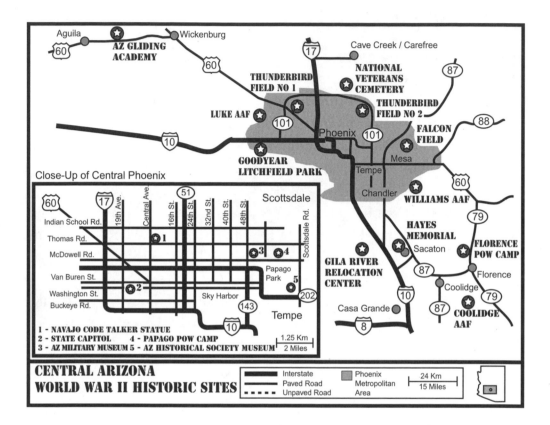

ARIZONA GLIDING ACADEMY
(Forepaugh Airport)
Founded as a civilian contract school for military glider pilots, the air field later switched to training for powered aircraft. Today a small, dilapidated hangar and numerous foundations are all that remain.

DIRECTIONS: From downtown Wickenburg, take US60 west for 15.6 miles and turn north on a short dirt road near a ranch. A local radio-controlled aircraft club now uses the field.

ARIZONA HISTORICAL SOCIETY MUSEUM AT PAPAGO PARK
This museum houses a wide range of permanent and changing displays on Arizona history topics. Their extensive "Views from the Home Front" exhibit

is an excellent description of life in Arizona during the war and its impact on the social and economic development of the state.

DIRECTIONS: The museum is located on the edge of Papago Park in north Tempe. From Scottsdale Road, take Curry Road west 0.4 mile to College Avenue, then turn north 0.1 mile to the museum.

ARIZONA MILITARY MUSEUM

The Arizona Military Museum houses an interesting collection of equipment, uniforms, and displays related to the military history of Arizona.

DIRECTIONS: From I-10, take exit 152 north and follow Arizona 143 (Hohokam Expressway) north to McDowell Road. Take McDowell Road 0.7 mile east to 52nd Street. The museum is in the Arizona National Guard complex on the northeast corner.

ARIZONA STATE CAPITOL BUILDING MUSEUM
AND WESLEY BOLIN MEMORIAL PARK

In addition to general Arizona history topics, the Arizona State Capitol Building Museum includes a large exhibit on the USS Arizona and its role during the attack on Pearl Harbor.

In front of the capitol building, the Wesley Bolin Memorial Park contains numerous memorials and monuments to various Arizona groups and individuals. Items related to World War II include memorials to the 158th Infantry Regiment (Bushmasters) and the Fourth Marine Division, as well as the seamen of the American merchant marine. Nearby, the mast and anchor of the USS *Arizona* form memorials to the men killed during the attack.

DIRECTIONS: From the I-10 Business Loop, take 19th Avenue (exit 143C) 0.3 miles south to Jefferson Street. Turn east on Jefferson Street and then immediately turn north into the visitor parking area.

COOLIDGE ARMY AIR FIELD
(Coolidge Municipal Airport)

Part of the Air Transport Command, Coolidge AAF was an important ferry service station for both army and navy aircraft before returning to civilian use in 1950. Today a nicely restored hangar and a single administration building

This beautifully restored hangar at the Coolidge municipal airport is the most striking reminder of the field's history as a ferry service station. Both the navy and the army air force used Coolidge as a fueling and maintenance stop on cross-country flights.

(now a private home) are the most visible reminders of the war years, although a walk around the area reveals numerous foundations, faint streets, and the abandoned camp swimming pool.

DIRECTIONS: From Arizona Boulevard (AZ87/AZ287) in Coolidge, take Coolidge Avenue east over the railroad tracks where it turns into Kenilworth Road. Follow Kenilworth east for 5.2 miles to the Coolidge Municipal Airport turnoff. From the turnoff it is approximately 3 miles to the air field.

FALCON FIELD, CHAMPLIN FIGHTER MUSEUM, AND CONFEDERATE AIR FORCE MUSEUM

Like Thunderbird, Falcon Field was not a true military installation but a civilian flying school contracted by the government to provide training to military pilots from the United States and England. Little remains from the war years except for a swimming pool, a stone fireplace from the pilots' lounge, and a hangar. The field is also the site of two World War II aircraft museums: the Champlin Fighter Museum and the Confederate Air Force Museum.

The famous Champlin Fighter Museum is home to the American Fighter Aces Association and contains histories and descriptions of every American fighter ace. Falcon Field is also home to the more recent Confederate Air Force Museum. The Confederate Air Force is a worldwide association of aviation enthusiasts who restore and fly World War II aircraft.

DIRECTIONS: From US60 in Mesa, take exit 185 (Greenfield Road). Follow Greenfield road north 4.5 miles to McKellips Road. The Confederate Air Force museum is on the northeast corner. To reach the Champlin Fighter Museum, go 0.5 miles east on McKellips road and turn north on Falcon Drive. After 0.2 miles, turn west on Fighter Aces Drive.

FLORENCE POW CAMP
(Florence Gardens Mobile Home Park)

Perhaps it is fitting that the home of Arizona's first state prison was also the site of the state's largest prisoner-of-war camp. Between 1942 and 1946 as many as fifty-one hundred Italian, and later German, prisoners were housed here. Very little remains of the camp, which is now covered by the Florence Gardens Mobile Home Park.

DIRECTIONS: The POW camp was located along the west side of Arizona 79 about 2 miles north of Florence. From Florence take Arizona 79 north toward Florence Junction. The POW camp was on the west side of the road just after the highway crosses over the Gila River.

GILA RIVER RELOCATION CENTER

Construction of the Gila River Relocation Center began in May 1942 on land leased, without tribe approval, from the Gila River Indian Reservation. The camp was divided into two subcommunities (Canal and Butte) which eventually held a combined population of more than thirteen thousand Japanese Americans. The camps were also referred to as Rivers and Sacaton camps.

Most of the camp structures were sold or torn down after the war, and no original buildings remain. However, both sites still contain faint streets, cement foundations, old irrigation ditches, and a few cement-lined basins that had once formed ponds for small Japanese gardens. Butte Camp also includes a monument to Japanese American soldiers, built by internees in 1944 and rededicated in 1995. The Gila River Indian Reservation strictly controls access to these sites, but the nearby Gila Indian Arts and Crafts Center contains an excellent display about the camps, as well as information on Pima war hero Ira Hayes.

DIRECTIONS: From Phoenix, take I-10 southeast approximately 30 miles to Sacaton (exit 175), then follow Casa Blanca Road 0.5 mile west to the Gila Indian Arts and Crafts Center.

GOODYEAR-ARIZONA PLANT AND NAVAL AIR FACILITY, LITCHFIELD PARK
(Phoenix Goodyear Airport; Lockheed-Martin Facility)

The Goodyear-Arizona aircraft modification plant was born in July 1941 when the Defense Plant Corporation began construction on land leased from the Southwest Cotton Company. In 1943 the navy also began making aircraft modifications at the Goodyear plant and in later years used the plant as a storage and ferrying stop. The current Lockheed-Martin facility at Litchfield Park occupies the site of the Goodyear plant and includes several of the original buildings.

DIRECTIONS: From central Phoenix, take I-10 west to Litchfield Road (exit 128). Take Litchfield Road 1.5 miles south to the Lockheed-Martin plant at Yuma Road. Continue about 0.5 miles south and then turn west on Central Avenue to reach the terminal.

LUKE ARMY AIR FIELD
(Luke Air Force Base)

Using AT-6 Texans, cadet training began in the summer of 1941, and by the end of the year more than 150 buildings had been built for a base population of more than three thousand. Eventually, Luke Field became the country's largest advanced single-engine flying school with a peak population of more than six thousand. Today, few original buildings survive on the base, which is still a major fighter-training facility.

DIRECTIONS: Luke Air Force Base is located 10 miles west of downtown Glendale. From I-10, turn on Litchfield Road (exit 128) and go about 6 miles north to the main gate (just past Glendale Avenue). The base is not open to the general public.

MATHEW B. JUAN–IRA HAYES VETERANS MEMORIAL PARK

As a member of the U.S. Marine Corps, Hayes served in the Pacific and was one of the soldiers in the famous flag-raising on Iwo Jima photograph. The town of Sacaton features a large monument to Hayes as well as a smaller monument to Mathew Juan, the first Arizonan to die in World War I.

DIRECTIONS: The Ira Hayes Memorial stands in the town of Sacaton on the Gila River Indian Reservation. From Phoenix, take I-10 south to Arizona 587 (exit 175). Immediately east of the exit, turn south on Casa Blanca Road and proceed for 6.3 miles to the town of Sacaton. The memorial park is across from the post office at the corner of Sacaton Road.

NATIONAL VETERANS CEMETERY OF ARIZONA

Originally known as the Arizona Veterans Memorial Cemetery, this large and somber memorial park contains the graves of hundreds of Arizona veterans from all wars. In the southwest corner is a collection of war memorials, including a large monument to sailors lost on America's submarines during World War II. A nearby flagpole came from the original USS *Arizona* memorial at Pearl Harbor.

DIRECTIONS: From Phoenix, take I-17 north to the Loop 101 exit. Take Loop 101 east for 4.5 miles to Cave Creek Road. Drive north on Cave Creek Road for 2 miles and turn east on Pinnacle Peak Road. The entrance to the cemetery is about 0.25 mile east.

PAPAGO PARK POW CAMP
(Papago Sports Complex)

Virtually nothing remains of the large prisoner-of-war camp that once occupied much of the area around Barnes Butte in Papago Park. Organized in 1943 to hold Italian POWs, the camp later became home to more than three thousand, mostly German, prisoners.

DIRECTIONS: From I-10, take Arizona 143 (Hohokam Expressway) north (exit 152) to McDowell Road. Follow McDowell Road east for about 2 miles to 64th Street. The majority of the prisoner barracks were located along either side of 64th Street between McDowell and Thomas Roads to the north.

THUNDERBIRD FIELD NUMBER 1
(American Graduate School of International Management)

Thunderbird Field was built in 1941 as one of several Arizona flight schools where civilian instructors provided basic flight training to military pilots from the United States, England, and China. Shortly after the war, the property was converted into the world-renowned American Graduate School of International Management.

Although the runways and flight lines are gone, two of the hangars and

The tower and flight administration building of Thunderbird Field Number 1, north of Glendale, is now part of the campus of the American Graduate School of International Management.

many of the other original base structures were incorporated into the school campus. The most striking is the control tower near the center of campus, which has been converted to a student lounge and offices.

DIRECTIONS: From central Phoenix, take I-17 north to Greenway Road (exit 211). Follow Greenway Road west for 4 miles to 59th Avenue. Take 59th Avenue south for about 0.3 miles to the school's main entrance.

THUNDERBIRD FIELD NUMBER 2
(Scottsdale Airport)

A younger sibling to Thunderbird 1, this air field also became an important civilian contract school that provided primary flight training for military pilots. Today the runways are part of the Scottsdale airport, and the original base grounds are occupied by a private school and businesses. There are plans to build an aviation museum on a portion of the site.

DIRECTIONS: Take the Loop 101 to Frank Lloyd Wright Boulevard (exit 38) and go west about 2 miles to Scottsdale Road. Follow Scottsdale Road south for 1.8 miles (past the airport entrance) to Thunderbird Road. The base was located to the south of Thunderbird Road about 0.2 mile to the east of Scottsdale Road.

WILLIAMS ARMY AIR FIELD
(Williams Gateway Airport)

Opened in 1941, Williams Army Air Field (better known as "Willie") was one of the largest air fields in Arizona by war's end. It trained both fighter and bomber pilots. After more than forty years of service, the base was closed in 1992 and transformed into Williams Gateway Airport. Most of the existing base structures date from the Cold War period.

DIRECTIONS: From US60 in Mesa, take Power Road (exit 188) south 5.5 miles to the main airport entrance near the intersection with Williams Field Road.

SOUTHWEST ARIZONA

Covering more than eighteen thousand square miles along the Colorado River, the California-Arizona Maneuver Area (CAMA) was the largest military training ground in the world and would eventually provide training for nearly a million troops. Four of the ten major encampments (Camps Bouse, Laguna, Hyder, and Horn) were located in Arizona. In addition to ground training, the sparsely populated deserts of southwestern Arizona also became home to several important air bases and the nation's largest bombing and gunnery range.

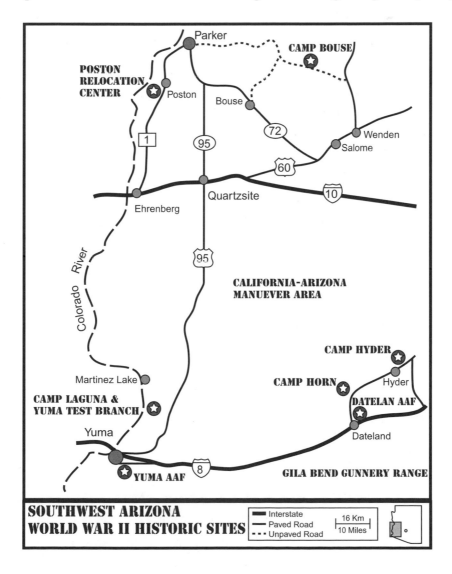

CAMP BOUSE AND CAMP BOUSE MEMORIAL PARK

Located in the remote Butler Valley, Camp Bouse was the most secretive base in the California-Arizona Maneuver Area. While the camp's isolation may have been hard on the thousands of men stationed here, it has helped preserve its extensive remains and it is by far the best-preserved of the Arizona CAMA sites that are open to the public. Like the other bases, Camp Bouse was a rectangular tent city laid out on a grid of gravel roads. Most of these original streets are still visible, and although no buildings survive, numerous rock outlines reveal their locations and that of the pathways that connected them. Special areas of interest include the circular roundabout at the northern end of the base where the hospital and headquarters were located and a small earthen amphitheater on the eastern edge that once served as a boxing arena.

In addition to the ruins at the camp itself, the nearby town of Bouse has created a small roadside park along Arizona 72 that includes several military vehicles and plaques dedicated to the units that trained in the area.

DIRECTIONS: The small community of Bouse is located along Arizona 72, approximately 26 miles southeast of Parker. To reach the site of Camp Bouse, take Main Street in Bouse east until it turns north and becomes Ravder Road. Follow the signs toward Swansea for about 16 miles until you get to the intersection and kiosk known as Midway. From Midway, head south approximately 9 miles. The camp was just east of where the road passes under a power line. You can also reach Camp Bouse by taking the Alamo Dam Road north from Wenden, then turning west on Transmission Line Road after crossing Cunningham Pass.

NOTE: Both routes include sections of rough dirt roads. A high-clearance vehicle, maps, and plenty of water are recommended, and visitors should inquire about road conditions, especially after bad weather. The remains of Camp Bouse are extremely fragile. Relic hunting is illegal and drivers should avoid off-road travel.

CAMP HORN

Camp Horn was another of the four major CAMA field camps in Arizona. Unfortunately, the entire area has been converted to farm land, and absolutely nothing remains of the camp except for a few piles of concrete rubble and a stone pyramid commemorating seven soldiers of the 81st Infantry Division who died while training.

DIRECTIONS: From I-8, take the Dateland exit and go north 8.8 miles on Avenue 64 until the road curves to the right (east). At the curve, turn left onto a dirt road that parallels the railroad tracks. After 1.5 miles, turn right (north) and cross the tracks to the stone monument, which was at the camp entrance.

Marking the site of Camp Horn in far western Arizona is this pyramid monument. More than a million men trained for desert warfare at this and other Desert Training Center camps.

CAMP HYDER

The most notable evidence of Camp Hyder are two stone pillars near the railroad tracks that once formed the gate into the base. The nearby ruins of Agua Caliente hot springs contain a large swimming pool constructed by engineers from Camp Hyder.

DIRECTIONS: From I-8, take the Sentinel exit (exit 87) and follow Agua Caliente Road north for 14.5 miles to Palmas Road. Turn left at Palmas Road and go about 2.6 miles to the Hyder Market. The pillars and camp ruins are on the north side of the railroad tracks just east of the store. The buildings at Agua Caliente are on private property and marked against trespassers.

CAMP LAGUNA AND THE YUMA TEST BRANCH
(Yuma Proving Grounds)

Unlike the other CAMA bases in Arizona, Camp Laguna enjoyed the relatively close comforts of civilization in Yuma. The ability to control the flow of water from nearby Imperial Dam led the Army Corps of Engineers to establish the Yuma Test Branch here in 1943 to test portable bridges. The camp was also home to more than eight hundred Italian POWs. During the Cold War, the camp evolved into today's Yuma Proving Grounds and continues to test new weapons and transportation systems.

Visitors cannot access the site of the original camp, but the Yuma Proving Grounds Heritage Center has an excellent collection of photographs and exhibits about the history of the base. Another interesting monument to the war period is a large stone paint locker near the base of the dam that was built in the shape of a castle (the symbol of the Army Corps of Engineers) by Italian POWs.

DIRECTIONS: Two huge cannons on the west side of US95, about 20 miles north of Yuma, mark the entrance to the Yuma Proving Grounds. From the entrance, follow Imperial Dam Road west for about 5 miles to the proving grounds office and heritage center on the north side. The paint shed is located near the California state line on the north side of Imperial Dam Road 1.5 miles farther west.

DATELAN ARMY AIR FIELD
(Dateland Air Field)

The Army Air Force established Datelan Army Air Field ("Dateland" was misspelled because of a transcription error) in the spring of 1943 as an auxiliary training base for the Yuma Aerial Flying School Gunnery Range and later developed it into a B-25 training site. Today I-8 runs directly across much of the camp's housing and administration area. Just east of Avenue 64 is a large concrete bunker that was once a target backstop used to calibrate guns on B-25 bombers.

DIRECTIONS: From Yuma take I-8 east to Dateland (exit 67). The base runways and flight line were to the northeast of the overpass. Foundations of buildings can be seen along the frontage road on the north side of I-8 immediately east of the Dateland overpass. The concrete backstop is visible to the east of Avenue 64 East a few hundred yards north of the overpass.

GILA BEND GUNNERY RANGE
(Barry M. Goldwater Bombing Range)

In the fall of 1941 the Army Air Corps established two large bombing and gunnery ranges in the sparsely populated deserts of southwest Arizona. The Gila Bend Gunnery Range and the Yuma Gunnery and Bombing Range were expanded to cover more than 2 million acres. Renamed the Barry M. Goldwater Bombing Range in 1986, it continues to serve as a bombing and practice range.

DIRECTIONS: The range covers most of the land between Yuma and Arizona 85 and between I-8 and the Mexican border. With the exception of the Cabeza Prieta Wildlife Refuge to the south, most of the area is not easily accessible to the public. For more information, contact the public affairs office at Luke Air Force Base.

POSTON INTERNMENT CAMP

With more than seventeen thousand internees, the Japanese American relocation center at Poston quickly became one of Arizona's largest communities. The residents, mostly California citizens, were divided into three subcamps (I, II, and III), spaced about 3 miles apart. Most of the Poston buildings were torn down after the war, and little remains except for portions of the large concrete sewer plants near each camp. A few classrooms and some foundations still survive at Poston I (near Poston Road); an elementary school occupies the site of Poston II; and farming has reclaimed Poston III. In 1992, internees and their descendants erected a monument just south of the Poston Road intersection with Route 1.

A somber monument beside Indian Reservation Route 1, south of Poston, memorializes the Japanese Americans who were interned here and their friendship with the surrounding Colorado River Indian tribes.

DIRECTIONS: From Parker, follow Indian Reservation Route 1 for about 2 miles southwest of town to the Colorado River Indian Tribes (CRIT) administration offices and museum. From the CRIT offices, follow Route 1 for an additional 13 miles to reach Poston. Those wanting to visit the sites should check with the CRIT office first (the museum there also includes a display about the camps).

YUMA ARMY AIR FIELD
(Marine Corps Air Station and Yuma International Airport)
The Yuma Army Air Field and gunnery school was established in June 1942 on the site of an earlier dirt landing strip. It soon became an important advanced

flying school for the training of pilots, radio operators, and gunners on the nearby Gila Bend Gunnery Range. Today the original runways are shared by the Yuma International Airport and the Marine Corps Air Station, but very little remains of the base itself.

DIRECTIONS: From I-8 take Avenue 3E (exit 3E) south for 1.2 miles to 32nd Street (I-8 Business Loop). To reach Yuma International Airport, go west on 32nd Street for 0.8 mile. To reach the Marine Corps Air Station, continue on Avenue 3E for another mile to the main gate. The air station is not open to the general public.

SOUTHEAST ARIZONA

Like central Arizona, the southeastern part of the state, including Tucson, attracted a large number of training air bases due to the excellent weather conditions. Marana Army Air Field became one of the country's largest single-engine training sites, and Douglas and Davis-Monthan Fields became important bomber-training bases. In addition to building air fields, the army

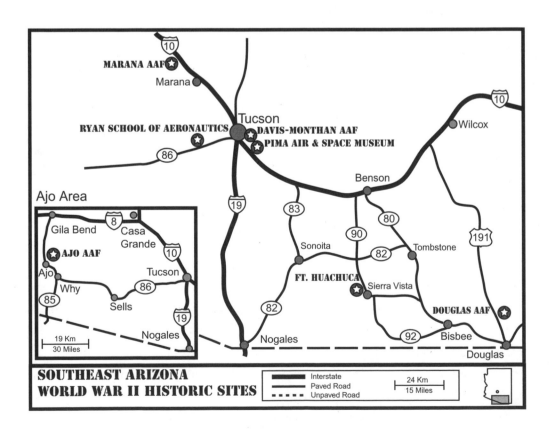

APPENDIX: A TRAVELER'S GUIDE ★ 199

also revitalized and enlarged the venerable old Fort Huachuca into the country's largest training center for African-American infantry units.

AJO ARMY AIR FIELD
(Ajo Municipal Airport)

Ajo AAF was opened in the spring of 1942 on the site of a small airport that consisted of little more than a dirt field. It soon developed into a significant single-engine flight-training and gunnery school with three runways and more than a hundred buildings. It is now the Ajo Municipal Airport. Little remains from the war period except for foundations and the concrete flight line.

DIRECTIONS: Take Arizona 85 north of Ajo about 10 miles. The Municipal Airport is on the east side of Arizona 85.

DAVIS-MONTHAN ARMY AIR FIELD
(Davis-Monthan Air Force Base)

Shortly before America's entrance into World War II, the Army Air Corps converted the Tucson Municipal Flying Field into a military air base. It soon became a major bombardment training center for B-24 and, later, B-29 crews. Little exists today from the war era except for an isolated hangar visible near Alvernon Road. Although still a major combat-training base, Davis-Monthan is perhaps best known today as the home of the Military Aircraft Storage and Disposition Center, commonly called "the bone yard."

DIRECTIONS: From downtown Tucson, take I-10 east to Alvernon Road (exit 265). Take Alvernon Road north for 1.5 miles to the intersection with Golf Links Road. Follow Golf Links Road around the northwest corner of the base for about 2.5 miles until you reach the main gate at Craycroft Road. The base is not open to the general public.

DOUGLAS ARMY AIR FIELD
(Douglas International Airport)

In 1942 the commercial air field north of Douglas was converted into an advanced flying school and eventually became a major multi-engine training base for bomber crews and one of the first to employ female pilots. The flight line area is now a civilian airport, while a state prison dominates the eastern end of the base. In addition to numerous foundations, the site still includes several original hangars and a remodeled armaments inspection building (now the airport terminal). Of special interest are the concrete vaults near the northern hangars where advanced Norden bombsites—one of the war's closely guarded secrets—were stored and guarded after each flight.

DIRECTIONS: From Douglas, take US191 north for 10 miles. The airport entrance is on the east side of the road. Visitors should check in at the terminal building and should not enter areas near the prison grounds.

FORT HUACHUCA

Named after the nearby mountains near the Mexican border, Fort Huachuca was founded in 1877 as an important army outpost during southern Arizona's Apache wars. During World War II the fort became the army's largest training center for African American soldiers and home of the Ninety-second and Ninety-third Infantry Divisions. The fort closed shortly after the war ended but was reopened in 1951 and has remained an important army base.

Fort Huachuca is one of Arizona's best-preserved military historic sites. Some buildings around the parade grounds date to the late 1800s. The base includes numerous buildings from both the frontier and World War II periods, as well as two excellent museums.

DIRECTIONS: Fort Huachuca is located on the northwestern edge of Sierra Vista where Arizona 90 meets Fry Boulevard. From downtown Sierra Vista, take Fry Boulevard west to the main gate.

MARANA ARMY AIR FIELD
(Pinal Air Park)

Marana Army Air Field was opened in 1942 as a basic flight school where cadets began their pilot training and made their first flights. By the end of the war Marana had become one of the nation's largest basic training centers for both American and Chinese pilots. The field was reactivated and rebuilt during the Korean War and now is a private airpark and maintenance facility. Two hangars and several smaller buildings still survive from the original base.

DIRECTIONS: The main gate for Pinal Air Park is located a few miles west of I-10 at exit 232, about 25 miles north of downtown Tucson. The field is not open to the public.

PIMA AIR AND SPACE MUSEUM

Located on the edge of the Davis-Monthan aircraft storage area, the Pima Air and Space Museum offers one of the largest collections of military aircraft available for public viewing. More than two hundred different aircraft from the first days of flight through the Cold War are presented in outdoor displays, as well as in several exhibition hangars. World War II exhibits include displays on the flight-training process, life at Arizona bases, a fully restored barracks building, and numerous period aircraft.

DIRECTIONS: From Tucson, take I-10 east to the Valencia Road exit (exit 267). Follow Valencia road 1.6 miles north to the museum gate.

RYAN SCHOOL OF AERONAUTICS
(Ryan Field)

Ryan Field was not an official military installation but one of several important civilian air fields that the government contracted to provide basic flight training to military cadets. Ryan School of Aeronautics provided training for American and Chinese pilots. The air field is now a private airpark and little remains from the war years except for photos hanging on the café wall.

DIRECTIONS: From downtown Tucson, take I-10 southeast to I-19 (exit 260). Take I-19 south approximately 1 mile to Ajo Way (exit 99). Proceed west on Ajo Way (where it transitions into Arizona 86) for about 12 miles until you reach the air field entrance at Waco Way.

SELECTED BIBLIOGRAPHY

PREFACE
Fairchild, Vernon. Personal interview with author, Flagstaff, Ariz., November 2001.

Flick, Luther. Personal interview with author, Flagstaff, Ariz., November 2001.

CHAPTER 1. PRELUDE TO WAR
Arizona Republic, misc. issues: 1930–1941.

Arizona Republican, misc. issues: 1930–1941.

August, Jack. "The Anti-Japanese Crusade in Arizona's Salt River Valley, 1934–1935." *Arizona and the West* (summer 1979).

Blair, Clay. *Hitler's U-Boat War: The Hunters, 1939–1942.* New York: Random House, 1996.

Cardozier, V. R. *The Mobilization of the United States in World War II: How the Government, Military and Industry Prepared for War.* Jefferson, N.C.: McFarland & Co., 1995.

Carlson, Raymond. "Continuing Our Correspondence with His Imperial Majesty, Mr. Hirohito, the Emperor of Japan." *Arizona Highways* (June 1942).

———. "Greetings from Arizona to the Emperor of Japan." *Arizona Highways* (May 1942).

———. "These Days of War." *Arizona Highways* (January 1942).

Cline, Platt. *Mountain Town: Flagstaff's First Century.* Flagstaff, Ariz.: Northland Publishing, 1994.

Collins, William S. *The New Deal in Arizona.* Phoenix: Arizona State Parks Board, 1999.

Faulk, Odie B. *Arizona: A Short History.* Norman: University of Oklahoma Press, 1970.

Flaccus, Elmer W. "Arizona's Last Great Indian War: The Saga of Pia Machita." *Journal of Arizona History* (spring 1981).

Gannon, Michael. *Operation Drumbeat: The Dramatic True Story of Germany's First U-Boat Attacks along the American Coast in World War II.* New York: Harper & Row, 1990.

Luckingham, Bradford. *Phoenix: The History of a Southwestern Metropolis.* Tucson: University of Arizona Press, 1989.

McFarland, Ernest W. *Mac: The Autobiography of Ernest W. McFarland.* N.p.: Privately printed, 1979.

Melton, Brad. "Arizona Highways Magazine: Tourism, Good Roads, and the Mythic West." Unpublished HIS 591 paper, Arizona State University, 1999.

Perkins, Maxine. Personal e-mail correspondence, January 2001.

Sato, Susie. "Before Pearl Harbor: Early Japanese Settlers in Arizona." *Journal of Arizona History* (winter 1973).

Smith, Dean. *The Best of Reg.* Phoenix: Arizona Republic, 1980.

———. *Glendale: Century of Diversity.* Glendale, Ariz.: City of Glendale Marketing Department, 1992.

———. *Tempe: Arizona Crossroads.* Chatsworth, Calif.: Windsor Publications, 1990.

Sonnichsen, Charles L. *Tucson: The Life and Times of an American City.* Norman: University of Oklahoma Press, 1982.

Trimble, Marshall. *Arizona 2000: A Yearbook for the Millennium.* Flagstaff, Ariz.: Northland Publishing, 1998.

———. *Arizona: A Cavalcade of History.* Tucson: Treasure Chest Publications, 1989.

Valentine, Richard. "Arizona and the Great Depression: A Study of State Response to Crisis, 1932–1937." Master's thesis, Northern Arizona University, 1968.

Workers of the Writers' Program of the Works Projects Administration in the State of Arizona. *The WPA Guide to 1930s Arizona.* Tucson: University of Arizona Press, 1989.

Ynfante, Charles. "Arizona during the Second World War, 1941–1945: A Survey of Selected Topics." Ph.D. dissertation, Northern Arizona University, 1997.

CHAPTER 2. DAY OF INFAMY

Baker, Leonard. *Roosevelt and Pearl Harbor.* New York: Macmillan, 1970.

Bergamini, David. *Japan's Imperial Conspiracy.* New York: William Morrow & Co., 1971.

Brownlow, Donald G. *The Accused: The Ordeal of Rear Admiral Husband Edward Kimmel, U.S.N.* New York: Vantage Press, 1968.

Butow, R.J.C. "Backdoor Diplomacy in the Pacific: The Proposal for a Konoye-Roosevelt Meeting." *Journal of American History* (June 1972).

Clark, Blake. *Remember Pearl Harbor!* New York: Modern Age Books, 1942.

Cosulich, Bernice. "The University of Arizona and World War II, 1949–1951." Unpublished manuscript. Special Collections, University of Arizona Libraries, Tucson.

Feis, Herbert. *The Road to Pearl Harbor.* Princeton, N.J.: Princeton University Press, 1950.

50th Anniversary World War II Commemoration. *World War II: A Listing of Resources and Information.* Program, N.p.: N.d.

Ickes, Harold L. *The Secret Diary of Harold L. Ickes.* Vol. III: *The Lowering Clouds, 1939–1941.* New York: Simon & Schuster, 1954.

Moore, Yndia Smalley. Personal interview with author, Tucson, December 1996.

National Archives. "Special War Problems." RG 59.

Nomura, Kichisaburo. "Stepping Stones to War." *United States Naval Institute Proceedings* (September 1951).

Perkins, Frances. *The Roosevelt I Knew.* New York: Viking Press, 1946.

Prange, Gordon W. *At Dawn We Slept: The Untold Story of Pearl Harbor.* New York: Penguin Books, 1991.

Robinson, Rhea. Personal interviews with author, Tucson, throughout 1996.

Roosevelt, Eleanor. *This I Remember.* New York: Harper & Brothers, 1949.

Toland, John. *The Rising Sun: The Decline and Fall of the Japanese Empire, 1936–1945.* New York: Random House, 1970.

Tucson Daily Citizen, February 26, 1942.

U.S. Congress. *Hearings before the Joint Committee on the Investigation of the Pearl Harbor Attack.* 79th Congress.

Yoshikawa, Takeo, with Lt. Col. Norman Stanford, USMC. "Top Secret Assignment." *United States Naval Institute Proceedings* (December 1960).

CHAPTER 3. ARIZONA DIVIDED

Burton, Jeffery, et al. *Confinement and Ethnicity: An Overview of World War II Japanese American Relocation Sites.* Washington, D.C.: National Park Service, 1999.

Caruso, Samuel T. "After Pearl Harbor: Arizona's Response to the Gila River Relocation Center." *Journal of Arizona History* (winter 1973).

Chanin, Abe, and Mildred Chanin. *This Land, These Voices: A Different View of Arizona History in the Words of Those Who Lived it.* Flagstaff, Ariz.: Northland Press, 1977.

Daniels, Roger. *Prisoners without Trial: Japanese Americans in World War II.* New York: Hill and Wang, 1993.

Kajikawa, Bill. Personal interview with Susie Sato, Tempe, Ariz., October 2000.

Sato, Susie. "Before Pearl Harbor: Early Japanese Settlers in Arizona." *Journal of Arizona History* (winter 1973).

————. Personal interview with author, Mesa, Ariz., March 1997

Tadano, Michiko. Personal interview with Susie Sato, Glendale, Ariz., October 2000.

Weglyn, Michi. *Years of Infamy: The Untold Story of America's Concentration Camps.* Seattle: University of Washington Press, 1996.

CHAPTER 4. WOMEN AND THE WAR EFFORT

Blanton, Elizabeth. Personal interviews with author, Phoenix, June–November 2000.

Cady, Dorothy. Personal interviews with author, Phoenix, June–November 2000.

Cahall, Rose. Personal interviews with author, Phoenix, June–November 2000.

Celaya, Laura. Oral history, Oral History Collection, Arizona Historical Society, Central Arizona Division, Tempe.

————. Personal correspondence with author, June 2001.

Fessler, Diane Burke. *No Time For Fear: Voices of American Military Nurses in World War II.* East Lansing: Michigan State University Press, 1996.

Fireman, Bert M. *Arizona: Historic Land.* New York: Alfred A. Knopf, 1982.

Garland, Georgiana. Personal interviews with author, Phoenix, June–November 2000.

Gleim, Edna. Personal interviews with author, Phoenix, June–November 2000.

Granger, Byrd Howell. *On Final Approach: The Women Airforce Service Pilots of World War II*. Scottsdale, Ariz.: Falconer Publishing Co., 1991.

Holm, Jeanne. *Women in the Military: An Unfinished Revolution*. Novato, Calif.: Presidio Press, 1982.

Jackson, Evelyn. Personal interviews with author, Phoenix, June–November 2000.

Johnson, Broderick, ed. *Navajos and World War II*. Tsaile, Ariz.: Navajo Community College Press, 1977.

McClendon, Fran. Personal interviews with author, Phoenix, June–November 2000.

Petsch, Roy. Personal interviews with author, Phoenix, June–November 2000.

Reinhold, Ruth. Oral history, Ruth Reinhold Aviation Collection, Arizona Historical Foundation, Hayden Library, Arizona State University, Tempe.

Rosenbaum, Polly. Personal interviews with author, Phoenix, June–November 2000.

Soza Michalec, Josephine. Personal interviews with author, Phoenix, June–November 2000.

Wiehrdt, Charlotte. Personal interviews with author, Phoenix, June–November 2000.

Williams, Gertrude. Personal interviews with author, Phoenix, June–November 2000.

CHAPTER 5. AMERICAN INDIANS AND THE WAR EFFORT

Arthur, Anthony. *Bushmasters: America's Jungle Warriors of World War II*. New York: St. Martin's Press, 1987.

Flaccus, Elmer W. "Arizona's Last Great Indian War: The Saga of Pia Machita." *Journal of Arizona History* (spring 1981).

Franco, Jere Bishop. *Crossing the Pond: The Native American Effort in World War II*. Denton: University of North Texas Press, 1999.

Gardiner, Harry. "Navajo Code Talkers." *Cobblestone* (July 1989).

Neuberger, Richard. "The American Indian Enlists." *Asia and the American* (November 1942).

Paul, Doris A. *The Navajo Code Talkers*. Pittsburgh: Dorrance Publishing Co., 1973.

Stewart, James M. "The Navajo Indian at War." *Arizona Highways* (June 1943).

Thomas, Estelle Webb. "America's First Families on the Warpath." *Common Ground* (1942).

Townsend, Kenneth William. *World War II and the American Indian*. Albuquerque: University of New Mexico Press, 2000.

Watson, Bruce, and Kenji Kawano. "Jaysho, Moasi, Debeh, Ayeshi, Hasclishnih, Beshlo, Shush, Gini." *Smithsonian* (August 1993).

CHAPTER 6. MILITARY BASES EVERYWHERE

Allen, Mary Moore. "Origin of Names of Army and Air Corps Posts, Camps, and Stations in World War II in Arizona." Hayden Library, Arizona State University.

Cook, James E. "Arizona and World War II." *Arizona Highways* (July 1988).

Harte, John Bret. *Tucson: Portrait of a Desert Pueblo*. Woodland Hills, Calif.: Windsor Publications, 1980.

Herman, George R. "A Bad Day at Douglas Army Air Field." *Journal of Arizona History* (winter 1995).

McLain, Jerry. "Warbirds' Swan Song." *Arizona Highways* (May 1947).

Pare, Madeline F., and Bert Fireman. *Arizona Pageant.* Tempe: Arizona Historical Foundation, 1974.

Preisler, Dennis. "Phoenix, Arizona, during the 1940s." Master's thesis, Arizona State University, 1992.

Provence, Jean. "Camp Horn, Arizona." Pamphlet in FE EPH HM, v. 11, 13, Arizona Historical Foundation archives, Arizona State University, Tempe.

————. "Davis-Monthan Air Force History." Tucson: Davis-Monthan AFB, 2000. Brochure.

————. "Luke Field During World War II." Brochure. Glendale, Ariz.: Luke AFB, 1954. Brochure.

Sheridan, Thomas. *Arizona: A History.* Tucson: University of Arizona Press, 1995.

Smith, Dean, ed. *The Great Arizona Almanac.* Portland, Ore.: WestWinds (a subsidiary of Graphic Arts Center), 2000.

Sonnichsen, Charles L. *Tucson: The Life and Times of an American City.* Norman: University of Oklahoma Press, 1982.

Tessman, Norm. "The Rescue of the Liberator 107 Crew." *Arizona Highways* (July 1997).

Trimble, Marshall. *Arizona: A Panoramic History.* New York: Doubleday, 1977.

See also the web pages of bases mentioned in the chapter:

Luke Field: www.luke.af.mil/

Davis-Monthan: www.dm.af.mil/default.htm

Fort Huachuca: http://huachuca-www.army.mil/

Marine Corps Air Station at Yuma: www.yuma.usmc.mil/

U.S. Army Yuma Proving Ground: www.yuma.army.mil/

Ryan Field: www.tucsonairport.org/ga/html/ga_ryan_ryanhistory.html

CHAPTER 7. THE WAR ON THE HOME FRONT

Ball, Phyllis. *A Photographic History of the University of Arizona, 1885–1985.* Tucson: Privately printed; distributed by the University of Arizona Press, 1986.

Cline, Platt. *Mountain Campus: The Story of Northern Arizona University.* Flagstaff, Ariz.: Northland Press, 1983.

————. *Mountain Town: Flagstaff's First Century.* Flagstaff, Ariz.: Northland Press, 1994.

Cole, Dawn, and Catherine Mendelsohn, eds. *As I Recall: Recollections from the Junior League of Tucson, 1933–1993.* Tucson: Junior League, 1993.

Curran, Eleanor. Oral history. Arizona Historical Society, Central Arizona Division.

Gart, Jason. *Papago Park: A History of Hole-in-the-Rock from 1848–1995.* Phoenix: Parks, Recreation, and Library Department, 1996.

Harris, Laura Dungee. Oral history. Arizona Historical Society, Central Arizona Division.

Hopkins, Ernest J., and Alfred Thomas, Jr. *The Arizona State University Story.* Phoenix: Southwest Publishing Co., 1960.

Kasun, Daisy. Oral history. Arizona Historical Society, Central Arizona Division.

Kober, Margaret. Oral history. Arizona Historical Society, Central Arizona Division.

Liu, Lily Valenzuela. Oral history. Arizona Historical Society, Southern Arizona Division.

Luckingham, Bradford. *Phoenix: The History of a Southwestern Metropolis.* Tucson: University of Arizona Press, 1989.

———. *The Urban Southwest: A Profile History of Albuquerque, El Paso, Phoenix, and Tucson.* El Paso: Texas Western Press, 1982.

Marin, Christine. "La Asociación Hispano Americana de Madres y Esposas (Tucson's Mexican American Women in World War II)." Renato Rosaldo Lecture Series Monograph, vol. 1, series 1983–84 (summer 1985).

———. "Mexican Americans on the Home Front: Community Organizations in Arizona during World War II." *Perspectives in Mexican American Studies,* vol. 4. Mexican American Studies and Research Center, University of Arizona, Tucson, 1993.

McAlister, Elsie. Oral history. Arizona Collection, Arizona State University Libraries.

Meier, Matt S., and Feliciano Rivera. *The Chicanos: A History of Mexican Americans.* New York: Hill and Wang, 1981.

Menetrey, Angela. Oral history. Arizona Historical Society, Central Arizona Division.

Osborn files. RG: Office of the Governor. Arizona Department of Libraries, Archives and Public Records, Archives Division, Phoenix.

Palmer, Bertha. Oral history. Arizona Historical Society, Central Arizona Division.

"Pattern for Living Suggested for American Women." *Arizona Republic,* March 5, 1942.

Redondo, Annie Garcia. Oral history. Arizona Historical Society, Central Arizona Division.

Reynolds, Jean. *"We knew our neighbors and it was like one family": The History of the Grant Park Neighborhood, 1880–1950.* Phoenix: City of Phoenix Historic Preservation Office, 1999.

———. "'We Made Our Life as Best We Could with What We Had': Mexican American Women in Phoenix, 1930–1949." Master's thesis, Arizona State University, 1998.

Robbins, Carolyn C., and Lew Davis. *"The Negro in America's Wars" and other Major Paintings.* Scottsdale, Ariz.: Scottsdale Center for the Arts, 1990.

Rothschild, Mary, and Pamela Hronek. *Doing What the Day Brought: An Oral History of Arizona Women.* Tucson: University of Arizona Press, 1992.

Sheridan, Thomas. *Arizona: A History.* Tucson: University of Arizona Press, 1995.

Snell, Frank. Oral history. Arizona Historical Society, Central Arizona Division.

Special Collections. Cline Library, Northern Arizona University.

Torres, Joseph. Oral history. Arizona Historical Society, Central Arizona Division.

White, Mrs. S. M. "Education and Understanding Will Solve the Race Problem." *Arizona Sun,* July 7, 1944.

World War II file. Personal reminiscences, newspaper clippings. Casa Grande Valley Historical Society.

Ynfante, Charles. "Arizona during the Second World War, 1941–1945: A Survey of Selected Topics." Ph.D. dissertation, Northern Arizona University, 1997.

CHAPTER 8. PRISONERS OF WAR

Anderlini, Elios. Telephone interviews with author, February 2001.

Cooper, Verna. Personal interview with author, Casa Grande, Ariz., June 1984.

Hoover, J. Edgar. "Here's How Uncle Sam Tracks Down Those Dangerous and Desperate Foes When They Escape." *American* magazine (April 1944).

Keppel, La Veta. Telephone interviews with author, January and February 2001.

Lammersdorf, Hans. Telephone interview with author, February 2001.

Moore, John Hammond. *The Faustball Tunnel: German POWs in America and Their Great Escape*. New York: Random House, 1978.

Moscardi, Luigi. Telephone interview with author, February 2001.

Papago Scout, no. 7 (March 1994) Phoenix: Papago Trackers.

Sroka, Marjorie. Telephone interviews with author, January and February 2001.

U.S. Army. *Army Almanac*. Washington, D.C.: U.S. Government Printing Office, 1950.

Wattenberg, Jürgen. Personal interview with author, Igls, Austria, May 1984.

Westerlund, John S. "Rommel's Afrika Korps in Northern Arizona." *Journal of Arizona History* (winter 1998).

Whittingham, Richard. *Martial Justice: The Last Mass Execution in the United States*. Chicago: Henry Regnery Co., 1971.

CHAPTER 9. ARIZONA'S WAR HEROES

Bradley, James, with Ron Powers. *Flags of Our Fathers*. New York: Bantam Books, 2000.

Cook, James. "Injuries Can't Stop GI at War or Home." *Arizona Republic,* May 17, 1991.

Hemingway, Al. "Ira Hayes." In *They Left Their Mark: Heroes and Rogues of Arizona History*. Wild West Collection, vol. 3. Phoenix: Arizona Highways Book Division, 1997.

————. *Ira Hayes: Pima Marine*. Lanham, Md.: University Press of America, 1988.

Lancaster, Roy. *Bushmasters*. Detroit, Mich.: Lancaster Publications, n.d. Copies available at Arizona Military Museum, Phoenix.

Lockhart, Vincent. *T-Patch to Victory*. N.p.: Staked Plains Press, 1981.

Lord, Walter. *Incredible Victory*. New York: Harper Row, 1967.

Lowe, Sam. "Battle of Ira Hayes." *Arizona Republic,* February 23, 1998.

Ropp, Thomas. "Reluctant Hero." *Arizona Republic,* August 29, 1985.

Turley, Wanda, ed. *Lt. Grant M. Turley: Ace Fighter Pilot, World War II*. N.p.: Privately printed, 1994.

CHAPTER 10. VICTORY AND BEYOND

Arizona Daily Star, misc. issues, 1944–1945.

Arizona Daily Sun, misc. issues, 1944–1945.

Arizona Republic, misc. issues, 1944–1945, 1993, 1995.

Ball, Phyllis. *A Photographic History of the University of Arizona, 1885–1985*. Tucson: Privately printed; distributed by the University of Arizona Press, 1986.

Brown, Carol Osman. "Phoenix, 1870–1970: 100 Years Young." *Arizona Highways* (April 1970).

Cline, Platt. *Mountain Campus: The Story of Northern Arizona University*. Flagstaff, Ariz.: Northland Press, 1983.

Harte, John Bret. *Tucson: Portrait of a Desert Pueblo*. Woodland Hills, Calif.: Windsor Publications, 1980.

Johnson, Wesley G., Jr. *Phoenix: Valley of the Sun.* Tulsa, Okla.: Continental Heritage Press, 1982.

Luckingham, Bradford. *Minorities in Phoenix: A Profile of Mexican American, Chinese American, and African American Communities, 1860–1992.* Tucson: University of Arizona Press, 1994.

———. *Phoenix: The History of a Southwestern Metropolis.* Tucson: University of Arizona Press, 1989.

Martin, Douglas. *The Lamp in the Desert: The Story of the University of Arizona.* Tucson: University of Arizona Press, 1960.

McFarland, Ernest W. *Mac: The Autobiography of Ernest W. McFarland.* N.p.: Privately printed, 1979.

Phoenix Gazette, misc. issues, May–September 1945.

Reynolds, Jean. "Battling for Justice, Freedom and Democracy: The Tony F. Soza American Legion Post, 1945–1950." Arizona Historical Society, Central Division.

Sheridan, Thomas E. *Arizona: A History.* Tucson: University of Arizona Press, 1995.

Sonnichsen, Charles L. *Tucson: The Life and Times of an American City.* Norman: University of Oklahoma Press, 1987.

Trimble, Marshall. *Diamond in the Rough: An Illustrated History of Arizona.* Norfolk, Va.: Donning Company, 1988.

Tucson Citizen, misc. issues, May–September 1945.

APPENDIX

Bowman, Martin W. *USAAF Handbook, 1939–1945.* Mechanicsburg, Pa.: Stackpole Books, 1997.

Burton, Jeffery F., Mary M. Farrell, Florence B. Lord, and Richard W. Lord. *Confinement and Ethnicity: An Overview of World War II Japanese American Relocation Sites.* Publications in Anthropology 74, Western Archaeological and Conservation Center, National Park Service, U.S. Department of the Interior, 1999.

Garner, John S. "World War II Temporary Military Buildings." Report Number CRC-93/01. Champaign, Ill.: U.S. Army, Corps of Engineers, CERL, 1993. Note: The text of this publication is also available online at www.cr.nps.gov/history/online_books/anthropolgy74/ (Accessed June 2002)

Iritani, Frank, and Joanne Iritani. *Ten Visits: Accounts of Visits to All the Japanese American Relocation Centers.* Los Angeles: Japanese American National Museum, 1999.

Kennedy, J., J. Lynch, and R. Wooley. *Patton's Desert Training Center.* Fort Myer, Va.: Council on America's Military Past, 1986.

Osborne, Richard E. *World War II Sites in the United States: A Tour Guide & Directory.* Indianapolis, Ind.: Riebel-Roque Publishing Co., 1996.

Pedrotty, Michael A., Julie L. Webster, Gordon L. Cohen, and Aaron R. Chmiel. "Historical and Architectural Overview of Military Aircraft Hangars: A General History, Thematic Typology, and Inventory of Aircraft Hangars Constructed on Department of Defense Installations." Report Number 98/105. Champaign, Ill.: U.S. Army Corps of Engineers, CERL, 1999. Available online from U.S. Army Corps of

Engineers Construction Engineering Research Laboratory website at
www.cecer.army.mil/td/tips/pub/details.cfm?PUBID=2023&TOP=1 (Accessed June
2002)

U.S. Army Corps of Engineers. Defense Environmental Restoration Program for Formerly
Used Defense Sites (DERP-FUDS) Inventory Project Reports. Available online at the
U.S. Army Corps of Engineers Project Information Retrieval Systems (PIRS) site at
pirs.mvr.usace.army.mil (Accessed June 2002)

NOTE: The DERP-FUDS program evaluates abandoned military sites to determine what
environmental impact, if any, remains from the military's occupation. The INP reports
often contain brief site histories and identify any military-related structures or remains.

ABOUT THE CONTRIBUTORS

ERIK BERG is a professional software engineer and avid historian. His interests include mining history as well as the social and industrial development of early twentieth-century Arizona. In addition to presenting at conferences, he has published articles in the *Journal of Arizona History* and contributed to the third volume of *History of Mining in Arizona*. Erik was the 2001 recipient of the Arizona Historical Society's James F. Elliot II award. He lives in Phoenix.

CAROL OSMAN BROWN is an award winning journalist whose work has appeared in *The Arizona Republic, Arizona Highways, Sunset, Westways, Native Peoples,* and many other regional and national magazines and newspapers. An Arizona resident since 1948, she has written many historical articles, including a 100-year history of Phoenix, published in *Arizona Highways,* April 1970. Formerly a faculty member of Arizona State University's Walter Cronkite School of Journalism and Telecommunications, she teaches writing courses for Rio Salado College. A Phoenix resident for many years, she now lives in Payson.

LLOYD CLARK is a journalist, lecturer, and tour guide. His column appears weekly in Sun City's *Daily News-Sun.* In 1966, he founded the Council on America's Military Past, which is a national organization interested in recording, preserving, and publicizing America's military heritage. He is a past board member for the

Arizona Historical Society and since 1994 has been the society's delegate on the Arizona State Board on Geographic and Historic Names. Clark is a retired army officer, public administrator, and teacher. He has written several articles, and he lectures extensively on the escape of twenty-five Germans from the Papago Park Prisoner-of-War Camp in December 1944. He lives in Surprise.

JANE EPPINGA is a member of both the Western Writers of America and the Society of Southwestern Authors and is a former president of Arizona Press Women. She has published three books, including *Images of America: Tucson, Arizona* and *Arizona Twilight Tales: Good Ghosts, Evil Spirits, and Blue Ladies.* One of her books, *Henry Ossian Flipper: West Point's First Black Graduate,* won a Spur finalist award from the Western Writers of America. A recipient of two degrees from the University of Arizona, she has published more than two hundred articles on the Southwest. She lives in Tucson.

DIANE BURKE FESSLER, author of *No Time for Fear: Voices of American Military Nurses in World War II,* graduated from Arizona State University with a degree in journalism. An Arizona resident since 1953, she has worked for the *Arizona Republic,* has promoted Arizona history as the former owner of Many Feathers Southwestern Books, and more recently has appeared on television and throughout the country speaking about military nurses. Diane is an editor with Primer Publishers. She lives in Phoenix.

SHARON S. MAGEE is an award-winning freelance writer who specializes in history with a heavy emphasis on the American Indian. She recently published *Geronimo! Stories of an American Legend* through Arizona Highways books. Magee's extensive publishing credits include *Arizona Highways, The Valley Guide, Priorities,* and *Phoenix Downtown Magazine.* She has won numerous awards and belongs to several professional organizations.

JOHN McCAIN graduated from the U.S. Naval Academy in 1958, beginning a twenty-two-year career as a naval aviator that included five and a half years as a prisoner of war in Vietnam. After retiring as a captain in 1981, McCain was elected as a member of the U.S. House of Representatives in 1982 and the U.S. Senate in 1985. He is the author of the best-selling book *Faith of My Fathers.*

MARY MELCHER, a curator of history at the Arizona Historical Society (AHS) Museum in Tempe, earned a Ph.D. in history at Arizona State University in 1994. She was a curator for the AHS Museum's recent exhibit "Views From the Home

Front: Arizona Transformed by World War II." Mary has published articles in the *Journal of Arizona History, Montana: Magazine of Western History,* and *Frontiers: A Journal of Women Studies.* She lives in Phoenix.

BRAD MELTON is a United Methodist youth and college minister as well as a freelance writer and editor. Before accepting the challenge of full-time ministry, he served as an editor for Northland Publishing, an editor for *Arizona Style* magazine, an assistant editor for *Documentary Editing,* and a research and copy writer for *Arizona Highways.* He has published articles in *Arizona Highways* and other publications, has presented papers on Arizona subjects at conferences throughout the West, and is listed in *Who's Who in the West.* In addition, he is a Prescott College graduate and a graduate student in public history at Arizona State University. He lives in Flagstaff.

ANDREW B. RUSSELL, a Ph.D. candidate at Arizona State University, currently teaches history at Albuquerque Technical Vocational Institute Community College. He earned his B.A. and M.A. from the University of Nevada, Las Vegas, and has published several articles and consulted on museum exhibits in Nevada and Arizona dealing with Japanese American experiences. Historian Susie Sato provided invaluable research assistance to Andy as he prepared his chapter. He lives in Albuquerque, New Mexico.

DEAN SMITH is the author of sixteen books on Arizona history and biography. He is a 1947 graduate of Arizona State University (ASU) and worked as a journalist for the *Glendale News, Mesa Tribune,* and *Arizona Republic* before returning to ASU as director of publications. After his retirement from the university in 1984 he served for three years as executive vice president of the Arizona Historical Foundation and continues to work as a freelance writer and editor. He lives in Tempe and Prescott.

MARSHALL TRIMBLE is Arizona's official state historian and the director of the Southwest Studies program at Scottsdale Community College, where he has taught Arizona history for more than thirty years. One of the state's most colorful personalities, he has appeared on ABC's *Good Morning America* and CBS's *This Morning.* He is the author of nineteen books on Arizona and the West. His stories and cowboy poems have appeared in *Arizona Highways, Western Horseman,* and *The American Cowboy.* He lives in Scottsdale.

ILLUSTRATION CREDITS

CHAPTER 1. PRELUDE TO WAR

The CCC camp at Portal, Arizona. Courtesy of the Arizona Historical Society, Central Arizona Division.

Worker at the construction of Hoover Dam. Courtesy of Cline Library, Northern Arizona University; NAU.PH.92.12.6245.

Raymond Carlson. Courtesy of the Herb and Dorothy McLaughlin Collection, Arizona State University Libraries.

Chinese flying cadet at Luke Army Air Field. Courtesy of Southwest Studies, Scottsdale Community College.

Reg Manning cartoon expressing the belief that the Allies would triumph. Courtesy of Dave Manning.

Reg Manning cartoon predicting America's entry. Courtesy of Dave Manning.

Reg Manning. Photo courtesy Dave Manning.

CHAPTER 2. DAY OF INFAMY

The USS *Arizona* under attack on December 7, 1941. Courtesy of Southwest Studies, Scottsdale Community College.

Abe Chanin selling war bonds. Courtesy of Abe Chanin.

Yndia Smalley Moore with her daughter, Dianne Bret Harte. Photograph by Jane Eppinga.

The USS *Arizona* Memorial. Courtesy of Southwest Studies, Scottsdale Community College.

Rhea Robinson. Photograph by Jane Eppinga.

Nagao Kita. Courtesy of the Library of Congress.

Japanese internees at the Triangle T Ranch. Courtesy of Rhea Robinson.

Otojiro Okuda. Courtesy of the Library of Congress.

Reed Robinson and Nagao Kita. Courtesy of Rhea Robinson.

Kokichi Seki and Nagao Kita. Courtesy of Rhea Robinson.

Takeo Yoshikawa, a.k.a. Tadashi Morimura. Courtesy of the Library of Congress.

CHAPTER 3. ARIZONA DIVIDED

Susie Sato holding her infant daughter. Courtesy of Susie Sato.

Japanese internees boarding a train. Courtesy of the Arizona Historical Society, Central Arizona Division; 1999.176.03.

Japanese farmers with truck. Courtesy of Susie Sato.

The Takeshi Tadano family. Courtesy of Michiko Tadano.

Bill and Margaret Kajikawa. Courtesy of Bill Kajikawa.

Butte Camp in 1942. Courtesy of Susie Sato.

Two girls in a relocation camp. Courtesy of the Arizona Historical Society, Central Arizona Division; 1978.67.04.

Eleanor Roosevelt being welcomed to the Gila camp. Courtesy of the National Archives.

Grandfather at the Gila camp with his two visiting granddaughters. Courtesy of the Arizona Historical Society, Central Arizona Division; 1978.67.01.

CHAPTER 4. WOMEN AND THE WAR EFFORT

Secretary during gas mask drill. Courtesy of Steve Hoza.

Army nurses training in the Arizona desert. Diane Fessler Collection.

Laura Celaya. Courtesy of the Arizona Historical Society, Central Arizona Division.

Charlotte Wiehrdt. Courtesy of Charlotte Wiehrdt.

African American army nurses at Fort Huachuca. Courtesy of the Crisis Publishing Company.

A civilian woman rigging parachutes. Courtesy of Steve Hoza.

Ina Petsch. Courtesy of Donna Petsch Donovan.

Ruth Reinhold. Courtesy of the Arizona Historical Foundation, Arizona State University.

Gertrude Williams. Courtesy of Gertrude Williams.

Rose Cahall. Courtesy of Rose Cahall.

Woman aircraft mechanic at Marana Air Field. Courtesy of Steve Hoza.

CHAPTER 5. AMERICAN INDIANS AND THE WAR EFFORT

A Navajo sailor visiting his family. Courtesy of the Museum of New Mexico; neg. no. 30 960.

The swastika, banned by the Apaches, Hopis, Navajos, and Papago. Bettmann/CORBIS.

Arizona American Indians undergoing machine gun training. Courtesy of Southwest Studies, Scottsdale Community College.

Marine Technical Sergeant Philip Johnston. Courtesy of Cline Library, Northern Arizona University, Philip Johnston Collection, NAD.PH.413.1299.

Navajo code talkers John Goodluck of Lukachukai and George H. Kirk. Marine Corps photograph, courtesy of the National Archives; no. 94236.

Marine Private First Class Carl Gorman. Courtesy of the National Archives; photo no. 127-MN-83734.

Corporal Henry Bahe, Jr., and Private First Class George H. Kirk. Marine Corps photograph, courtesy of the National Archives; photo no. 127-MN-69889B.

Bushmasters with a captured a Japanese soldier. Courtesy of the National Archives.

CHAPTER 6. MILITARY BASES EVERYWHERE

Bill Mauldin. Courtesy of Southwest Studies, Scottsdale Community College.

Bill Mauldin cartoon. Courtesy of Southwest Studies, Scottsdale Community College.

Senator Carl Hayden with Col. John A. Des Portes. Courtesy of the Arizona Collection, Arizona State University Libraries; CP CTH 1087.

Four pilot instructors. Courtesy of Harry Maryan.

Evan Mecham. Courtesy of Evan Mecham.

African American soldiers receiving instruction in firing mortars. Courtesy of Southwest Studies, Scottsdale Community College.

An M-5 light tank at the Desert Training Center. Courtesy of the Arizona Collection, Arizona State University Libraries.

AT-6 trainer. Photograph of a painting by Gerry R. Maryan; courtesy of Harry Maryan.

Major John J. Rhodes and other senior officers welcome Major General Hodges. Courtesy of John Rhodes.

Major Barry Goldwater. Courtesy of Southwest Studies, Scottsdale Community College.

Hogan at the Navajo Ordnance Center. Courtesy of Cline Library, Northern Arizona University, Navajo Army Depot Collection, NAD 1985.

CHAPTER 7. THE WAR ON THE HOME FRONT

Tucson women serving as home guards. Southwest Studies, Scottsdale Community College.

Reg Manning cartoon on the plight of Arizona farmers. Courtesy of Dave Manning.

Newspaper advertisement calling on women to "help win the war." Courtesy of Arizona Historical Society, Central Arizona Division.

Tucson residents collecting for scrap drives. Courtesy of Southwest Studies, Scottsdale Community College.

Red Cross canteen volunteers in front of the Phoenix Union Station. Courtesy of Arizona Historical Society, Central Arizona Division; 1978.43.01.

Announcement for a servicemen's recreation center. Courtesy of Arizona Historical Society, Central Arizona Division; 1978.58.

Lew Davis. Courtesy of the Arizona Historical Society, Central Arizona Division.

Lew Davis's poster about black servicemen. Courtesy of the Arizona Historical Society, Central Arizona Division.

CHAPTER 8. PRISONERS OF WAR

German POW escape tunnel. From the collection of Mrs. Lawrence C. Jorgensen.

Officers' quarters at the Papago Park camp. Courtesy of Steve Hoza.

Stockade at the Papago Park Prisoner-of-War Camp. Lloyd Clark Collection.

German POWs at the Papago Park camp. Courtesy of Southwest Studies, Scottsdale Community College.

Jürgen Wattenberg at the London Bridge. Photograph by Lloyd Clark.

Italian prisoners at Florence POW camp. Courtesy of Steve Hoza.

Guard tower at the Florence POW camp. Courtesy of Steve Hoza.

CHAPTER 9. ARIZONA'S WAR HEROES

Bushmasters training in Panama. Courtesy of Southwest Studies, Scottsdale Community College.

Silvestre Herrera memorial. Photograph by Marshall Trimble; courtesy of Southwest Studies, Scottsdale Community College.

Silvestre Herrera receiving the Congressional Medal of Honor. Courtesy of Southwest Studies, Scottsdale Community College.

Lieutenant Grant Turley with his P-47 Thunderbolt and crew. Courtesy of Stan Turley; Southwest Studies, Scottsdale Community College.

A Douglas SBD Dauntless dive bomber. Navy photograph, courtesy of Southwest Studies, Scottsdale Community College.

Ensign John C. Butler. Navy photograph, courtesy of Southwest Studies, Scottsdale Community College.

Irene Butler at the christening of the USS *John C. Butler*. Courtesy of Southwest Studies, Scottsdale Community College.

The American flag being raised over Mount Suribachi. Photograph by Joe Rosenthal, courtesy of Southwest Studies, Scottsdale Community College.

Ira Hayes. Arizona State Library photograph, courtesy of Southwest Studies, Scottsdale Community College.

The Mathew B. Juan–Ira Hayes Veterans Memorial. Photograph by Marshall Trimble; courtesy of Southwest Studies, Scottsdale Community College.

CHAPTER 10. VICTORY AND BEYOND

Reg Manning's "Peace" cartoon. Courtesy of Dave Manning.

Polly Rosenbaum. Courtesy of the Arizona Historical Foundation, Arizona State University.

Senator Ernest W. McFarland with D. Worth Clark. Courtesy of the Ernest W. McFarland Library and Archives, McFarland Historical State Park, Florence, Arizona.

The first Veterans Administration hospital in central Arizona. Courtesy of the Phoenix Veterans Administration Medical Center; photo no. 29188.

Bob Hope and Jerry Colonna visiting patients. Courtesy of the Phoenix Veterans Administration Medical Center; photo no. 29188.

Ronald Reagan with John F. Long. Courtesy of John F. Long.

Lieutenant Lincoln Ragsdale. Courtesy of the Lincoln Ragsdale family.

Reg Manning cartoon about jet plane noise. Courtesy of Dave Manning.

APPENDIX. A TRAVELER'S GUIDE TO ARIZONA'S WORLD WAR II SITES

All maps and photographs in the Appendix are by Erik Berg.

INDEX

Note: Page numbers in italics refer to illustrations.